MW00908335

SOCIETY FROM THE INSIDE OUT

SOCIETY FROM THE INSIDE OUT

Anthropological Perspectives on the South Asian Household

Edited by
JOHN N. GRAY
DAVID J. MEARNS

SAGE Publications
New Delhi/Newbury Park/London

First published in 1989 by

Sage Publications India Pvt Ltd
M–32 Greater Kailash Market I
New Delhi 110 048

Sage Publications Inc
2111 West Hillcrest Drive
Newbury Park, California 91320

Sage Publications Ltd
28 Banner Street
London EC1Y 8QE

Published by Tejeshwar Singh for Sage Publications India Pvt Ltd., phototypeset by Mudra Typesetters, Pondicherry, and printed at Chaman Offset Printers.

Library of Congress Cataloging-in-Publication Data
Society from the inside out: anthropological perspectives on the
   South Asian household / edited by John N. Gray, David J. Mearns.
      p. cm.
   Includes index.
      1. Households—South Asia.   2. Family—South Asia.   3. Kinship—
South Asia.   I. Gray, John N., 1945–   II. Mearns, David J., 1948–
   HQ666.5.S58   306.85'0954—dc20   1989   89–31724

ISBN 0–8039–9609–8 (US)
         81–7036–146–X (India)

For
Jacki and **Lesley**

Contents

Acknowledgements

T HIS VOLUME is the outcome of an idea originally developed by the editors for an Honours Seminar in the Department of Anthropology at the University of Adelaide, South Australia. We owe a continuing debt of gratitude to the students who participated in the seminar during 1983, 1984 and 1985. They provided the first forum for examining the approach. It was their critical appraisal of our idea which inspired us to refine the approach and to organise a series of papers by other anthropologists interested in the South Asian household. We are also deeply grateful to Professor T.N. Madan. Although he was unable to contribute a paper because of other commitments, he gave us his moral and professional support throughout the process of completing the volume and kindly contributed its Foreword. We would also like to thank the Department of Anthropology at the University of Adelaide for their willing support of the project, especially Rebecca Anderson and Wendy Fisher who prepared the manuscripts and Marian Thompson who compiled the index. Finally, we thank the authors for their contributions and their patience.

John N. Gray
David J. Mearns

Foreword

Yesterday's discoveries and analytical breakthroughs are, as is very well known, today's truisms. Thus, it hardly bears repetition that cultural reality is socially constructed and not externally given. This is no more or less true of the manner in which sociologists and cultural anthropologists construct representations of the societies and cultures they study than of the people themselves who constitute these societies and are the bearers and creators of their respective cultures. Representations of socially constructed reality are fabricated in the light of prevailing and often competing paradigms which are themselves historical products. Max Weber drew pointed attention to this is his essay on 'Objectivity' when he wrote: 'Any knowledge of cultural reality . . . is knowledge from *particular points of view*'. Needless to add, as paradigms change so do the representations. What seems important within one theoretical framework loses significance in another.

Now, the importance of the 'household' in the study of society in India has been evident for a fairly long time. The apprehension of this importance has, however, arisen from different perspectives.

For the census takers of a hundred years ago, and their successors to the present day, the household has been the concrete unit of social organisation, so identified by the people and the enumerators alike. The fact that the house-household equation did not always hold did not pose serious problems because the cultural emphasis was on the hearth or the kitchen and the commensal group. Individuals as such did not matter. Among the Hindus, particularly upper caste Hindus, the individual was either the householder (*grihastha*), in which case he or she lived in and through a household-based web of kinship and marriage ties, or a renouncer (*sannyasi*), in which case he lived outside society. To say that the household 'is the next bigger thing on the social map after the individual', as is often done, may make sense elsewhere but in India it is true only in a banal way.

What the census takers gained by way of concreteness or empirical validity, they unfortunately squandered by getting bogged down in terminological confusion. A false or, in any case misleading, typological question emerged which has not yet disappeared: Is the joint family, believed to be characteristic of traditional societies, in decline? The debate has raged while the size though not the kin composition of the household has remained almost constant. The confusion arose because the distinction between the family and the household was not clearly drawn by the outsiders, administrators as well as academics (the people themselves were of course aware of it), and also because anything larger or more ramified than the so-called nuclear family, characteristic of contemporary Victorian society, was seen as being not only backward but also perhaps in some sense artificial and unstable. Words such as 'joint', 'extended', and 'undivided', which came to be prefixed to the family in India, particularly the Hindu family, are quite revealing.

Sociologists and social anthropologists have also been handicapped by definitional short-sightedness, searching for a supposedly universal 'nuclear family' in every cultural nook and corner (if only the Nayar were not real people!). Fieldwork, however, saves us from many errors of commission and omission and is a sobering experience. While indologists and sociologists (such as P.V. Kane and K.M. Kapadia) had given us descriptions of the family and domestic organisation on the basis of texts and other secondary materials, anthropologists turned from the general to the specific and rediscovered the importance of the household through fieldwork. Tl .r interest in the concrete was rooted in the ethnographic method: it was similar to but not the same as that of census administrators.

Thirty years ago, the objective of rendering the social reality of everyday life sociologically intelligible led me to hold up the household as the focal group among the Pandits of rural Kashmir. There was nothing outside or beyond it that one's study of it did not illuminate. While extra-domestic kinship and marriage ties had obvious structural significance, everyday life was lived in all its vividness within the setting of the household. Economic activities and an emerging interest in politics also were rooted in the household and to a lesser extent in wider kin groupings.

Around the same time and in the following years some other scholars (including Pauline Kolenda, Ramkrishna Mukherjee, Jyotirmoyee Sarma, Milton Singer, Sylvia Vatuk and, above all, A.M. Shah) also stressed the importance of the household, though they did not always use this term and preferred to speak of 'the family'. Not only were definitional issues discussed, the compositional, functional, and processual aspects of the household also received attention. Besides, the behaviour of households and families in the context of the new economic opportunities, particularly in urban areas, was studied.

Interest in the study of the household, clearly defined, did not, however, become widespread enough nor did it deepen sufficiently. Concern with wider groupings (caste) and with wide-ranging networks of relationships (extra-domestic kinship) overshadowed interest in the household. The structuralist approach *à la* Claude Lévi-Strauss and Louis Dumont never became really dominant in anthropological studies of India. Even so, some scholars who had earlier shown an interest in the household turned to studies at a higher level of abstraction, exploring relations between relations. The ethnosociological approach of more recent years has been preoccupied with general cognitive categories, and the household too became a 'fluid sign' along with other expressions of 'dividualism'.

Yet it is the post-structuralist phenomenological turn in theoretical orientation which holds the promise of a revival of interest in the concrete. The present volume of essays focusing on the household, it seems, is a fruit of this development. It is very welcome. The editors have characterised the approach underlying these essays as one of giving 'ethnographic priority' to the household and of studying 'society from the inside out'. This 'strategy' is differentiated from the 'outside-in' approach. They advocate the strategy not only on methodological grounds (it will produce new insights) but also on empirical grounds ('the cultural centrality of the householder's way of life'). They rightly complain that the householder's status as 'pivotal persona' has not received enough attention from the scholars concerned. I have myself drawn attention to this deficiency in *Non-Renunciation: Themes and Interpretations of Hindu Culture* (1987).

The editors invite us to look at the data on domestic organisation in some well-known ethnographic 'outside-in' studies from the complementary 'inside-out' perspective. I find their emphasis on the complementarity of the two points of view wholesome. The widespread tendency to claim exclusive merit for one's own theoretical standpoint is crippling and impoverishes our understanding of social reality. The contributors to this volume do not deny that social actors or small-scale groups are located in broader social contexts which are external to and exert constraint upon the former. But they rightly question the illegitimate inference that micro-level phenomena are mere 'epiphenomena' or 'social sequiturs to the encompassing principles, processes and/or institutions'. They urge us to explore with them the ways in which the wider social structure is sustained, altered or generated by social actors operating through small groups such as the household. Their interest is not in the household by itself, for it is not the locus of walled-in phenomena. They present it as an institution that mediates between the social actor and society, both of which require each other, as it were. In other words, the essays comprising this volume seek to steer clear of both kinds of reductionism, psychological and sociological.

The authors do, however, underline the primacy of the household in everyday life and in intersubjective experience. They are, it seems to me, advocating a shift of emphasis from structure to consciousness, from function to meaning. This, too, is welcome. In the past we have had excellent portrayals of the meaningfulness of domestic life but only in novels (Rama Mehta's *Inside the Haveli* readily comes to mind) and autobiographical and biographical narratives (see, for example, Ursula Sharma's *Rampal and his Family: The Story of an Immigrant*, 1971). It is time they found their place in social science writing also. Let me quote the editors: 'while we do not advocate analysing all social units as different formations of linked households, we do suggest that because the household is the primary context in which people constitute their experience and knowledge of society and its basic principles, they also bring such knowledge and experience to bear upon their understanding of and practices in these other social contexts.'

Society from the Inside Out is an important and interesting volume of essays on South Asian (Indian, Nepalese, Sri Lankan and Malaysian-Indian) households, contributed by scholars all of whom are esteemed colleagues and some of whom are also my personal friends. Between themselves they combine the experience of the older generation and the enthusiasm of the younger. They bear witness to the vigour of South Asian studies on three continents. I have benefited much by reading the essays and enjoyed them too. It is a pleasure to recommend the book to students of South Asian culture and society everywhere.

T.N. Madan

Introduction

Household and Domestic Group— Society from the Inside out

John N. Gray
David J. Mearns

The Project

IN ORGANISING this volume, we proposed to all the contributors a general analytic strategy which we thought would operationalise an approach we are developing for the understanding of complex societies which gives 'ethnographic priority' to the household. The strategy entails an analysis of the household, including definitional issues, which attempts to reveal its particular characteristics, whether relational, structural, conceptual, and/or behavioural, which recognises that these characteristics are not merely manifestations of the encompassing society writ small in the domestic domain, and which focuses on the centrifugal implications of domestic relations and processes for social domains of a larger-scale. Hence the phrase 'inside out' which we adopt to describe the approach. The basic aim of the book was to provide a forum in which several experienced anthropologists could explore and critically assess the approach in relation to their own ethnographic material.

The areal focus of the book is a consequence of the fact that both editors did fieldwork among South Asian social groups—one with Hindus in Nepal and the other with south Indians in Melaka. Not surprisingly, then, it was in this context that we began to develop the approach. Further, we could do so in direct relation to the complementary 'outside in' ethnographic strategy which has been particularly dominant in South Asia thanks to Dumont. For all these reasons we thought it best to confine the first rigorous exploration of the approach to the ethnographic region we knew best. Hence the focus on South Asia.

Moreover, culturally and analytically South Asian society is especially fertile ground for exploring the household and its implications for wider society. Classical Hinduism recognises four stages (*aśrama*) or ways of life: the celibate pupil (*brahmacharya*), the householder (*grihastha*), the forest hermit (*vanaprastha*), and the renouncer (*sannyasa*). Unlike the others, the householder is 'the man-in-the-world' (Dumont 1960: 37), the archetypal social being, and the typical way of life for most people. The householder encompasses three of the main ethical goals that orient social life in the world: *artha* (wealth, material possessions and power), *kama* (desire, physical and erotic love), and *dharma* (righteous duty). The householder's duties and obligations are to marry and beget children, to perform sacrifice which sustains the cosmos, to produce wealth which materially sustains the family and community, and, as the only producer of material goods, to give alms which sustain the pupil, hermit and renouncer. Thus the householder is the pivotal persona in Hindu society because by maintaining the sacred cosmos through sacrifice and the earthly community through material and biological reproduction, he is the 'upholder of the dharma' (Heesterman 1982: 253).

While ethnographers of South Asia rarely refer to this cultural centrality of the householder way of life, their analyses resonate with it in the extensive sections devoted to understanding the domestic realm and its relation to the encompassing society.[1] However, it was not until the distinction between 'household' and 'family' was firmly established by Mayer (1960: 182) in South Asia and by Bender (1967) more generally, that ethnographers began to analyse the household as a distinct social realm with its own characteristics. One of first and still one of the finest ethnographies in which the household is the dominant focus is Madan's analysis of Kashmiri Brahmans (1965). In addition to the intricate account of the kinship principles, the economic activities and developmental processes characteristic of Kashmiri Brahman households, there is in the very structure of his ethnography—which begins with the household and works outward to wider kinship structures—the seeds of the inside-out approach we are advocating as a complement to most other studies which place the household in the analytic location of sequitur to processes and principles of wider society. The hints provided by Madan were not pursued in later studies in which two dominant themes are discernible, one ethnographic and the other analytic. When juxtaposed these themes seem somewhat contradictory and yet together they form the 'received wisdom' about the household in South Asian society. The first theme is ethnographic and identifies the household as one of the most

[1] See Shah (1974) for an informative and complete annotated bibliography of studies which include major sections on the family and household. In addition to the references cited in Shah, see Beck (1972), Bennett (1983), Berreman (1972), Fricke (1987), Khare (1976), Parry (1979), Sharma (1980, 1986), Srinivas (1976), and Vatuk (1972).

significant social groups in people's lives; relations with other household members are usually more intimate, intense and important than any others a person may establish outside the domestic domain; it is the primary place for socialisation and for the constitution of a person's identity in South Asian society (see Daniel 1984); and it is the location and beneficiary of a majority of the rituals performed by members of South Asian society. Yet the second theme, which is analytic, is that the household is a domain whose structure, functions, operation and meaning are primarily seen as manifestations of abstract society-wide principles. In this sense it is analytically treated as epiphenomenal thereby implicitly diluting the importance given to it ethnographically. We illustrate the incorporation of these two themes, the insights enabled by them and the conceptual problems engendered by them in two major ethnographies of South Asian society.[2]

Brenda Beck (1972) proposes a series of concentric social-territorial realms descending in scale from the region through the sub-region, village and hamlet to the household as a way of analysing the Konku region of south India. Working from the largest-scale regional caste down to the smallest-scale domestic group, she demonstrates with rich ethnographic material how a basic structural principle of south Indian society—the left/right division of castes—differentially organises groups and their relations in each of the social-territorial domains. The smallest of her socio-territorial units is the household/family complex (KuTumpam). For Beck the specificity of the KuTumpam as a distinct social unit is culturally defined by the confluence of commensality and marriage within a ritually demarcated living space. However, once this specificity is presented, she is immediately drawn into the usual analysis of the household as one manifestation of abstract society-wide principles—in this case the left/right division of castes in south India. Following Kolenda (1968) and foreshadowing the major issue of Netting, Wilk and Arnould's volume (1984), her ethnography focuses on explaining how and why households vary within Konku society. She cites the left/right division of castes and the concomitant Kshatriya and Brahmanic models of socio-religious life to explain variations in household structure and practices according to the differential application of Dravidian kinship terminologies, cross-cousin marriage preferences and gift exchanges between affines. One of the unintended consequences of adopting this form of explanation is that Beck implicitly devalues the particular nature of the household in its own right for the sake of its cultural coherence with all the other social-territorial realms as the various manifestations of a single social principle. There is a

[2] Instead of reviewing the large numbers of ethnographies which devote significant sections to the household in South Asia in terms of these two themes, we feel that a more extended critical discussion of two major ethnographies by Beck (1972) and Parry (1979) provides a better presentation of our views.

complementary analytic strategy potential in her material which recognises
that the household has a character which is not totally determined by wider
societal principles and processes. Such an ethnography would give greater
emphasis to the distinctive nature of the household by tracing the implications of its endogenous core cultural characteristic (i.e., as the basic
commensal unit preconditioned on the husband-wife dyad) for the relations,
functions and meanings that constitute it as a particular kind of social group.
Then Beck could have developed an understanding of the larger social
groups (e.g., lineage, clan and sub-caste) constitutive of the wider social-
territorial realms (e.g., hamlet, village, and sub-region) on the basis of the
ways in which Dravidian kinship and marriage differentially link the households that make up these larger social groups (cf. Gray in this volume).

Parry's (1979) ethnographic strategy is similar. He too begins with an
encompassing principle—in this case Dumont's (1980) hierarchy—which
for him structures Kangra society at all levels. The trajectory of his analysis is
summarised by the following progression of oppositions which descend in
scale from the cosmic to the domestic:

men : gods :: low castes : high castes :: wife-givers : wife-takers ::
junior agnates : senior agnates (cf. Parry 1979: 6)[3]

For Parry the cultural and sociological 'location' of the basic hierarchical
principle is the widest-scale cosmic realm of religion as indicated in his
privileging the 'men: gods' opposition (1979: 6). From here he shows in a
succession of social levels of descending scale how inter-caste relations,
intra-caste relations between *biradaris*, and domestic relations are all manifestations and analytic sequiturs of hierarchy.

Yet in his examination of domestic relations, Parry explicitly admits that
status as revealed in marriage is ultimately a matter for the household (1979:
280). However, he does not pursue the implications of this insight about the
endogenous nature of the household for relations between households and
for the constitution of larger-scale social domains. Instead, like Beck, he
works in the other direction, explaining the hypergamous relations between
households that result from marriage as a product of encompassing principles that exist 'outside' the households. As Beck did, Parry's rich ethnography provides the necessary material about marriage patterns which
would enable one to explore the centrifugal vector of the household, i.e.,
how larger-scale social units (i.e., hamlets, biradaris) may be conceived as
particular ways of organising smaller-scale units (i.e., households) which are

[3] We have reversed the order in which Parry actually presents the series of oppositions
because we felt it more accurately reflects his argument and the underlying outside-in analytic
framework of his ethnography.

emergent from the nature of these units.[4] Both Parry and Beck move away from this style of analysis because they unwittingly adopt what we call an 'outside-in' approach.

An outside-in ethnography implicitly assumes a concentric model of society. Smaller-scale social phenomena (i.e., the person, the household) are encompassed spatially, conceptually, and analytically by larger-scale social phenomena (i.e., society, the state, the market, religion) which are accorded more political, economic, and sociological power seemingly just because of their greater social scale. The concentric model can range in complexity from the simple dual encompassed-encompassing notion (cf. Dumont 1980 and Levi-Strauss 1963) to one with a greater number of levels and/or multiple nestings of realms within a single whole. Whatever the degree of complexity, the implications of an outside-in approach are fourfold:

a. Phenomena of or at the smaller-scale ('inside') manifest, confirm and are explained by phenomena of larger and encompassing scale ('outside'), whether these latter are conceived as abstract principles or concrete social processes and institutions. This mode of analysis is evident in both Parry's and Beck's ethnographies where the household was explained in terms of the principle of hierarchy in the former and the left/right division of castes in the latter.

b. There is the assumption that all levels of society are neutral in relation to the interpenetration of the encompassing. Thus, for example, the abstract social principle is the same and has a monolithic structuring effect no matter what the nature and scale of the social unit in which it is seen to be operating. Together, these two implications constitute the smaller-scale phenomena as epiphenomena in that they are analysed as the sociological sequiturs to the encompassing principles, processes and/or institutions.

c. As a result, the particular nature of each level of society is analytically devalued. The ethnographer tends to show how the encompassing principle is manifest in and explains smaller-scale social phenomena. In this way smaller-scale social units are denied any autonomy. Thus he or she is diverted from examining in detail how the specific structures, processes and meanings are emergent in, and become characteristic of, these smaller-scale phenomena. Further, the ethnographer is prevented from revealing how the endogenous nature of smaller-scale social phenomena might significantly affect the way encompassing principles and processes operate in these domains.

d. Finally, an outside-in approach assumes that important social principles do not emerge in small-scale domains of intense social relations. We are

---

[4] For an illustration of this type of analysis specifically related to hypergamous relations within a caste, see Gray (1980).

suggesting that it is precisely in this kind of social realm that important social principles and processes *experientially* emerge and are given specific cultural shape and meaning for actors.

This outside-in ethnography strategy has an eminent pedigree. The most obvious and recent for South Asia is Dumont's (1980) encompassing-encompassed model for Indian caste society. For him the principles of the purity-impurity opposition, hierarchy, separation and complementarity are sociologically located in religion and in the minds of Indians, both of which encompass society as a whole and structure relations at all levels of Indian society. This is the basis of Dumont's claim that there are 'no privileged levels' in the caste system at which the principles exist and operate. His analysis is an outstanding example of the enlightenment to be gained by viewing society from the outside in.

However, the foundations of this approach are embedded more deeply than this in anthropology. Marx and Durkheim each proposed a sociology based on the assumption of society-wide principles having analytic priority and thus structuring smaller-scale social phenomena. For Marx, dialectics and the principles organising the economic infrastructure define the nature of society and its history. In capitalist society, for example, the state, the market, the division of labour, the social units of production as well as the family are 'in the last resort' (to paraphrase Engels) sequiturs to the forces and relations of production characterising the social whole. So too for Durkheim but in a different way. The collective conscience and the moral authority of the social it represents are external, constraining, and general forces of the whole society on the individual. Thus they provide not only the explanation but also the genesis of social groups, relationships between persons, and modes of thought at all levels of society.

When incorporated into ethnography as an outside-in approach, this perspective bestows a particular kind of reality onto societal principles and institutions. They are the result of abstracting common phenomena from a myriad of forms of social practice which can be done either by the actors themselves or by an outside investigator. Whichever the case, these sociologically derived principles and/or institutions take on a separate and holistic reality. Since this reflects one way in which actors may confront these principles and/or institutions, the approach has legitimacy. However, we are suggesting that there is a complementary mode of analysis which reflects another aspect of social reality. We call this an 'inside-out' approach.

While accepting the insight afforded by some form of concentric social model, too thorough-going an outside-in approach devalues the endogenous processes of small-scale social domains which are constitutive of actors' experiences. In these respects our reasons for emphasising the domestic as a more important small-scale domain are aptly put by Hammel (1984) and

Kunstadter (1984): 'A household, in fact, is the next bigger thing on the social map after an individual' (Hammel 1984: 40–41); '. . . most people in most societies at most times live in households . . .' (Kunstadter 1984: 304). It is in such domains where, rather than showing how abstract holistic principles are sociologically manifest, we may examine the social process by which they are constituted. Moreover, we can explain the particular form such principles take in actors' consciousness by relating them to the particular structure and meaning characteristic of the domestic domain. The experience and knowledge which people develop of the social in these smaller-scale realms have a centrifugal vector in the sense that individuals often draw upon such knowledge for their action in larger-scale domains. Accordingly, an inside-out approach examines the distinctive intersubjective reality that is generated in the intimate social relations that characterise smaller-scale social domains and analyses the way the social features of the domains affect the constitution of this intersubjective reality.

In focusing on the constitution of actors' consciousness, an inside-out ethnography draws upon Weber's sociology and Schutz' phenomenological critique of it. Weber (1978) views society as the subjectively meaningful and socially probable result generated by the successive layering of individual social action and interaction that constitutes collectivities and associations of increasing social scale. For Weber the basic social reality is not society writ large as it is for Durkheim and Marx but the social interaction of individuals. Taking up Weber's themes of subjective meaning and social interaction as the building-blocks of society, Schutz (1972) proposes that the precondition for the very existence of sociality is the intersubjectivity of the Self and the Other. His social phenomenology is, in part, an explanation of the processes of human consciousness which generated the intersubjective knowledge that enables social interaction and ultimately society. Thus, both Weber's and Schutz' explanatory strategy begins with the smallest-scale social unit—the Self and the Other—and traces its consequences for principles and institutions of increasing social scale.

By recognising the centrifugal vector inherent in Weber and Schutz we are not obliged to adopt their starting point of the Self and the Other which, as Dumont (1980) pointed out, may have a Western bias. In this respect we were inspired by Sahlins' notion of a Domestic Mode of Production (1972). Sahlins adopts a two-stage strategy in order to analyse the particularity of the household as a social domain and its centrifugal effects. In the first he isolates the domestic domain to enable him to describe the social, economic and kinship processes particular to the household *qua* household. In the second stage he returns the household to its place in society but now is able to trace the effects of the distinctive processes of the household for larger-scale political and economic structures. An important implication of Sahlins' work for what we are calling an inside-out perspective is that it fosters an emphasis on the specific nature of smaller-scale units as building-blocks with endogenous characteristics. Accordingly, we ask how the structure, practices and meanings of the South Asian household as a distinct social unit have implications for larger-scale social realms such as the hamlet, village, region, state and cosmos?

This question is important for anthropologists because most ethnographic practice involves an experiential and analytic confrontation with the household. For ourselves as analysts and for the people whose society we investigate, the household is a significant context for the constitution of our consciousness of the social world. To say the least, methodologically a great deal of knowledge and data about a range of topics is generated in the domestic domain. Whether our own or our informants, the household is the place where anthropologists often meet informants and learn about a variety of socio-cultural phenomena—not only those pertaining directly to domestic life but also those relating to aspects of ritual practice, economic production and political process in the extra-household 'public domain' (Rosaldo 1974). As a significant locus of fieldwork, the household is a primary context in which our experience and understanding of another culture is constituted. This is a feature of our methodology that usually goes unnoticed in our ethnographies. Moreover, it is true not only for our encounter with the other, but it also holds for how members themselves encounter their own cultural world. And here too Kunstadter's remark cited earlier is apposite. In this sense the household is the primary context for everyday action and experience. Thus it is one of the most important social arenas for learning the principles and assumptions that enable social relations both within and beyond the household.

In both cases, since the household is a recognised social unit with distinctive characteristics, it is not a socially neutral context for this constitution of experience, whether it be the members' or the ethnographer's. Thus we need to examine what is particular to the household in South Asia, its structure, its social relations, its functions and the meanings enacted within it in order to reveal the inflection these features impart to members' knowledge. From our perspective, as a 'domicile' (see Kondos in this volume) the household punctuates or brackets people's forays into other, and usually larger-scale, social domains. Further, from Sahlins' work there is some legitimacy in viewing such larger-scale domains as a set of households linked in specific ways that are partly the consequences of endogenous domestic structures and processes.[5] Such a view of the household also suggests that

---

[5] Just how much the endogenous character of the household affects the ways households are linked in the formation of larger-scale domains is also an important derivative issue that needs to be explored ethnographically.

the particular experience of abstract social principles—which are analytically constituted by the ethnographer—emergent in it has implications for members' interpretations of, and actions in, these larger-scale realms. There-fore, the household becomes a significant framework for analysing the nature of socio-cultural principles and institutions which spatially and con-ceptually may be seen to exist 'outside' it.

Our approach, therefore, involves a double analytic movement. First, like the perspective taken by Netting, Wilk and Arnould (1984), we emphasise the identification of the structure and processes particular to the domestic domain. However, for them the basic issue is to explain the variations in households both within and between societies and to do so they look to the endogenous structural, behavioural and conceptual dimensions as the source of such variations. That is, they limit themselves to social factors *within* the household to explain its variations. Thus their perspective is susceptible to the problems associated with treating any social realm as an isolated unit.

While our approach maintains the focus on the household, it shifts the analytic problem away from its variations as that which is to be explained to its particular structure, practices and cultural logic as that which explains some important aspects of wider society. Thus, far from being an isolated unit, we treat the household's particularity, its location in, and relations to, wider society as central to its analysis. However, as argued earlier in relation to the ethnographies of Beck and Parry, by adopting an inside-out approach, we are also reversing the usual conception of the household's relation to wider society.[6] This is the second analytic movement; and it necessitates developing a way of describing the household which allows the recognition of its particularity and partial autonomy while at the same time enabling the discovery of its consequences for larger-scale social domains.

Yanagisako (1979) provides an excellent review of the issues involved in defining the 'family', 'household', and 'domestic group'. She argues that in the constant focus on genealogical relationships there has been a continuing implicit assumption that the essential function of the family, household or domestic group is 'the reproduction of society's members' (ibid.: 199). She advocates that 'we abandon the search for an irreducible core of the family and its universal definition' and not deny the cross-cultural structural and functional diversity of what these 'odd job words' describe (ibid.: 200). Yanagisako is able to advocate a tolerance of odd-job descriptive concepts in ethnographic analysis because she too tends to assume an outside-in perspective. When the household is understood as a manifestation of general

---

[6] One way of establishing the legitimacy of this inside-out approach is based upon its replication of the phenomenological understanding of the social processes by which human culture is constituted as a shared set of interpretive schemes that enable social life.

principles—whether these be religious, political or economic—there is no
necessity to distinguish it rigorously from other social domains because the
aim of the explanation is to show how it is similar to others in that all are
sequiturs of the same principles. However, an inside-out approach does
require a clear conception of the household and its features as a distinct and
distinctive social domain if we take it as a significant locus for ethnographic
fieldwork, the constitution of the socio-cultural world and members' knowledge of it. Still we take the import of Yanagisako's argument and avoid a
conception oriented only by genealogical relations and aimed at accommodating every empirical instance of what people term the 'household'.
Instead we attempt to provide a heuristic conception which allows scope for
exploring the particularity of South Asian households.

Provisionally, we suggested to the contributors that the household in
South Asia is a specific confluence of three forms of social relations—kinship,
production, and consumption—including the functions and meanings co-
implicated by them. Together they entail a territorial dimension, which is
usually manifest in 'co-residence',[7] as the locus for the practise of these
relations. Singly, each of these forms of social relatedness orients domains
other than the domestic. Thus it is the specific way they mutually interpenetrate which constitutes the household as a distinct social group and its
particular endogenous characteristics.

Most ethnographic accounts of South Asian households involve identify-
ing a genealogical matrix of membership and social relations. In some way
or other domestic groups are meaningfully, if not structurally, oriented by
kinship reckoning. But this does not imply that kinship is either a necessary
or sufficient condition of membership. It provides the 'core' of the structural and conceptual dimensions of the household while allowing other
people to be incorporated on the basis of other types of social relatedness. In
this respect we concur with Carter's notion that the domestic is composed of
two dimensions: the 'familial' and the 'household':

> . . . the familial dimension of the domestic group is distinguished from
> the household dimension. The former is defined by the origin of the
> links between its members, links that have their source in culturally
> defined relations of birth, adoption, and marriage regardless of whether
> those who are so linked live together or engage in any shared tasks.
> The household dimension of the domestic group, on the contrary, is
> defined by shared tasks of production and/or consumption, regardless
> of whether its members are linked by kinship or marriage or are co-
> resident (1984: 45).

[7] Co-residence is one form the territorial dimension of the domestic domain may take. It is
the usual one in South Asia. However, in other societies the specific realisation of the territorial
locus of domestic social practices may vary.

Further, just as concepts of **genealogical** relatedness do not by themselves necessarily entail co-residence or co-activity, neither do they imply procreation as the basic function of the household. Kinship forms a central dimension of other large-scale social groups (e.g., clans, tribal groups) without procreation as the essential *raison d'être*. Moreover, Godelier (1978) and Sahlins (1972) have persuasively demonstrated the variety of functions kinship groups may fulfil in society, and there is no reason to deny this variety to the household. Thus it is necessary to look beyond kinship in order to describe the particularity of the domestic.

Production is a second structural matrix of the household. In rural South Asia, there are two aspects of production that are central to the domestic group. These are the relations entailed by rights of access to productive resources—principally land but also including crafts skills—and the division of labour—principally organised by gender. Both are appropriated into the kinship nexus of the domestic groups such that it is culturally difficult not to see them as integral parts of the genealogical framework. Sharma's description of the household in northwest India in terms of the genealogically-based male dominance in relations to productive resources and the primary economic dependence of women (1980: 198) seems to hold generally for most of the South Asian region. Again we do not imply that rights of access to productive resources and labour relations are dimensions unique to the household. Yet the domestic productive matrix is perhaps distinctive because it is essentially intended to directly provide for the consumption needs of its members. And this makes it integral to the third relational matrix—consumption.

Conceptually the household is constituted by the 'hearth group'—those people who have rights to eat food prepared at a common hearth. That is, domestic commensality concerns the rights members have to the produce or income generated from household productive resources. The importance of the notion of the hearth group in South Asia is not so much the empirical necessity that household members always eat together. Rather, it encapsulates the common rights to the product of household resources which is manifest whenever members eat together. In the practice of sharing food cooked at a common hearth, members of the household physically and conceptually constitute their selves as a distinct social unit who consequently share a common bodily substance. Further, commensality is the metonym of the more general right of members to household income for the provision of all culturally defined subsistence needs. Thus domestic commensality is a 'total social fact' (Mauss 1954) enacting the special ethos of the household which is not limited *a priori* to a particular functional or structural orientation.

As implied in the reference to Mauss' notion of the total social fact, while it is necessary to identify these relational ingredients of the household, it is not sufficient because they are parts of an encompassing whole which South

Asians themselves recognise and which effects the way they are practised
and interrelated. Thus, in order to fully describe the particularity of the
domestic domain there must also be a holistic conception of the household.
Happily, as we noted at the start, for Hindu South Asia, such a conception is
explicit in the notion of the *grihastha asrama*—a conception which highlights
and gives a particular meaning to the procreative, sacrificial, productive and
distributive functions of the household; all are in service of sustaining the
social and cosmic worlds which figuratively may be understood as the
dharma of the household.

The ethnographic analysis of the household as a distinct social unit is only
the first stage of an inside-out approach. The second stage involves un-
covering the implications of the domestic for the structural, behavioural and
conceptual nature of larger-scale social realms. If, as we suggested previously,
the household is a significant context for the generation of intersubjective
experience and knowledge of society, then the particular holistic configuration
of the kinship, production, and consumption matrices that constitutes the
household must be seen to inflect that experience and knowledge. Further,
there are large-scale social realms which may be profitably conceived as
different formations of households linked together in specific ways. Hamlets
and villages in South Asia are the immediate examples which suggest that we
explore how the intersubjective experience and knowledge generated in the
household is extended analogically or homologically to the interpreting of
relations in these larger-scale contexts. This is the strategy taken in Gray's
paper.

However, while we do not advocate analysing all social units as different
formations of linked households, we do suggest that it is because the
household is the primary context in which people constitute their experience
and knowledge of society and its basic principles that they also bring such
knowledge and experience to bear upon their understanding of, and practices in, these other social contexts.

By taking this approach, we do not deny the complementary outside-in
perspective in which basic principles and processes particular to, and
generated in, larger-scale encompassing social domains impinge upon the
nature of households and other smaller-scale social units. It is just that the
latter has been the dominant mode of ethnography which, while powerful, is
not exhaustive. It is in complementarity to this that we propose an inside-out
approach with a focus on the household, though for other societies, the
'inside' may be a different small-scale and relational intensive social unit.

The Papers

In compiling this volume, we have deliberately tried to assemble work by writers whose perspectives and interests complement each other. Their papers, of course, could have been arranged in a number of ways depending upon which of a variety of analytical points we felt it most appropriate to highlight. In the end we decided not to privilege any particular theme in our arrangement. Rather, we feel that in conjunction with our introduction, the more 'active' reader of this volume could be left to establish his or her own view on which of the themes are worthy of emphasis. As a result, the sequence of essays is designed to take the reader simply from the core issues and locations of northern and southern India to the comparative ethnography of the margins of the region and beyond. The goal is to present the arguments in such a way as to allow the problem of the analysis of the household to be addressed from a range of viewpoints. We have also tried to present the reader with an opportunity to consider the relationship between an author's style of analysis and the nature of the chosen 'problematic'.

Thus, the papers have a tri-polar organisation. Some, like McGilvray's and Vatuk's take the case study style in order to present the fine-grained ethnography so important to the understanding of the variety of forms the domestic takes in South Asia. Other papers, like Kondos', Gray's and Mearns', begin with an analytical issue about the household which is critically explored in the ethnography. Still others, like Kolenda's and Sharma's show how the variety and dynamism of domestic form in South Asia is related to historical, geographic, economic and social conditions in which it is constituted. Clearly, a concentration upon the household does not predict either a single approach or point of focus for the specific analysis of the relationships encompassed within its social space.

As we have said, the 'household' has been the subject of much debate in recent years (see for example Netting, Wilk and Arnould 1984 and Smith et al. 1984). However, as we have also already noted, much of that debate has been at a very general level and has chosen empirical material from an extremely diverse set of societies. Where the debate has focused on the function of the household in relation to the processes at work in the larger social system, the conclusions have all too often had to remain rather general and unilluminating precisely because the forms and functions of the household in their particular contexts are highly variable.

Thus, for example, the assessment that the domestic group is a primary location for the reproduction of labour power in a world dominated and penetrated by the forces of International Capital may well be to identify a major and growing function of the household in many parts of the world. What inevitably remains to be explained, and what is at the heart of the Netting volume, is precisely the astounding variety in form of the household even if one were to agree that reproduction of labour power is its major contemporary function. We of course would add that in this essentially Marxist approach explanations are often also lacking for the *other* functions the domestic group performs; for the varying ranges of relationships which the household encompasses: for its capacity to mediate the effects of capitalist penetration; for its relevance to the processes of cultural transformation and, above all, for its role in shaping experience. In the papers in this volume, these issues are discussed in a number of different ways, but always in terms of households which have a location in social and cultural systems originating in the Indian sub-continent.

The advantages of discussions of a problem in terms of a sphere of geographical, social and cultural contiguity are manifold. Perhaps the single most obvious one to emerge from this volume is that it enables us to see and develop a more positive and less contradictory relationship between the analytical and the experiential significance of the household in general and for understanding South Asian society in particular. We began to develop our perspective in response to what we saw as the risk of 'premature delivery' resulting from too rapid an evaluation of the theoretical relevance of a particular social form. To make too quick a judgement on the social and cultural significance of the household may be to beg a lot of logically prior questions as to the very nature of that form and whether it is indeed identifiable as a single logical entity. This danger is evident even in the cases available from the one region on which we focus here. We do need to consider some basic questions about the essential similarities and differences in the sets of relations which analysts have chosen to identify as 'household' or 'domestic'. We hope that this volume provides a useful comparative starting point for such considerations.

In the course of analysing the various contexts from which they derive the substantive material of the following chapters, the authors inevitably do address the relevance of concepts of kinship and the family (see Kolenda, Sharma and Vatuk), the role of women and gender relations (see Kondos), the dynamics of the domestic cycle (see Vatuk), and ideas related to production, consumption and the use of labour (see Mearns). As our authors' citations indicate, in the works of earlier writers each of these issues has been central to particular versions of how those analysts believe the role of domestic relations should be represented in anthropological attempts to characterise social organisation. While the conclusions of our writers often differ with regard to the significance of the household, because, in part, they have set themselves different problems, each adds to our capacity to consider the extent to which it is worthwhile to argue for a single or even dominant meaning to be attached to the social processes entailed in living in a South Asian domestic group.

The conclusions a reader may draw then will undoubtedly have a wider relevance than merely the obvious ones for people interested in natives of the Indian subcontinent. What are raised are indeed some fundamental and general questions for our theoretical understanding and our methodology.

Many of these general questions are the very subject of our first paper by Ursula Sharma, which explicitly undertakes to examine some of those core issues which lie at the heart of the analysis of the household. She renders problematical the very assumption of the household as a bounded and collective group; an assumption upon which she believes the moral concept of the domestic group held by South Asians themselves is based as well as the analysis of it by anthropologists. Accordingly, she presents a 'frankly methodological' discussion which takes account of recent arguments in relation to the household in general and in South Asia in particular. She notes the seductive attraction that the moral force and cultural emphasis given to the household by South Asians themselves engenders and the effect that this has had on previous analyses. She suggests that a useful starting point for testing the 'taken-for-granted' nature of the household is to focus on the relationship of the individual to the household.

After providing some case histories, Sharma concentrates on the relative position of women and men with regard to choices and decision making, especially with respect to the possibilities of personal mobility. The ambivalence of north Indians to women in wage labour is also examined. Finally she suggests that a combination of processual analysis and the 'new approaches' to the household should prove productive.

In the following chapter, Pauline Kolenda examines the household in relation to its definition in the Indian census in terms of the sharing of food production and consumption. Noting the prevalence of nuclear or supplemented nuclear families in this context, she asks 'So what of the much vaunted Indian joint family?' She observes that the nuclear family is commonly reported as being locked in a matrix of kin relationships in a given locality. She warns against the assumption of simple patterns of organisation derived from logic rather than from fine-grained accounts of practices. Kolenda moves to the analysis of a sample of the 1961 Census data in order to consider the social variables which lie behind the pattern of joint family distribution which she is able to identify in Rajasthan. Her data are examined in detail in terms of the social, geographic, and kinship relations which affect the particular form they take. An important point clearly identified by Kolenda is that while the singular term 'joint family household' implies a single domestic phenomenon, she is able to specify three distinct characteristic types of joint family: the protective joint family, the well-team joint family, and the egalitarian joint family. Kolenda attempts to show how the particularity of each type emerges from the interaction of domestic processes and principles with varying social, economic and ecological processes to which it is adapting.

Sylvia Vatuk's paper is also based on not assuming that the concept of joint household refers to a monolithic phenomenon. She focuses her paper on data collected in 1984 from the south Indian cities of Madras and

Hyderabad. She sets out to examine the cultural, religious and regional heterogeneity of Indian life as witnessed in the activities of the household. Very conscious of the problems of generalisation, Vatuk surveys those offered by other scholars on the difference between north and south India and between Hindu and Muslim households. She finds that her particular data on Muslims from the south tend to show greater degrees of difference than other writers appear to have allowed. She also addresses the issues of social change and the effect this has on models such as that of the 'domestic cycle' which assume a basic social stability. The history of the central Urdu-speaking lineage of the 150 households—which form the basis of analysis—is traced in detail and her analysis suggests that we may have to reconceive the 'domestic cycle' as a 'domestic spiral' to incorporate the changes occurring in the contemporary domestic domain. Patterns of contemporary marriage and household organisation in the face of considerable labour migration of young males are considered as a significant transformational force. The consequent and parallel changing roles of women and the need to examine households in terms of their new situation and context form the final section of the chapter.

A Hindu, but strictly non-'Indian' context, is the basis of our next paper. John Gray elaborates the concerns expressed in the first part of this intro-duction when he examines the Nepalese household as a distinctive context of social life of which neither the form nor significance is determined in some simple and direct manner by wider social processes and principles. He goes on to consider the centrifugal effect of household formation on the structure and economic processes of the hamlet and village. Reviewing the work of Brenda Beck, Gray offers an alternative approach based on the social theory of Weber and Schutz which focuses first and foremost on the interaction within the household. The role of the household as primary context for the experience, transformation and conscious attention to struc-tural principles of South Asian social life—such as hierarchy and equality—is stressed. The ethnographic locus comprises the Brahman-Chetri households of southern Kathmandu Valley. A detailed examination of the composition and interaction of these households is undertaken through discussion of a series of dyadic relationships encompassed within them. These are the father-son, the husband-wife, the brother-brother and the brother-sister relations, each of which is dealt with in terms of the cultural loading inherent in its form. Functional relations with respect to land and hearth are matched with cultural understandings of hierarchy and equality in providing evidence for the conclusions drawn in regard to the central place of house-hold dyadic relationships in constituting social meaning. The analysis broadens out to a discussion of the hamlet as a set of households and looks at its and the village's essential replication of the configuration of household relationships. The analysis concludes with a linking of the village system to the regional caste system.

Vivienne Kondos' paper both complements and contrasts with the preceding chapter. It also focuses on Nepalese households but specifically addresses them from the perspective of the lives of high caste women. Noting that complementarity is not necessarily incompatible with inequality, Kondos discusses some work on gender relations which she finds inadequate for application to the Nepalese context. She too suggests that an over developed concern with aspects of the male 'outside' world tends to undervalue the cultural and social significance of the female and the domestic. The critical focus for understanding the disadvantages faced by Parbatiya (high caste Hindu) women is the analysis of the position of both affinal and consanguinal women in the household. We must beware, says Kondos, of the indiscriminate use of the purity/pollution opposition as a 'catch all' explanation; other, no less Hindu, concepts may be invoked to account for household social relationships. In considering the 'domicile', as she calls it, Kondos invokes the theory of the three *gunas*. She goes on to consider the range of strategic options available to women and finds that there are few that do not entail subordination to other males or more general servility, there being so few opportunities for economic or legal independence. Women's success is predefined and failure an everpresent threat.

Moving away from the South Asian mainland, Dennis McGilvray's paper takes us to the Hindu and Muslim town of Akkaraipattu in the eastern province of Sri Lanka. McGilvray sets the background of the ethnic differences between the two matrilineal populations, the 'Moors' (Sunni Muslims) and the 'Tamils' (Shaivite Hindus), and the divisions within the categories, all of which are reflected in spatial organisation. A detailed account of the form of the local houses in relation to the social organisation of family structure follows. This in turn leads to a discussion of the essentially identical matrilineal kinship structures of the two basic populations. Preference for bilateral cross-cousin marriage and the existence of exogamous matriclans serve as a basis for discussion of marriage practices which show tendencies for repetition of alliance patterns. The patterns of post-marital residence are shown to involve men marrying out and parents moving domicile frequently as they give their house as dowry at the marriage of a daughter. The inbuilt dynamics of the local household are further traced in the changing personnel and leadership roles through time. The control of household and family affairs devolves upon the senior son-in-law who is carefully recruited for this purpose. His importance is culturally marked in a number of ways. All males are shown enjoying much greater freedom of movement than the women whose cultural universe is generally much smaller.

The linkage between households amongst Hindu Tamils is shown to include the vertical stratification of caste attachments. Moorish groups are not marked by this sort of arrangement, though they do employ low caste Hindus for some purposes. Amongst Moors, class status appears to play a more prominent role. The domestic ritual obligations of Muslims and Hindus are compared and shown to have similar orientations. Unlike patrilineal India, the concept of death pollution appears underdeveloped for these matrilineal groups. Also, in Akkaraipattu mixed caste marriages are shown to result in the offspring inheriting the mother's caste affiliation. The final section of McGilvray's paper examines several case studies illustrating the dynamics of household forms. Among these is a fascinating example of how education and out-migration of both young males and females is presently altering relationships within the domestic context. The data analysed here parallel those offered by Vatuk in particular and provide us with some interesting comparative material. They clearly place contemporary Sri Lankan domestic forms in a direct relationship with the global economy and raise questions about the effect of such forces at the local level.

The paper by David Mearns shifts the focus to overseas South Asians in the multi-ethnic nation of Malaysia. The discussion is one which returns us explicitly to the consideration of the processes by which the household is constituted rather than beginning by assuming its constitution and integration prior to the analysis. It examines the relationship between membership of a household located within a system of politically imposed ethnic categories and the creation and maintenance of social identity. These issues are further considered in relation to the processes of re-production of larger social structures all the way up to the international economy. The role of cultural factors and their interpretation in the creation of Hindu social understandings and meanings are seen as central to the analysis of the position of Indians in the town of Melaka. The ways in which households are formed and domestic space ordered is considered for two of the major, self-defining subsets of the Indian population, the middle class 'Ceylonese' and the Indian labourers. Using the further example of the Malay-speaking Melaka Chitty Hindus, there follows a discussion of the underlying structural principles of the cultural organisation of household space, which, it is argued, is essentially the same for all the Hindu 'Indians'. The implications of these patterns for relationships within and beyond the domestic context are then pursued. Ritual and cultural understandings of space are seen as fundamental to the creation of social identity but do not stand in grand isolation. Class and status in the wider 'Indian' and non-Indian society are found to be related to caste and linguistic identity within the Indian population. These themselves are found to be formed and re-formed in the relationships within and between domestic groups. It is argued that processes in both the wider social system and the household must be understood, therefore, if we are to explain the failure of a solidary Indian ethnic identity to emerge in a situation which would seem to demand it.

The Findings: The Domestic Mediation of
the Individual and Society

The social and cultural processes which constitute the household are perhaps given greater emphasis in the works of Sharma, Kolenda and McGilvray, while the papers by Vatuk, Gray, Kondos and Mearns emphasise the socially constitutive force of household processes. However, all the authors seek to show how the social world of South Asians is given shape in the interrelationships of prior but evolving social circumstances with the small-scale forces at work in domestic inter- and intra-action. What each of the papers demonstrates and what emerges from them all collectively is that the household remains absolutely central to bringing together the experiential and analytic interpretations of complex societies just as it has taken a basic role in the accounts of smaller-scale societies with less elaborated technologies and forms of social division. Indeed, one can go much further. To paraphrase Sahlins (1972), while there may not strictly be a Domestic Mode of Production in South Asian society, there is a domestic mode of cultural constitution. These papers demonstrate that for the purpose of advancing our analytical understanding it is vital that we adopt a methodology sensitive to the micro forces at work in social life. Without a sophisticated consideration of this dimension of social experience we are constantly at risk of producing grand generalisations and assertions about social life which are 'true' for no particular person living within that social system. The more 'complex' the system becomes, the more it seems necessary for anthropologists to generate such grand abstractions. So the household, while ethnographically and experientially significant, becomes analytically epiphenomenal. We are, after all, dealing with human society and any analysis which omitted consideration of the role specifically located people play in the evolution of the complex system would be denying the essential humanity it entails. As this collection shows, the more we are able to detail the way in which people are affected by and *are able to affect* the social world they inhabit, the better will be our understanding of that social world. Large-scale structural forces may appear

external but they get their energy from people who are continually gene-
rating and regenerating the social system from within their own experiential
realms.

For the writers represented here then, the recognition of the household as
part of a dynamic set of processes does entail a need to consider the *history*
of the form and content of household relationships as well as their context.
The simple 'domestic cycle' model does not any longer seem adequate, if
indeed it ever was, to describe the major trends in household formation and
transformation. Our authors do all wish to argue for an approach which
allows the complexity and sensitivity of the domestic group in relation to
wider social processes to emerge and so they have in fact all dealt with the
household as part of a larger set of relationships and each has argued in
some sense that the social identity of household members is predicated on a
dialectical relationship between the domestic context and the social and
cultural processes within which it has its being.

A recurrent theme in this approach has been the way in which inequality
is generated and experienced. Whether referring to gender, class or caste,
the analyses generally support the point that inequality and hierarchy are
endemic in relations within and between households. Moreover, it is not
simply a matter of the effects of one or more 'outside' systems which is the
source of status and/or power differences in and through intra- and inter-
domestic relationships. Just as much as it is a matter of the effects of an
external class system or the manifestation of abstract cultural principles,
inequality like other social forces is given its reality in the collective experience of life within this most intimate context of social interaction as well as
between this context and others similar and dissimilar. Put another way, on
the evidence of these papers it is household relations which may be said to
be the major experiential mediator between the 'individual' and 'society'. It
is also the primary context through which both are reproduced. Domestic
relationships are not then seen by our authors to be a separate 'domain' in
any simple sense. They are inextricably bound up with the processes which
constitute and reconstitute social experience at all levels.

● ● ●

References

Beck, B.E.F. 1972. *Peasant Society in Konku: A study of Right and Left Subcastes in South India.*
    Vancouver: University of British Columbia Press.
Bender, D. 1967. A Refinement of the Concept of Household: Family, Co-residence, and
    Domestic Functions. *American Anthropologist* 70: 309–20.

Bennett, L. 1983. *Dangerous Wives and Sacred Sisters: Social and Symbolic Roles of High-Caste Women in Nepal.* New York: Columbia University Press.

Berreman, G.D. 1972. *Hindus of the Himalayas.* Berkeley, California: University of California Press.

Carter, A.T. 1984. Household Histories. *In* R. McC. Netting, R.R. Wilk and E.J. Arnould (eds.), *Households: Comparative and Historical Studies of the Domestic group*, pp. 44–83. Berkeley, California: University of California Press.

Daniel, E.V. 1984. *Fluid Signs: Being a Person the Tamil Way.* Berkeley, California: University of California Press.

Dumont, L. 1960. World Renunciation in Indian Religions. *Contributions to Indian Sociology* 4: 32–62.

Dumont, L. 1980. *Homo Hierarchicus.* Chicago: University of Chicago Press.

Fricke, T.E. 1987. *Himalayan Households: Tamang Demography and Domestic Process.* Ann Arbor, Michigan: UMI Research Press.

Godelier, M. 1978. Infrastructures, Society and History. *Current Anthropology* 19 (4): 763–71.

Gray, J.N. 1980. Hypergamy, Kinship and Caste Among the Chettris of Nepal. *Contributions to Indian Sociology* (ns) 14 (1): 1–33.

Hammel, E.A. 1984. On the *** of Studying Household Form and Function. *In* R. McC. Netting, R.R. Wilk and E.J. Arnould (eds.), *Households: Comparative and Historical Studies of the Domestic Group*, pp. 29–43. Berkeley, California: University of California Press.

Heesterman, J.C. 1982. Householder and Wanderer. *In* T.N. Madan (ed.), *Way of Life: King, Householder, Renouncer*, pp. 251–71. New Delhi: Vikas Publishing House.

Khare, R.S. 1976. *The Hindu Hearth and Home.* New Delhi: Vikas Publishing House.

Kolenda, P.M. 1968. Region, Caste and Family Structure: A Comparative Study of the Indian 'Joint Family'. *In* M.Singer and B.S. Cohn (eds.), *Structure and Change in Indian Society*, pp. 339–96. New York: Wenner-Gren Foundation for Anthropological Research.

Kunstadter, P. 1984. Cultural Ideals, Socioeconomic Change, and Household Composition: Karen, Lua', Hmong, and Thai in Northwestern Thailand. *In* R. McC. Netting, R.R. Wilk and E.J. Arnould (eds.), *Households: Comparative and Historical Studies of the Domestic Group*, pp. 299–329. Berkeley, California: University of California Press.

Levi-Strauss, C. 1963. *Structural Anthropology.* Garden City, New York: Doubleday and Company, Inc.

Madan, T.N. 1965. *Family and Kinship: A Study of the Pandits of Rural Kashmir.* New Delhi: Asia Publishing House.

Mauss, M. 1954. *The Gift: Forms and Functions of Exchange in Archaic Societies.* London: Routledge and Kegan Paul.

Mayer, A.C. 1960. *Caste and Kinship in Central India: A Village and its Region.* Berkeley, California: University of California Press.

Netting, R.McC., R.R. Wilk, and E.J. Arnould. 1984. Introduction. *In* R.McC Netting et al. (eds.), *Households: Comparative and Historical Studies of the Domestic Group*, pp. xiii–xxxviii. Berkeley, California: University of California Press.

Parry, J.P. 1979. *Caste and Kinship in Kangra.* London: Routledge and Kegan Paul.

Rosaldo, M.Z. 1974. Woman, Culture, and Society: A Theoretical Overview. *In* M.Z. Rosaldo and L. Lamphere (eds.), *Woman, Culture and Society*, pp. 17–42. Stanford, California: Stanford University Press.

Sahlins, M. 1972. *Stone Age Economics.* London: Tavistock Publications.

Schutz, A. 1972. *The Phenomenology of the Social World.* London: Heinemann Books.

Shah, A.M. 1974. *The Household Dimension of the Family in India.* Berkeley, California: University of California Press.

Sharma, U. 1980. *Women, Work, and Property in North-West India.* London: Tavistock Publications.

Sharma, U. 1986. *Women's Work, Class and the Urban Household: A Study of Shimla, North India.* London: Tavistock Publications.

Smith, J., I. Wallerstein, H.E. Evers (eds.). 1984. *Households and the World Economy.* Beverly Hills: Sage.

Srinivas, M.N. 1976. *The Remembered Village.* Berkeley, California: University of California Press.

Vatuk, S. 1972. *Kinship and Urbanization: White Collar Migrants in North India.* Berkeley California: University of California Press.

Weber, M. 1978. *Economy and Society.* Berkeley, California: University of California Press.

Yanagisako, S.J. 1979. Family and Household: The Analysis of Domestic Groups. *Annual Review of Anthropology* 8: 161–205.

1

Studying the Household: Individuation and Values

Ursula Sharma

THE INTENT of this paper is frankly methodological rather than ethnographic. This may disappoint some readers but my experience of researching the household in South Asia has made me aware that some critical assessment of this concept is due.

Recent work on the domestic domain in South Asia has tended to favour the concept of the household at the expense of that of the family. The domestic group was formerly analysed mainly in terms of its role structure, the way in which it socialised individuals into these roles and the rules which governed its composition and development. Social scientists now seek to ground this normative work within a unit whose basis is prosaically material. The domestic group (both in Western and in 'Third World' societies) is now treated as being constituted through the exchange of concrete goods and practical time-consuming services.

This tendency is not confined to any one discipline. In anthropology it had taken the form of a new emphasis on the systematic properties of the household. The household, argue the editors of a recent volume of anthropological and historical papers on the subject, 'is the fundamental social unit . . . 'the next biggest thing on the social map after the individual" '. Households have 'an emergent property which makes them more than the sum of their parts' (Netting, Wilk and Arnould 1984: xxii). Other anthropologists have recognised the problems of treating the household as a bounded unit, but nonetheless continue to refer to it as though it were an unproblematic social agent. Thus Wallman, in a recent study, discusses the household as a resource system but recognises that households may be 'differently bounded in respect of different resources available to them, the resources they choose to deploy, and the kind of value they vest in them for particular purposes in local or cultural contexts of various kinds' (Wallman 1984: 21). And the boundaries of a particular household group may change over time in the course of the domestic cycle (ibid.: 24). All the same, households are treated as real units which 'assess options' 'use resources' or 'see themselves' in a particular way.

Another influential manifestation of this general tendency is the approach which applies microeconomics to the household, analysing it as though it were a kind of small-scale firm or production unit. 'The basis of the new economic theory of the family is that the household is a productive unit—not necessarily in the sense of producing physical goods and services, though this may be one of its functions, but in the sense of producing benefits of all kinds for its members' (Papps 1980: 14).

My own view is that this shift from studying families to studying households is a constructive change since it enables us to ask questions which the functionalist framework made it difficult to pose. Yet the new approach leaves a number of problems unsolved, two of which I have selected for discussion here. One is the problem of the relationship between the individual and the household and the whole question of whether the systemic nature of the household has not been over-estimated. The second issue is that of how to accommodate norms and values within a model of the household which tends to view household processes in terms of the economic costs and advantages of various courses of action, and the interests of individuals or groups within the household. I shall subject the notion of the household as a primary unit in society to critical assessment in the light of work which has been done on Hindu society in north India since that is the limit of my expertise, but I should be surprised if what I write does not have wider application.

The Household as a System

One of the problems for researchers in South Asia, whether they be South Asians themselves or foreigners, is the fact that local ideology itself gives much emphasis to the collective nature of the domestic group, and it is difficult not to be influenced by this. The solidarity and positive value of the household receives strong moral emphasis by the people who are studied themselves. In both the rural and the urban areas where I have done fieldwork,[1] people generally feel sorry for an individual who is obliged for lack of kin to live alone or in an institution. A strong, and preferably large, household group based on kinship is regarded as indisputably the most

---

[1] The fieldwork I shall refer to in this paper was conducted in Ghanyari, a village in Himachal Pradesh (1966–67 and at intervals since), in the villages of Harbassi (Punjab) and Chaili (Himachal Pradesh) (1977–78), and in the Himachal city of Shimla (1982–83). The second two projects were funded by the Social Science Research Council.

effective and most legitimate way of satisfying personal needs, both material and emotional. It is quite in order for this group to demand the subordination of individual members' desires or inclinations in the interests of its own integrity or continuation, and members must be ready to accede to this discipline in their own long-term interest. This ideology is not unlike ideologies of the household that exist in other societies, but it is very persuasive and pervades discourse about the domestic domain in South Asia. What we as social scientists have to ask is whether we really *know* that the household is some kind of system, and not simply a conglomeration of individuals whose life trajectories throw them together for a longer or shorter period of time. We need to question the taken-for-granted nature of the household unit, rather in the way that Barrett and Macintosh have questioned the taken-for-granted nature of family life in Western societies in their book *The Anti-Social Family.*

A useful way to tackle this question might be to take the relationship between the individual and the household as our point of departure. What circumstances are conducive to individuals being prepared to accept the discipline involved in household living, and under what conditions are individuals (or groups of individuals) within the household likely to decide that independent living will best suit their needs?

There is of course an established body of research which attends to the relationships among the sub-groups which constitute the 'joint family' household, in particular the way in which such households cohere or succumb to partition (e.g., Madan 1965: 164ff, Parry 1979: 150ff). Much of this literature is dominated by a concern with the relationship between household form and modernisation (urbanisation, industrialisation, or some other characterisation of the spread of the social relations typical of industrial capitalism in the West). On this count, one can do no more by way of summary than state that there are evidently local circumstances in contemporary South Asia which favour the maintenance of large complex households, while others discourage such arrangements. What the literature does suggest very strongly, however, is that the scale of household which it is easy to maintain where resources are scarce is very small. Where anthropologists have recorded household size, there is usually a manifest tendency for the average size of households among the poor or low castes to be smaller than that among the more substantial castes (e.g., Lewis 1958: 16). In particular, 'joint' households seem uncommon among groups where chronic landlessness and economic insecurity are the norm.

Mandelbaum, for example, cites Gough's material from south India and Cohn's data from a Chamar community in north India to demonstrate how the very weak economic power which the father is able to wield over his adult sons (when he lacks land and his earning power as a labourer is reduced in middle age) makes it difficult for him to force them to remain under his roof (Mandelbaum 1972: 47–51). Another factor in the fragility of the low caste household which is mentioned by Mandelbaum is the earning capacity of low caste women. Where women are permitted by caste norms (or obliged through economic necessity) to take wage work outside the home they are likely to wield greater economic power within the household. Being more economically 'self-sufficient' they can divorce relatively easily, and not being secluded they are less amenable to the control of elders. Therefore disagreements among the female members of a joint family household are more likely to lead to its partition than in socio-economic groups where women are completely dependent on men (ibid.: 48–50).

According to this brand of conventional wisdom then, the household is a unit composed of determinate roles, governed by powerful norms about what it is to be a dutiful son, obedient wife, etc. But economic factors 'interfere' to make these ideals difficult to attain for people in the lowest strata of society since they lack the property and other resources which bolster the control which elders and males are expected to exert over juniors and women. This view represents a great advance on that which simply saw the differences between castes in terms of different norms, degrees of Sanskritisation, etc. But perhaps it does not go far enough. Is the 'independence' of women in low castes really independence, for instance?[2] If divorce is more acceptable in such communities, is this because women are exercising some kind of autonomy, a 'right to choose' in respect of sexual partner, or is it because they are liable to be abandoned by their husbands and, being abandoned, their best hope of survival is to find another partner as soon as possible? If landless men are under little constraint to stay with their parents if they choose not to do so (as Mandelbaum suggests), then may not the same apply to their relationships with their wives?

More evidence on the processes by which marital or parental relationships break down is needed, and as far as rural communities are concerned, this is very scanty. The ethnography of the dislocated urban poor does provide some hints. The work of writers such as Gulati (1981) and the Majumdars (1978) suggests that whilst the desertion of the household group by the husband is possible, the desertion by the wife is less likely. It would be most unusual for a wife at this level of society to have the kind of earning power that would make it an easy proposition to set up a household with her children independently of a husband for whom she did not care. Nor would it make her an attractive proposition to an unattached man seeking a partner. Indeed, if the husband's response to extreme poverty is to attempt to abandon his responsibilities to the wife and their children, then the fact

---

[2] See Karlekar (1984) for a useful discussion of this issue in relation to sweeper women.

that she is capable of earning a few rupees a day on her own account presumably makes it easier for him to do so, not harder. In a case cited by the Majumdars, Radha earns an occasional sum by building huts for other squatters in the slum colony where she lives. Her husband found it increasingly difficult to support their family on the Rs. 9 per day which he received as a labourer. Eventually he simply walked out on Radha, presumably knowing that she would either return to their village or somehow struggle along on her own earnings (1978: 73ff).

In situations like this, and particularly where the household has migrated from elsewhere and is without a local group of caste fellows or kin who might put moral pressure on either partner, there is little a woman can do to oblige her husband to share what he earns with her or with other members of the household. The Majumdars cite the case of Sita, a sweeper woman, who feeds her family on what she earns through rag picking and scavenging, since her husband seldom brings home any of the money he earns as a *chaprassi*. Sita claims that she stays with him only because 'in a city like Delhi it is better to live with a bad husband than without one' i.e., she would not be safe living on her own (1978: 86).[3]

At a certain level of poverty and insecurity it may be just as difficult for parents to oblige sons to contribute their earnings to the household pool of resources. Sara, the fish vendor described by Leela Gulati, cannot force her son Stellas to abandon his insistence that he take a 'clean' occupation and not dirty his hands doing manual work, in spite of the fact that Sara's husband Jose is permanently disabled and the household relies on Sara's income as a vendor and on the limited earnings of two younger brothers (Gulati 1981: 79ff). Kishni, the elderly sweeper woman described by the Majumdars (1978: 51), had no recourse when her sons robbed her, refused to support her and turned her out of their house to fend for herself. Although my own research did not concern groups suffering extreme insecurity, I often heard poor women express a sense of the conditionality of sons' contributions to the household budget. One sweeeper household in Shimla was, on the face of it, doing rather well since four of its members (including two adult sons) were earning as well as the two parents. But Shila, the mother, regarded this comfortable situation as a matter of provisional good fortune. 'My elder son will probably take his wife and set up his own household, and who knows how long my other son will go on giving me his wages?' she told me. In either of these eventualities Shila and her husband would have to support the younger children on only half the budget they commanded now. Whether this insecurity simply reinforces the preference

---

[3] For other cases of poor women whose husbands refuse to share their wages see Karlekar (1984: 84), Per-Lee (1984: 195).

for sons (after all, among a really large family of sons one at least is likely to prove loyal to his elderly parents) or whether it eventually will favour poor families' reliance on the aid or earnings of daughters, is a matter of speculation.

Poverty can of course, have the effect of producing a more concentrated household effort to cooperate and survive. The fragmentation of individual interests I have discussed above seems to occur only when the household appears to offer earning members no long-term benefits to offset what they contribute from their wages to the welfare of their dependents. An earning son, for instance, would be ill advised to cut himself off from his parents and siblings if he can count on his parents to arrange and pay for an advantageous marriage for him, or if he can expect his brothers and sisters to offer services, information, or concrete help in the future. In the absence of such guarantees or of any form of community control, there is less to hold a large group together and the individuation of the interests of earning members is liable to manifest itself.

Cash Wages and the Individuation of Interest

These anecdotal examples from studies based on very limited samples can hardly be said to demonstrate conclusively any particular trend in household organisation. Certainly it is not useful to speculate whether in some hypothetical 'good old days' even the most poverty stricken were constrained to acknowledge their own. It may well be that were the data available we might be able to identify quite different conditions at other levels of the socio-economic hierarchy which favour individuation for quite separate reasons. However, one general sociological question which I believe it is useful to ask and which has already stimulated some worthwhile discussion is whether or not wage labour favours the individualisation of resources in the household. Do not personal earnings increase the capacity for individuals or sub-groups within the household to establish separate funds which need not be pooled with other household resources or even divulged to other household members?

Hitherto this question has been discussed mainly in relation to the joint family household. Bailey regards the existence of new opportunities to earn money outside the village as one of the main reasons for the partitioning of the joint household in the area where he conducted fieldwork, since 'the joint family cannot survive divergent interests and disparate incomes among its members' (Bailey 1957: 92). Both Rao and Madan have pointed out that there are circumstances when a man employed in wage labour outside his own village finds the joint household an attractive arrangement, since there is material and social advantage to be gained if his wife and young children remain under the same roof as his brother while he is earning elsewhere (Madan 1965: 153; Rao 1972: 104ff). The most sophisticated discussion of this issue is provided by Parry (1979: 150ff) who holds that whether or not individual earnings drive a wedge between the members of a joint family household will depend on 'the balance of advantage' enjoyed by a particular sub-group within the complex household. The mere fact of a man's being employed outside the village need not predispose him to either joint or nuclear family living in itself; much depends on how many other members of the joint household are so employed, the amount he receives in comparison with other earners, what other economic activities are also going on in the household, etc.

It would be useful to open out this discussion so as to consider the effect of wage labour on the household in general rather than in relation to the joint family household alone. Where wage labour is associated with long distance migration, for instance, there is always the possibility that earning members through an adaptation of the existing division of labour, but there is In many parts of South Asia we find areas where a local economy is adjusted to the periodic or long-term absence of many adult males, whether their destination is some other part of India or one of the Gulf states.

In the majority of cases the household survives the lengthy absence of key members through an adaptation of existing division of labour, but there is always the risk that the absent member may fail to return. In the course of my 1977 fieldwork in Punjab I met or heard about a number of women (usually from families with little land) whose husbands had long since disappeared to Canada, Britain or some other foreign country. When the remittances became few and far between and eventually ceased, the assumption was that 'he has found himself a white girl over there'. One does not have to travel as far as Vancouver or Coventry to effect a desertion of this kind, only far enough to put a distance between oneself and any coercive attempts on one's kin or affines. In recent fieldwork in Shimla I came across the following two cases.

Mary, a well educated Christian woman had married a man of her own choice, a doctor in a well-known hospital. When their daughter was still a baby, he decided that he would migrate to Britain, where he had no difficulty in getting a job. Mary was to follow when he had established himself there and bought a house. However, his remittances to her became irregular and eventually ceased, and he never invited her to join him. He said that he had found an English woman whom he wished to marry. During a brief visit to India he set divorce procedures in motion, but Mary was never able to obtain the maintenance which the court ordered her husband to pay, and she never received any replies to her letters.

Rattana was a young woman from a farming family who had married at the age of 18. She returned to her parents' home for the birth of her child, a little girl, but her husband, who was employed in the army, never came to fetch her after the baby was born. He had been posted in a distant part of India and seldom returned even to visit his brothers (their parents were dead). Rattana decided that he had 'more or less left her' and turned her attention to finding a job near her parents' home. She still lives with her parents and saves as much as she can from her wages as a seamstress to pay for the education and marriage of her daughter.

I am not trying to suggest that such cases of divorce or desertion could only occur when the husband was earning away from home; simply that such circumstances made it easier for the husband to drift into a situation where he was in practice no longer supporting his wife and children, a unilateral break being made by default. There were, of course, many other forms of marital breakdown (see Sharma 1980: 155ff for an account of 'ruptured marriages'). Wives could always be repudiated, or ill treated to the extent that they no longer wished to live in their in-laws' houses. But such lines of conduct would be difficult for a locally resident husband to effect without the tacit consent or even cooperation of his own kin. Labour migration makes unilateral withdrawal more of a possibility.

Individual wages are also liable to complicate the relationship between a man and his parents. In a household producing for its own needs (or even for the market) without reliance on wage labour, the expectation that at least one son will stay at home and work the land as his parents grow older is likely to be fulfilled (although widows are vulnerable to the effects of conflicts between themselves and their daughters-in-law; see Sharma 1980: 171ff). Where a son is engaged in wage labour he may use his earnings (either as an individual or in collusion with his wife) to establish a private fund which is not pooled or made available to his parents and siblings. In a Himachal village I studied in 1977, for instance, there was the case of Devi, whose son Madan Lal was employed as a forest guard in another village. His young wife Kamala lived with Devi and helped her parents-in-law cultivate their land. Devi, although a mild enough woman, did not get on with her daughter-in-law and suspected that Madan Lal was giving Kamala most of his pay since his remittances to his mother were not as large as she felt they ought to be. She did not know for sure, however, how much he earned. One day Madan Lal was fired from his job because he had allegedly been caught taking a bribe. He wrote to his mother that he would be coming home shortly, bringing the money he had saved from his employment. When he arrived, however, he told his parents that he was penniless. He had, he claimed, had his pocket picked as he came home in the bus and lost the entire sum. Devi found this difficult to believe, not because such crimes are unknown, but because having one's pocket picked is a rather common excuse for not pooling one's cash. Madan Lal should have thought of a more original excuse. Devi felt sure that he and Kamala had secreted the money or deposited it in the bank without telling her. She feared that eventually they would use Madan's earnings to build a house of their own and demand partition of the family land.

In another case, three brothers lived jointly with their parents, who owned about 7 acres of land. One of the sons was fortunate enough to obtain a job as a driver in Dubai and for several years sent home sums of money beyond the dreams of his family. On the proceeds of his earnings the family bought land, a tractor and trailer, and built themselves a smart new house. Much credit accrued to the son who had provided for his parents and brothers so handsomely. More recently, however, he has sent less money home. Yet his wife always seems to have ready cash to buy herself and her children ample supplies of clothes and other necessities, which makes his mother and sister-in-law suspect that instead of sending money to his parents he now sends remittances separately to his wife. His mother had searched the wife's trunks and cupboards and had discovered neither bank book nor cash, but is still convinced that she has a secret fund of money which the couple do not wish to share with the wider group.

In these cases the existence of personal funds within the joint family household is a matter of contention and conflict, but some individuation of funds may be accepted as a normal practice in complex households. Among the urban households I studied in Shimla were a few wealthy joint family households, mostly business families or fairly well paid professionals. In a number of cases, examination of the way in which household budgets are decided and household funds organised revealed that a married couple would have individual or joint bank accounts in which they saved cash which was not destined to be shared by the whole household group but which was intended for their own present or future use. Where wives were in employment they frequently established post office or bank accounts from which they saved small amounts from their pay. In some cases these were earmarked for special purposes, e.g., the education or marriage of their own children. There did not seem to be anything particularly secret or contentious about such funds; it seemed to be accepted that individual wages gave people the right to save on their own account, provided they were prepared to chip in when some general expense had to be met by the entire group. In many cases the couple were quite open about the fact that they were accumulating funds to buy land or a house in which they would eventually live separately. In such cases the financial security of the parents was independently assured and the fact that their sons and daughters-in-law did not pool all their earnings was not in itself seen as a threat to domestic harmony.

My urban research (1982) suggests that there is often a resigned acceptance on the part of parents that when the entire structure of the household depends on the wages brought in by its different members, there is little they can do to force a recalcitrant son to hand over all his pay to their control. By extension even the wages of a daughter-in-law may also be beyond their control if the son is more disposed to economic collaboration with his wife than with his parents. The case is quite different with unmarried daughters. The wages of sons are outside the scope of parents' control to the extent that parents can only have limited control over adult sons' general activities and movements, whereas the activities and movements of grown daughters will be subject to quite strict scrutiny. This being so, it is not surprising that there is some evidence that in certain urban communities where unmarried women routinely take wage work, daughters are often regarded as more reliable contributors to the household budget than sons. There are data from various parts of Asia to support the view that if wage work has the potentiality of liberating sons from their parents' control, it also has the potentiality of reinforcing the control which households already seek to exert over their earning daughters (see, for instance, Trager's material on Philippine migrants, Trager 1984: 1274).

The partition of the joint family household is experienced as something which is painful, even traumatic (see Bennett 1983: 209) and indeed is often preceded by personal tensions or quarrelling. Perhaps it is for this reason that the detachment of the nuclear family from the joint family household has received so much attention from anthropologists, and the contrast and discontinuity between the two kinds of households emphasised. Yet what the foregoing discussion has demonstrated is that in fact there is a continuum of corporateness or collectivity of effort. At one pole we have the household (whatever its actual composition) in which there is minimal individuation of the interests of particular members or sub-groups. At the centre we have a unit in which there is incipient separation of funds or interests. At the opposite pole we have a situation in which a number of individuals or smaller household groups live separately and have separate budgets but may continue to cooperate in certain spheres.[4]

Communality and Cohesion

Instead of asking about the circumstances which favour individuation and the subdivision of interest within the domestic group, we can turn the question around and ask about the conditions in which it is relatively easy to maintain communality of purpose.

[4] For numerous descriptions of the cooperation of separate but related household groups see Shah (1974).

Clearly there are phases in the domestic cycle of some cultivating house holds when there are mutual benefits for a large and possibly complex group of kin to live together and cooperate in the farming of their land. This collective interdependence is likely to be particularly intense when there are few opportunities for members to earn income through wage labour and the welfare of individuals depends entirely on the success of the group in its productive efforts. I would conjecture that the collective effort is also likely to be more intense when the household cannot afford to hire servants and the women of the household therefore constitute a work-team which operates on both the domestic and the agricultural front. Such a situation does not, of course, preclude tension and quarrels within the household (if anything the reverse is likely to be true), but it does mean that the possibilities for the concrete expression of separate interests is strictly limited. The only way for individuals within the group to acquire and accumulate 'personal' funds would be to sell off the grain or other assets belonging to the household and convert the money so obtained to their private use (see Bennett 1983: 207).

Another situation in which household interdependence and internal cooperation is likely to be particularly pronounced is when the household is socially (and usually also geographically) mobile. In an expanding bureau-cratic town in north India where I conducted fieldwork in 1982, this was the experience of a number of households at various levels of the class hier-archy. Most of the workers here (mainly employed in the white collar, service and professional sectors) had migrated to the city. Most of them came from families which practised subsistence farming in their home areas but had managed to educate a few sons (and occasionally daughters also) to the level where they could expect to find urban employment. Many such workers not only experienced 'sideways' mobility (from the rural to the urban sector) but also upward mobility, since the bureaucratic hierarchies they joined often provided considerable scope for advancement, given the local shortage of educated and professionally trained personnel. In the case of upward mobility, many male workers relied heavily on their wives not only for ordinary domestic services (cooking, cleaning, child care, etc.) but also to help them construct and service networks which would enable the family to establish itself more firmly at a higher level in the hierarchy. This meant cultivating useful contacts at work and in the neighbourhood, with all the entertaining and social activity that this would involve. Information becomes a crucial resource in finding work, housing and schooling for the children, and other vital urban resources. In such a position households fared best where both partners could cooperate in the husbandry of useful contacts and each was prepared to put their networks at the disposal of the other. Where households are geographically mobile as well, the services of the wives of other members of the household might be essential in maintaining contacts with village kin, supervising property held in the village or elsewhere, locating friends or kin in the urban environment who could help the newcomers settle in, and so forth. Husband and wife in such households are likely to undertake many social activities jointly and I have argued elsewhere (Sharma 1986) that whilst it is possible to see this as evidence of more 'joint' conjugal roles and a new, more westernised, pattern of companionate marriage, it is probably more appropriate to see it as evidence of the strict degree of cooperation between the activities of husband and wife which the household requires. This kind of domestic group is not likely to be very large (many informants explicitly stated that they did not desire many children since the effort and expense of bringing them up in such a way that they maintained the progress made by the parents outweighed the advantages of a large family). This kind of urban household will operate, for a time at least, as a compact group, each member having a considerable investment in the social and economic resources of the others, 'human capital' being particularly important.

Summarising the argument so far, I have tried to show that rather than take the household for granted as a unit already constituted by nature or through general economic conditions, the anthropologist should attempt to identify the conditions in which the household is more or less of a corporate entity. It should be viewed as a group which is differentiated according to the roles, functions and degrees of domestic power of its various members, but possibly also according to the degree of commitment of its different members. The idea that the household is the next social unit above the individual is a useful one, provided only that we employ it with critical alertness to the various forces which favour or disfavour collective effort.

Morals and Interests

Having welcomed the treatment of the household as a resource system with its own economy of costs, rewards and interests, have we no need to refer to the norms regarding household roles and solidarity which I mentioned earlier?

There are models for the discussion of kinship which bypass norms, or rather treat them as manifestations of local culture subordinate to global trends. There has been for instance the 'modernisation' approach which sees certain types of family and household organisations as the inevitable consequences of economic and political integration into the world economy or industrialisation (e.g., Goody 1976: 108). There is also a Marxist version of this tendency, according to which capitalism necessitates certain patterns of interaction or organisation among kin which local norms and national cultures modify only minimally (e.g., Stivens' [1978] observations about kin relations among women in capitalist societies). One could argue that Goody's attempt to make cross-cultural generalisations about household organisation and the transmission of ·property belongs to this family of approaches. South Asian household organisation is viewed by Goody as a particular manifestation of a general pattern of organisation which tends to go with an economy based on agriculture such as has been widespread in Europe and much of Asia (Goody 1976).

If these approaches have been a healthy corrective to the propensity of some anthropologists to treat Hindu society as though it were a law unto itself, they still do not help us resolve the relationship between norms and interests. Can we retain the model of the household as a resource system without rejecting the idea of the social person who follows culturally prescribed rules and evaluates actions.

This is a major problem which cannot be resolved by a neat and tidy formula. It can be illuminated however by examining how norms and interests interact in particular situations, especially situations of crisis or choice.

An appropriate example might be the question of how households resolve the problem of families which include no sons. To be without a son is a real problem for any couple in north India because of the strength of the norm that daughters leave their parents' households on marriage and transfer their responsibilities to their husbands' kin. Daughters therefore are not in a position to care for their parents in their old age—indeed in many communities their marriage expenses and the gifts that in-laws are liable to expect will constitute a drain on resources which cannot easily be compensated. Needless to say there is little public provision for the elderly in the way of pensions and welfare entitlements. What possibilities are open to couples in this unfortunate position?

In the course of fieldwork in a Himachali village I came across the case of Hari Chand, a Brahman with five daughters but no son. For many years he and his wife have hoped that 'the next baby will be a boy' but in the course of her many pregnancies Hari Chand's wife Raksha lost the boys she conceived either at or soon after birth. Raksha urges that the solution to their problem is to wait until the eldest daughter is of an age to be married and then find a *gharjawai*, i.e., an uxorilocal son-in-law, who would be prepared to come and live with them with a view to eventually inheriting their land (about 30 acres and therefore well worth inheriting). Hari Chand has no brothers of his own or he might be in a position to adopt a nephew to bring up as his own child. His neighbours (especially his cousins' wives) urge that a better solution to the problem is to take a second wife by whom he might be more lucky and conceive a son, and most of those who press this idea can suggest suitable parties from among their own acquaintances and kin.

In the same village a distant relative of Hari Chand's, Moti Lal, also failed to get any sons by his first wife. He owns a shop in a distant city of Punjab and has employed many of his village kin in this prosperous venture, but like Hari Chand he has no brothers of his own. As in the case of Hari Chand, both the idea of a gharjawai and of a second marriage were suggested by his kin, and in the end he did take another wife. This new bride is a very young girl who appears to be slightly mentally retarded, and has recently borne him the son he desired.

A third household in the same village did resolve the problem of having no son by acquiring a gharjawai, but their circumstances were rather peculiar. Sethu and his wife had originally migrated to the village, having inherited land in the locality. As they were outsiders, not related consanguinally to anyone else in the village, their daughter Swarana they argued, need not strictly speaking be regarded as a 'sister' to the other village boys and a match was arranged for her with Lakshmana, a man of the same village (a practice which would normally be regarded as deviant, even incestuous). This man, Lakshmana, was to help them cultivate their land and eventually inherit it. This gharjawai did not come to live with his wife's parents in a literal sense—his house was only a few hundred yards from theirs so it was not necessary—but he and the daughter were able to take some responsibility for the elderly couple and see that they were comfortable in their old age. Lakshmana has since died and his wife Swarana and their sons have inherited the estates of both Sethu and Lakshmana.

In a sense, it is the differential value placed on sons and daughters in the Hindu cultural scheme which makes the lack of a son into a problem in the first place. If norms about the transfer of daughters' rights and responsibilities to their husbands' households on marriage were less rigid, then sons-in-law might care for parents in their old age just as well as sons. Modern legislation has made it possible for a daughter to inherit shares of her parents' land and property, but popular feeling decrees that she has already received her share of her parents' estate when they paid her dowry and marriage expenses and therefore she is not morally entitled to more. The gharjawai arrangement represents a kind of sanctioned modification of these norms, a kind of institutionalised 'second best' option in the situation of being unable to produce sons. It is 'second best' not so much in the sense that there is anything wrong with *having* a gharjawai if you cannot manage to have a son, but in the sense that to *be* a gharjawai is a very second best role, since he is seen as having given up some of the authority he might expect to exercise in his own household and village in order to adopt a subordinate role to his father-in-law. The only man who would eagerly undertake such a role must presumably be a very poor man whose own father has little or no land, and what parents would happily marry their daughter to a man with no resources or prospects? The best hope, if such a course is to be taken, is to find a boy from a family of some substance and standing who has too many brothers to stand in hope of inheriting much himself. Only such a family would be able to 'spare' a son to become someone else's gharjawai whilst also being able to offer something in terms of status and assistance. Nowadays, however, a much better option for such young men would be to get as much education as they could and seek their fortune on the job market rather than the marriage market. The reason why Lakshmana was prepared to become a gharjawai was because, for the reasons explained, he did not actually have to move from his own place of residence and from among his own kin.

If there is opprobrium attached to the role of gharjawai, there is none attached to that of second wife. To become the second wife of a man who has no sons is not a 'bad match' for a girl, provided that the man has the characteristics which would make him a desirable husband in any other circumstances, i.e., he has land or a good job, comes from a respectable family, etc. Given that most men who need and can afford to make second marriages are older and better established than 'first time' bridegrooms, they will normally fulfil these criteria anyway. Onlookers may feel sorry for the girl who has to contend with a *sonkhan* (co-wife) as well as a mother-in-law, but they will not feel that her parents have done anything shameful. It is not uncommon for a man who takes a second wife to marry a girl who is retarded, dumb, or who has some other disability of a kind which will not affect her capacity to bear healthy children. It seems that this is not, as I had formerly thought, because such a girl cannot find a 'better' match, but because she will be considered more manipulable and less likely to disturb domestic harmony by quarrelling with the first wife.

There is always the possibility that the problem of having no sons can be solved through adoption rather than through marriage strategies.[5] Adoption is a culturally approved but less commonly chosen option presumably because it is not easy in practice to find a child who is available for adoption. One might think that destitute or orphaned boys would find it easy to secure

And, of course, hope never dies that medical technology may provide a solution to the problem of lack of male issue. Newspapers and street vendors advertise all kinds of medicines supposed to ensure the conception of healthy sons and more recently, it seems, the development of amniocentesis in private clinics provides a means by which the wealthy can find out the sex of a foetus and ensure, by abortion, that unwanted girls are not born even if there is still no scientific means of guaranteeing sons.

adoptive homes in a society where male issues are at a premium, but to adopt a stranger's child is regarded as a bad risk. A brother's son has, after all, the same 'blood' and if he does not turn out well is at least unlikely to spring any unpleasant surprises because of his unfamiliar ancestry. Yet what brother is likely to have an interest in giving up his own son to a childless relative? It goes without saying that it would only be a brother with a large enough number of sons of his own to feel secure about his own future welfare and security. Before changes in the Hindu inheritance law made it possible for wives and daughters to inherit shares in a man's land, it was liable to revert to collaterals in the absense of a male issue, and so there can have been little incentive for brothers to exercise benevolence by providing their childless brothers with an issue.

Neither Hari Chand nor Moti Lal had brothers of their own who might have offered them adoptive sons, nor in Hari Chand's case were there any other close agnates. Moti Lal had a number of first cousins living in the village but as long as he was prepared to offer their sons employment in his shop (and therefore guarantee income for his cousins' households) there was little incentive for them to give up a child to him. Nor is there great moral prestige to be gained from the gift of an adoptive son such as might compensate for the loss of such a son's economic and social protection in later life. Adoption remains 'on the books' as an approved possibility but is seldom chosen, for the reasons I have outlined.

This discussion hints at the dialectic by which values and interests interact. Both norms (about the marriage of daughters) and economic conditions (lack of pensions or other social security arrangements outside the household) make sons a necessity and the lack of sons a problem. Norms further limit the kinds of options which are available to couples with no son by defining the extent to which existing values may be stretched to cover the exceptional case. The kinds of options which are actually available to any particular couple are further limited by the social and economic interests of those other parties on whom they depend to resolve their dilemma (by offering brides, sons-in-law or adoptive children).

Social Change and the Elasticity of Norms

So far we have treated values and culture in a very static manner. Yet there were hints in the foregoing discussion that new conditions (changes in the law, changes in employment opportunities) will cause shifts in the range of options available to a household obliged to make choices at some critical juncture in its development. One generation may not be offered precisely the same set of choices as the next, and if the second generation makes choices that were not open to the first, then these options may become part of the 'normal' experience of the third generation. This certainly is one way of interpreting urban households' varying practices with regard to women's wage work, a matter which initially I found puzzling.

Attitudes to women's employment in north India vary with class, caste and locality, but in most communities they could quite fairly be described as ambivalent. Wage work for women is acceptable in case of dire necessity or in case really prestigious work is available to them; otherwise it is not regarded as women's primary duty to bring income into the household, this being the business of fathers and sons. On the other hand, in areas such as Himachal Pradesh there is some cautious acceptance of female employment; women enjoy the independence and extra income it gives them and men do not resent sharing their own economic responsibilities provided that domestic comfort and notions of female modesty and respectability can be maintained. Wage work is therefore accepted in a conditional sort of way (so long as there is a need for it, so long as women can continue to fulfil their domestic duties, etc). The situation is complicated, but this is the best that can be done by way of summary.

Analysing interviews conducted in 1982 among a sample of married women, which included both women in wage work and women who were not in employment, I found that there were at least two distinct types of ethos to be found among white collar Himachali families (assuming that the women's own accounts of their upbringing were accurate). In one kind of household girls were encouraged to train for clerical or professional jobs and were given energetic support in their search for employment. Eventually they would be married to young men who sought or valued a working bride. In another kind of household girls might be urged to pursue their education as far as household resources permitted but they were not encouraged to think of themselves as future workers. In the latter type of household, the idea of the accomplished but essentially domesticated female was the dominant role model. The two kinds of households seemed to differ little from each other in other respects; at least, from the interview data one could deduce no neat correlations between household ethos and, say, origin or occupation of parents, caste, etc. In a considerable number of cases where women reported that they had been brought up in an atmosphere which viewed daughters' wage work positively, there were examples of senior women in the household having been employed before, often aunts or older sisters, and not necessarily with the initial consent of their own elders. Or other senior members of the household had been exposed to the experience of women working in some favourable context and had transmitted a positive response to their daughters' aspirations. Few of the women who described their parents' attitudes to women's employment as negative could remember any examples of senior women in their own households working, though a number of them were in fact in employment themselves at the time of the interview. The majority of the latter group stated that they rejected their own elders' evaluation of women's wage work and proposed to encourage their own daughters to think in terms of training for white collar or professional employment.

One might characterise what has happened as follows. Before Independence and perhaps for some time after that, the employment of urban women in Himachal was an entirely hypothetical option for most households, and one which even as hypothetical was not looked upon favourably. With the increased demand for white collar workers and the traditionally 'female' professions, the option became less hypothetical. There were some jobs which women were qualified to do and there were employers willing to give them work. A few women took these new opportunities with or without their families' approval, but the gains in both economic and other terms were considerable. In such households, women's employment presents itself to the next generation as a tolerable or positively approved option. But in those households where no women have had the experience of wage work, the costs of women not having jobs are not yet so great as to cause a rapid reappraisal of the existing evaluation of women's employment. Therefore, at the particular point in the process of change at which I conducted my study, the situation was one in which there were a variety of what might be called household 'cultures' regarding women's education and employment. Norms and experience therefore interact (although at variable rates) to produce diverse standards of behaviour. The range of permissible options in terms of which individuals or household groups pursue their goals and interests shifts from time to time and place to place.

Summary

In this paper I have been dealing with a classical antinomy of social anthropology. Norms and cultural values are an essential aspect of society and we cannot understand the behaviour of individuals or groups without reference to the normative sphere. If an anthropologist tries to analyse the household without reference to value he/she will end up doing a job which a sophisticated microeconomist will probably do better. On the other hand, a whole generation of anthropologists railed at the limitations of functionalist anthropology which tended, in its less satisfactory forms at least, to be incapable of accommodating the fact that any society is actually made up of individual persons, each acting in pursuit of variously defined and often conflicting interests. In the context of the study of domestic groups, how can anthropologists incorporate the insights of the 'New Household Economics' without abandoning the insights gained from their own normative analyses.

I think that my discussion of the individual and the household in South Asia indicates that values can be accommodated to the useful model of the household as a resource system on certain conditions. Households in India can be understood in terms of the interacting interests of individual members and we certainly should not accept the household as a cultural 'given' just because its integrity is a particularly powerful cultural norm. Yet values are a crucial ingredient in the situations I have described, not in the sense that individuals respond to problems as cultural automata, their behaviour simply *determined* by their 'values', but in the sense that current versions of an existing culture contribute to the definition of what is to be regarded as a problem in the first place. (Having no sons or being an abandoned wife is a problematic situation because of the way in which values and resources are *already* structured.) Cultural values also help people to rank the various possibilities available to them when they are obliged to make choices. I hope that I have shown how cultural imperatives interact with grosser economic trends which affect the household (urbanisation, growth of industry, changes in occupational structure, opportunities for migration, etc.) to produce a range of possible outcomes and much local or sub-cultural variation.

This being so, it is not surprising that anthropological studies have illuminated the domestic domain best (both in South Asia and elsewhere) when they have adopted a processual approach rather than attempting grand sociological generalisations (the joint household is/is not declining, joint conjugal roles are/are not on the increase). In my view it is the alliance of an established tradition of processual analysis at the micro level with the new approach to the household as a resource system which offers the most promising programme for the systematic study of the domestic domain.

● ● ●

References

Bailey, F. 1957. *Caste and the Economic Frontier*. Manchester: Manchester University Press.
Barrett, N. and M. McKintosh. 1982. *The Anti-Social Family*. London: Verso.
Bennett, L. 1983. *Dangerous Wives and Sacred Sisters*. New York: Columbia University Press.
Goody, T. 1976. *Production and Reproduction*. Cambridge: Cambridge University Press.
Gulati, L. 1981. *Profiles in Female Poverty*. Delhi: Hindustan Publishing Corporation.

Karlekar, M. 1984. Sweepers. *In* J. Lebra, J. Paulson and J. Everett (eds.), *Women and Work in India,* pp. 78–99. New Delhi: Promilla and Co.

Lewis, O. 1958. *Village Life in Northern India.* New York: Vintage Books.

Madan, T.N. 1965. *Family and Kinship. A Study of the Pandits of Rural Kashmir.* Bombay: Asia Publishing House.

Majumdar, P. and **I. Majumdar.** 1978. *Rural Migrants in an Urban Setting.* Delhi: Hindustan Publishing Corporation.

Mandelbaum, P.G. 1972. *Society in India.* Berkeley and Los Angeles: University of California Press.

Netting, R. McC., R.R. Wilk, and **E.J. Arnould,** (eds.), 1984. *Households: Comparative and Historical Approaches.* Berkeley and Los Angeles: University of California Press.

Papps, I. 1980. *For Love or Money: A Preliminary Economic Analysis of Marriage and the Family.* London: Institute of Economic Affairs.

Parry, J. 1979. *Caste and Kinship in Kangra.* London: Routledge and Kegan Paul.

Per-Lee, D. 1984. Street Vendors. *In* J. Lebra, J. Paulson and J. Everett (eds.), *Women and Work in India,* pp. 184–200. New Delhi: Promilla and Co.

Rao, M.S.A. 1972. *Tradition, Rationality and Change.* Bombay: Popular Prakashan.

Shah, A.M. 1974. *The Household Dimension of the Family in India.* Berkeley and Los Angeles: University of California Press.

Sharma, U.M. 1980. *Women, Work and Property in North West India.* London: Tavistock.

Sharma, U.M. 1986. *Women, Class and the Urban Household.* London: Tavistock.

Stivens, M. 1978. *Women and Their Kin. In* P. Caplan and J. Bujra (eds.), *Women United. Women Divided,* pp. 157–84. London: Tavistock.

Trager, L. 1984. Family Strategies and the Migration of Women: Migrants to Dagupan City, Philippines. *International Migration Review,* 18(4): 1264–77.

Wallman, S. 1984. *Eight London Households.* London: Tavistock.

2

The Joint Family Household in Rural Rajasthan: Ecological, Cultural and Demographic Conditions for its Occurrence

Pauline Kolenda

O NE OF the most characteristic social institutions of Rajasthan is the rural joint family household. Often considered to be one of the most characteristic social institutions in India as a whole, the joint family takes its place beside caste and the arranged marriage as close to universal in India.

Acknowledgements: A brief version of this paper was read at the Annual Conference on South Asia at the University of Wisconsin-Madison, 8 November 1986. Fieldwork in Rajasthan was supported by Faculty Research Fellowships of the American Institute of Indian Studies, and by grants from the National Science Foundation and the University of Houston. Statistical analysis of the data was supported by the University of Houston through computer time and two Grants-in-Aid.

This study would not have been possible without the work of Lorraine Haddon, who calculated measures of over 60 variables for 326 districts and territories of India from the statistics in the 1961 Census, and Indira Sapru, who served as research assistant on the project in Rajasthan. Others who contributed to the statistical research and analysis were Albert Ballinger, Diane Ballinger, Nancy Bernard, Pam Brown, David Cohen, Gary Dworkin, Christopher Kolenda, Carolyn Lewis, Kevin Olive, Leslie Pinter, Moniker Reuter-Echols, and Rebecca Story. I am also grateful to Joseph E. Schwartzberg for having called my attention in 1965 to the C-I Tables of the 1961 Census of India.

Help in obtaining the scores of census volumes used in the study was given by a number of individuals at several libraries: Gene Jackson, Helen Tatman and Michael Biggs at the University of Houston Library, T. Tsuchiyama and Merry Burlingham at the University of Texas Library, Richard Martin at the University of Virginia Asia Library, and anonymous but helpful librarians at the Louisiana State University Asia Library and the Library of the University of Texas at Arlington.

Thanks are hereby extended to Thomas Rosin and others who made significant suggestions for improving earlier versions of this paper. Ved Vatuk helped me with a calendrical reference. William Skinner's unpublished papers on Chinese demography which he kindly made accessible to me gave me courage to apply ethnographic evidence for Rajasthan.

The 1961 Census of India was one of the first to collect data on household composition, enabling comparative analysis of family household structure between different states, regions and districts. A comparison of the 1961 household composition tables for 326 districts and territories was reported in an earlier paper (Kolenda and Haddon 1987). Mapping of various measures of the occurrence of joint family households revealed that in proportion to the population, there were more rural joint family households in Rajasthan than in any other state (ibid.: 227–38; see also Maps 1 and 2 in this paper).

What accounts for this high occurrence of joint family households in Rajasthan? That is the problem that I try to solve in this paper. I draw on three kinds of data—cultural, derived from ethnographies of various villages in Rajasthan, most done by Census ethnographers, some by other anthropologists and by myself; demographic, namely, statistics derived from a variety of tabulations in the 1961 Census; and ecological, derived from Census District Gazetteers, geographical works, and especially important, from mapping done by A.K. Sen of the Central Arid Zone Research Institute (CAZRI) in Jodhpur, Rajasthan.

The Concept of Joint Family Household as Used in the Census of India

There are two aspects to the definition of the joint family household, that of composition—who belongs to a joint family?—and that of location and boundaries—how does one locate a joint family and distinguish it from other families and other social units? There has been much more agreement about the functional location and boundaries of the family than about its composition. The problem of definition of family structure is one I addressed in the past (Kolenda 1968: 344–49; see also Kolenda 1987: 8–16); the conclusions of that effort are briefly stated here and are used in the present analysis.

The functional definition of the joint family established by the Census of India more than a hundred years ago is relatives who eat from the same kitchen (*chulha* in Hindi), or the 'hearth-group'. This definition has been used by many social scientists, as well as the Census, and its use has made for consistency, enabling comparability between studies. This is not the ideal definition of joint family for all research purposes, as a chulha-group is almost always linked socially and economically to others, and it is a wider *set* of chulha-groups that functions in many contexts as the joint family. The households in the C-I Tables of the Census of India, central to this study, are chulha-groups, however, and the ethnographers who studied hundreds of villages in the 1960s for the Census also used that functional definition. Thus, the problem of this paper more precisely is: why were there, in proportion to the population, more joint family hearth-groups in Rajasthan according to the Census of India 1961, than in other Indian states?

As for the composition of the joint family household, while Indians are often inconsistent in their use of the term 'joint family', they are usually referring to a household consisting of two or more related couples. Usually a joint family is composed of parents and one married son, his wife and their children (the patrilineal joint family), but there can also be more than one married son (the patrilineal-collateral joint family). Consistent with my previous work (1967, 1968, 1987: 1–154; Kolenda and Haddon 1987), I will follow the above definition: a joint family is a household composed of two or more related couples. While anthropologists might consider the Indian joint family to fall under their more general rubric of 'extended family', I prefer to be consistent with Indian usage here.

While English-speaking Indians generally use 'joint family', there are various terms in Indian languages for it. The villagers in the village I studied in Jaipur district used the expression *puna parivar* (literally, 'the complete family').

While most Indians trace their descent and structure their families along the father-son line, the culturally prescribed structure among some communities in the northeast and southeast is along the mother-child line (the matrilineal joint family). In Rajasthan, the norm is the patrilineal joint family.

Household Tables in the Census of India—1961

The 1961 Census examined a 20 per cent sample of all households (hearth-groups) within every district and territory of India, tabulating their composition under the rubrics of head, spouse of head, other married relatives (sons, other males, other females), unmarried relatives (never married, widowed or divorced, separated) and unrelated persons. The data are presented in the C-I Tables of the Census, entitled 'Composition of Sample Households By Relationship to Head of Family Classified by Size of Land Cultivated'.[1] That table divides each district or territory's population into rural and urban. In this paper, I am concerned only with the statistics for rural populations. Since over 80 per cent of the Indian population lived in rural areas in 1961, we are concerned with the households of the vast majority of Indians at that time.

[1] While these tables are consistently labeled 'C-I', the title for the C-I Table varies among different states.

The reader may ask why I report a study done with data from the 1961 Census rather than the 1981 Census. One answer is that conditions in Rajasthan a generation ago were probably closer to those which fostered joint family households in past centuries than are the changed conditions of the 1980s. For example, land reform, which began in Rajasthan in 1952, significantly affected household structures, at least as these were reported to Census-takers in 1961, and it is likely that it continued to stimulate changes for a decade or more. While it would add significantly to this study to compare the 1961 figures with those of 1981, this study involved references to scores of different volumes of the Census of India 1961, and sufficient comparable volumes from the 1981 Census have only recently become available in United States libraries. It might be possible at present to replicate this study with 1971 Census data if the enterprise proved worthwhile. The 1961 analysis should, in any case, serve as a 'baseline' against which to compare changes in household distribution in 1971 and 1981 and in subsequent censuses.

The 1961 data showed marked regional differences in family structure. These were revealed by mapping two indices derived from the C-I Tables. By dividing the total rural population in the 20 per cent sample of all households in a district into the number of Married Sons residing with the heads of those households, the resulting percentage was used as an index of the prevalence of the patrilineal joint family, as one can expect that where a larger percentage of the persons in the sample households are married sons of the household head, there are more patrilineal joint families. In the same way, the total number in the 20 per cent sample of households was divided into the total for Other Married Relatives (excluding the spouse), as one can also expect that where a larger proportion of the persons in the sample households are Other Married Relatives, there is a larger proportion of lineal, collateral, lineal-collateral and other types of joint families. (Note, of course, that one kind of Other Married Relative is the married son.)

The method used for mapping these two variables and others based on census data depends upon ranking all districts and territories on the variable and then dividing them into quintiles. The 326 districts and territories of this study[2] are divided into four quintiles of 65 districts each, and one quintile

[2] Not all the districts and territories of India as it was in 1961 are included in the study. Excluded are Daman, Diu, Goa, the Yenam portion of Pondicherry, and the divisions of the Northeast Frontier Agency for which data were not available to us. The three divisions of Nagaland are merged and treated as one unit, as are the Laccadive, Amindivi and Minicoy Islands. The protectorate of Sikkim is included. Note that in 1961, the state of Haryana did not yet exist, nor did a number of subsequently designated districts (Rupar, Punjab; Jind, Haryana; Bulsar, Gujarat; or Rajura, Maharashtra), and that some districts now in Himachal Pradesh were in the Punjab (Simla, Lahaul and Spiti, Kangra, and Kulu). Finally, since these data are only for rural populations, entirely urban districts (Bombay, Madras, Calcutta, and Bangalore) have been omitted.

Map 1: Proportions of Joint Families in India from Census of India 1961 as Measured by Proportions of 'Married Sons' in 20% Sample of Households.

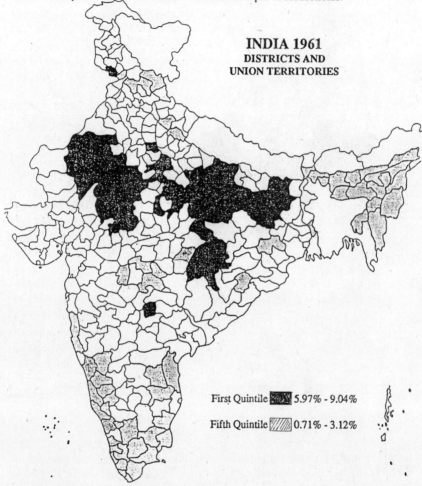

INDIA 1961
DISTRICTS AND
UNION TERRITORIES

First Quintile [shaded] 5.97% - 9.04%

Fifth Quintile [hatched] 0.71% - 3.12%

(Quintile 3) with 66 districts. The districts with the highest values on a variable are in Quintile 1, those with the lowest in Quintile 5. Thus, Maps 1 and 2 show the districts in Quintile 1 and Quintile 5 for the two measures of joint family, the *proportions of Married Sons* and the *proportions of Other Married Relatives* in the household sample populations. Mapping of these two indices of joint family should be a reasonably sound guide to those regions where joint families occur with high frequency and those where they are more rare.

Looking first at Map 1, we see that districts in Quintile 1 on proportions of Married Sons, indicating high proportions of patrilineal joint families,

Map 2: Proportions of Joint Families in India from Census of India 1961 as Measured by Proportions of 'Other Married Relatives' in 20% Sample of Households

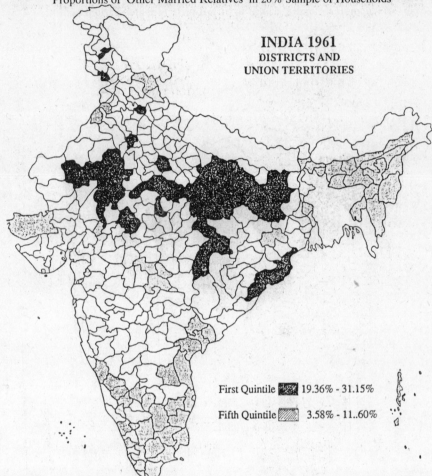

INDIA 1961
DISTRICTS AND
UNION TERRITORIES

First Quintile 19.36% - 31.15%

Fifth Quintile 3.58% - 11..60%

form a belt of 62 districts across northern India—15 in Rajasthan, contiguous with 14 in Madhya Pradesh, 25 in Uttar Pradesh, and eight in Bihar. Districts in Quintile 5 cluster in two blocks, one in the northeast, composed of all the districts of Assam, some territories beyond Assam, and some of the districts of West Bengal, the other in the southwest, composed of Kerala and parts of Madras, Andhra Pradesh and Mysore. Map 2, showing quintiles based on Other Married Relatives, indicating high proportions of all types of joint families, shows a similar pattern of a Quintile 1 belt across the waist of India and two Quintile 5 clusters, one in the northeast and one in the south, with a few Quintile 1 and Quintile 5 districts scattered elsewhere.[1]

¹ Regional differences in family structure in various European countries both in the present and the past are beginning to be recognised by social historians (Laslett 1977: 16–27; Wall 1983: 52–60).

Map 3: Joint Family Districts in Rajasthan as Measured by the First Quintile Rankings on Proportions of Married Sons in 20% Household Samples (Census of India 1961)

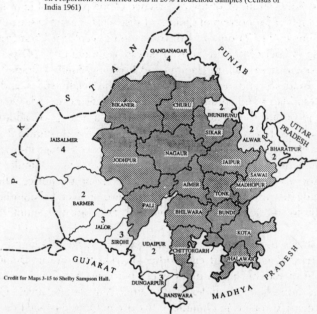

Credit for Maps 3-15 to Shelby Sampson Hall.

Map 4: Joint Family Districts in Rajasthan as Measured by the First Quintile Rankings on Proportions of Married Relatives in 20% Household Samples (Census of India 1961)

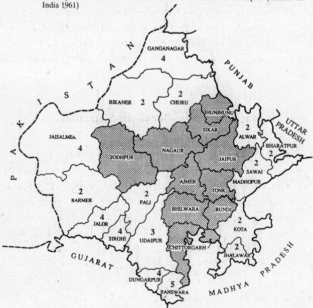

Map 3 shows the 15 districts out of Rajasthan's 26 which fall in Quintile 1 on Married Sons, an index of the occurrence of the patrilineal joint family. This is the highest proportion of Quintile 1 districts for a single state (58 per cent), as compared to 25 out of 54 districts (46 per cent) for Uttar Pradesh, 14 out of 43 (33 per cent) for Madhya Pradesh, eight out of 17 (47 per cent) for Bihar, one district each for Jammu and Kashmir, Andhra Pradesh, and Himachal Pradesh, and no districts in the other eight states and nine territories. On Map 3 and on subsequent maps, each district outside Quintile 1 has within its outline the quintile number to which it belongs. In addition to the 15 districts of Rajasthan in Quintile 1, there are five in Quintile 2. Thus, 20 out of Rajasthan's 26 districts (76 per cent) are above average in frequency of joint family households in the all-India perspective, since Quintiles 1 and 2 are together the upper 40 per cent of all districts and territories. Three of the remaining districts in Rajasthan are in the third or 'average' quintile, and three in the fourth, a below average quintile; none are in Quintile 5, the lowest.

Map 4 shows the 11 districts in Rajasthan which fall in Quintile 1 on Other Married Relatives, and eight other districts that are in Quintile 2. Thus 19 out of Rajasthan's 26 districts (73 per cent) are above average in joint family households as indexed by Other Married Relatives. Of the remaining districts, one is in Quintile 3, five are in Quintile 4, and one is in the lowest, Quintile 5.

Thus, according to the figures of the 1961 Census, there were at that time more rural joint family households (hearth-groups) in Rajasthan in proportion to the population than in any other state of India. What accounts for this high proportion? The remainder of this paper is devoted to exploring this question through an analysis of demographic, cultural and ecological factors.

Ethnographic Fieldwork in Rajasthan

My own ethnographic fieldwork in Rajasthan was guided by preliminary, incomplete versions of Maps 1 and 2 that I prepared in the summer of 1966, using the 1961 Census volumes then available. On the basis of these maps, I chose six districts in various parts of India in which to do fieldwork, one of them Jaipur district in Rajasthan. By observation of families in their villages, I hoped to discover the essential conditions for joint family structure. In this paper, I draw on my field notes and published and unpublished articles (Kolenda 1978a; 1987: 178–213) concerning the linked villages of Maharajapur-Kishanpur, 13 miles west of the city of Jaipur, where my research assistant, Indira Sapru, and I worked for five months in 1966–67. Mrs. Sapru has gone back to Maharajapur-Kishanpur several times to gather further data, and we have worked there together for brief periods in 1969, 1974, 1978 and 1985.

In Maharajapur-Kishanpur (henceforth M-K), with a population of 367 in 1966, consisting almost entirely of two well-known Rajasthani ethnic groups, Jats (63 per cent of the population) and Minas (25 per cent), I expected to find high proportions of joint families. There were indeed high proportions— 31 per cent of the Jat families and 49.5 per cent of the Jat population lived in joint families, as did 21.5 per cent of the Mina families and 46.5 per cent of the Mina population (see Tables 1 and 2 for the full distributions).

Table 1
Family Structure Among the Jats of Maharajapur-Kishanpur

Type of Family	Families		Persons	
	No.	%	No.	%
Joint	12	31	131	49.5
Supplemented Nuclear	9	25	66	24
Nuclear	12	31	51	20
Polygynous	1	3.25	6	3
Supplemented sub-nuclear	1	3.25	3	1.5
Sub-nuclear	1	3.25	3	1.5
Single-person	1	3.25	1	0.5
	37	100	267	100

(Kolenda 1978: 243; 1987: 179)

An unexpected factor emerged, one not previously highlighted in Indian or other ethnography: the existence of very high proportions of sibling-set and collateral-set marriages. This was the custom of a set of two or three brothers marrying a set of two or three sisters or 'cousin-sisters' (father's brother's daughter to each other), or other sets of women who were close relatives.[4] The male set might be 'cousin-brothers' (father's brother's son to

---

[4] One of the founding fathers of modern cultural anthropology, Lewis Henry Morgan, did conceive of sibling-set joint families. According to Morgan, the second in a series of five successive forms of marriage throughout human evolution was the Punuluan. He described it as follows:

It was founded upon the intermarriage of several sisters, own and collateral, with each others' husbands not being necessarily kinsmen of each other. Also, on the intermarriage of several brothers, own and collateral, with each others' wives, in a group; these wives not being necessarily of kin to each other, *although often the case in both instances* (Morgan 1964: 325–26, emphasis added).

My thanks to the anthropologist Edward Norbeck who mentioned this old reference to me.

each other) or other sets of men who were close relatives. Almost two-thirds (63 per cent) of M-K Jat daughters were married in sibling- or collateral-sets (Kolenda 1978a: 253; 1987: 190), as were 60 per cent of Mina wives (Kolenda 1969: 53). This very strong marital pattern double-bonded the joint families of M-K, so that not only were the adult males of a family brothers, but the adult females were sisters or cousin-sisters as well as sisters-in-law (brothers' wives). A newly in-married woman would not be entirely among strangers, because her older sister might be in the same household; her aunt (father's sister) might live in a household nearby, as might other women from her village. She could thus, presumably, make an easier adjustment to her life as a married woman and be less likely to develop hostile relations with her sisters-in-law. Such double-bonding might ensure greater harmony between women and, hence, a joint family would be less likely to fragment into its component nuclear units.

Table 2
Family Structure among the Minas of Maharajapur-Kishanpur

Type of Family	Families		Persons	
	No.	%	No.	%
Joint	3	21.5	39	46.5
Supplemented nuclear	3	21.5	22	26
Nuclear	5	35.5	19	22.5
Single-person	2	14	2	2.5
Other	1	7.5	2	2.5
	14	100	84	100

(Kolenda 1969: 29)

The villagers themselves did not emphasise joint family double-bonding through sibling-set or collateral-set marriages; rather, they emphasised the economy in affinal ties thus established. The expenses of the wedding and of subsequent gift-giving and hospitality are indeed curtailed if two married daughters share the same set of affinal kin, or two daughters-in-law share the same set of natal kin. Furthermore, the difficulty of seeking bridegrooms for daughters is less if two or three marry into the same family. Despite the villagers' ability to cite some instances of sisters married into the same family who quarrelled, my comparison of Jat joint families in M-K indicated that families in which sisters or cousin-sisters were sisters-in-law endured longer (Kolenda 1978a; 1978b: 265; 1987: 201; see also Rosin 1987: 26).

Other anthropologists have noticed sibling-set marriage. Brij Raj Chauhan, in his book on a village in Chitorgarh district, mentions that it is 'permissible in southern Rajasthan, to find two brothers marrying two sisters' (1967: 212). Drs. Anandlaxsmi and Carol Henderson have mentioned to me the prevalence of the custom in the villages they have studied in Jaipur and Jodhpur districts, respectively (personal communication). Bhargava and Gupta, writing about Rangmahal village in Ganganagar district, refer to the Scheduled Caste Meghwals and Nayaks (together composing 54 per cent of families) 'among whom younger sisters of a grown up girl are sometimes married along with her. This is done with a view to economise' (1965c: 20). Similarly, writing about Mudh village (in Bikaner district), a multi-caste Hindu village in which 31 per cent of the population was Scheduled Tribe Meghwals, the same authors say that 'a person having more than one daughter may arrange their marriages simultaneously in order to effect economy. In such cases girls even of tender age might be married along with his elder daughters' (1965a: 22). Thomas Rosin mentions that 'The high frequency of sibling- and cousin-set marriages strengthens joint family solidarity', in the Nagaur village he studied (1978: 490).

Rosin (1987), in the only other analysis of sibling-set and collateral-set marriages in Rajasthan, found that 24 per cent of all married couples in Undhyala village in Nagaur district were married in sibling- or collateral-sets in 1964–65. This proportion of such marriages is much lower than the three-fifths or more of such marriages among the Jats and Minas of M-K. This comparison raises the question of why there were higher proportions of sibling- and collateral-set marriages in the one village rather than the other. Similar to M-K, Undhyala Jats, the largest caste group in the village (22 per cent of the total population), have : (i) relatively high proportions (40 per cent) of such marriages (ibid.: 3, 19), (ii) their joint families composed of such sets tend to endure (ibid.: 26), and (iii) their motivation for such marriages is 'cost cutting' in performing weddings (ibid.: 25). Sibling- or collateral-set marriages occur in Undhyala among all the larger castes (ibid.: 11). Rosin is especially concerned with the relationship between sibling- and collateral-set marriages and the endurance of joint families. When his analysis is ready for publication it will undoubtedly shed much light on this relation-ship.

In Jaipur district (Agarwal and Gupta 1965: 16) and other parts of Rajasthan (Rosin 1987: 4 for Nagaur district, Singh and Pendharker 1967: 15 for Jodhpur district), it is customary to hold all weddings on only a few specific days during the year. In M-K, the two wedding days were Akha Tij (the third day of the bright half of the month of Baisakh) and Pipal Purnima (the full-moon day in Jeth). In 1967, Akha Tij fell on 12 May, when there were five weddings of M-K children and, according to newspapers, thou-sands in and around Jaipur city, and Pipal Purnima fell on 22 May, when there were four weddings of M-K children.

As a result of this custom, a wedding guest invited to more than one wedding has to stay at each wedding only briefly or else must choose among his invitations. The many weddings occurring on the same day in a region therefore helped save on wedding costs by limiting the number of guests. The reason villagers gave for having weddings only on these two days—that they were auspicious and hence one did not have to consult a Brahman pandit to find an auspicious day—appears to be another economy measure.

In addition, there are many double or triple weddings. In M-K, there have been as many as seven weddings taking place together. Sisters and/or cousin-sisters are often married at the same time.

One cannot reconstruct a precise composition of families from the C-I Tables of the Census, and it is therefore not possible to find sibling-sets or collateral-sets in joint families there. However, as we will see later, the factor with which the Census measures of joint family ('married sons' and 'other married relatives') correlates most strongly is young adolescent marriage. As Bhargava and Gupta suggest, and as I have found in M-K, the practices of sibling-set and collateral-set marriage and of multiple weddings on the same day tend to encourage the marriage of much younger girls along with their older sisters or cousin-sisters. The matching bridegrooms are often similarly apart in age. Thus, these customs contribute to the high proportions of married young adolescents in Rajasthan. Young adolescent marriage, in turn, contributes to the high proportion of joint families in Rajasthan, as the high correlations between the indices of joint family structure and the proportions of males or females aged 10–14 who are reported as married show.

Young adolescent marriage or even child marriage is prescribed by some influential Hindu law books. Some speak of brides as young as 6 (Kane 1958: 614), 8 and 12 (Buhler 1886: 355). A frequent prescription is that a daughter should be married before or immediately after her first menstruation (Kane 1941: 438–47). As Kane points out, with respect to the recommended young ages (6–12) for brides, 'There was no question of consummation which took place only after puberty' (ibid.: 446), and some law books prescribe celibacy for the married couple for some time after marriage (ibid.: 441), which is consistent with the continuing physical immaturity of one or both members of the couple for some time after the wedding.

Traditionally, Rajasthani Hindu custom has tended to be consistent with the law books. In the mid-1960s it was customary in M-K and in surrounding villages for marriage to be celebrated by two major sets of ceremonies, usually a year or more apart, the *shadi* and the *muklava*. The first established an alliance between the two families, and often took place before a girl reached puberty. The second usually took place one or more years later, usually after the bride had reached puberty, and preceded the couple's commencement of sexual relations.

Among the Jats of M-K, the custom was for the shadi to take place before the age of 12 for both sons and daughters, and for the muklava to take place one to seven years later; exactly how soon after the muklava a bride began to live with her husband and his family depended upon her age and physical maturity. For example, one Jat wife who had come to live with her husband four years before told us that she had been married at the same time as her older sisters, 15 years before, and the muklava for both had been one year later. While the older sister came to live with her husband's family imme-diately, our informant, married at age '5 or 7,' did not come until 11 years after the muklava. We may guess that the older sister was 11 or 12 at the time of the shadi and 13 at the time of the muklava, and that her younger sister probably did not come to reside with her marital family until the age of 16. Another girl of about 12 had still not gone to her mother-in-law even though she had had her muklava four or five years earlier, again as the junior bride in a double sibling-set marriage with her sister. True to their proclivity for economising, many Jats dispense with the muklava ceremonies entirely and allow one or more men from the groom's family to come and escort the bride to her mother-in-law when she is mature, or if the bride is already mature at the time of the shadi, the muklava takes place immediately after the shadi, before the bride departs with the new husband and his party for his village.

Lushington wrote about the weddings of the royal Jats of Bharatpur:

> On the expiration of her three days residence at the home of her lord and master, the bride returns to her relations for a period of one, three or five years, and she is then brought home by the bridegroom to assume the duties of the married state. This second bringing home of the wife is termed *gona* or *gaman*, and is usually the consummation of the marriage; but the *gaman* may be altogether dispensed with by the performance of *phir-pattah*, or changing the stools of the bride and bridegroom, when the *hom* is celebrated (1833: 294–95).

The customs Lushington described for royal Jats are consistent with those followed by M-K Jats 133 years later.

Thus, both Hindu domestic law and long tradition support the M-K Jats in their child marriages. Since there is no real lower limit in age for marriage, and a considerable feeling that there must be something wrong with an unmarried person who is over the age of 16 (for girls) and 20 (for boys), the custom of sibling-set or collateral-set marriages for children several years apart in age makes good sense, especially in the context of Jat penury and adherence to Brahman advice. I should add that some families are so poor that sons among them may not marry until they are mature, when a man can earn enough to pay a brideprice himself.[5] We attended one Jat wedding in M-K at which the bride appeared to be 12 and the groom 25 or 30 years old. There are some men who get only a leviratic bride when a brother dies; some men never marry.

Among the Minas, on the other hand, there appeared to be two patterns. Among the wealthier Minas, the grooms tended to be 17 to 20, and the brides 15 to 16; among poor Minas, grooms tended to be 25 to 30 and brides 10 to 14. Among both Jats and Minas, the marriages of men in their twenties to young girls were likely to be brideprice marriages in which a very poor man gave his daughter to a bachelor, also from a poor family, who had managed to raise enough money (about 2,000 to 4,000 rupees in the mid-1960s) to pay the brideprice. Especially important in evaluating a bridegroom's status was whether his family owned land and how much land, and whether the men of the family had outside jobs from which they earned money.

The first factor discovered to be related to joint family households, then, was sibling-set and collateral-set marriages, and the second was child or young adolescent marriage. Both are facilitated by the Rajasthani custom of holding multiple weddings on the one or two days a year deemed by astrological almanacs to be auspicious for them to take place. A third factor was one often mentioned by anthropologists: the joint family as work-team. This was a factor I was aware of from writings about Japanese families (Johnson 1964: 846; Nakane 1967). In M-K, the joint family functioned as a well-team consisting of two adult men, who were almost always related, either as father and son, or as brothers, plus one of their wives and some of their older children. I described the system as follows:

> . . . an incline is built in front of a well down which a pair of bullocks is driven, their downward movement pulling a leathern pouch (*charas*) full of water from the well. One man drives the bullocks, a second man empties the pouch of water into a sink from which it drains along dried-mud channel-bunds built above the fields. A third person, often a woman or older child, releases the water from the channel at the desired point to enter the fields . . . . Almost three-quarters of the Jat well-teams (74 percent)—seventeen out of twenty-three—are composed of patrilineally-related men. Two-thirds (65 percent)—fifteen

[5] Space does not permit a discussion here of the subject of brideprice or dowry in Rajasthan. Careful examination of the 24 Census village surveys treated later as well as other ethnographic evidence indicates that brideprice is much more prevalent in Rajasthan than is dowry. Neither seems to influence in any obvious way the timing of weddings.

out of twenty-three—are composed either of brothers or of father-son combinations. Thirteen, 56 percent, are composed of brothers or of father-sons who share the same house and eat from the same kitchen. There is thus a majority tendency for Jat men who compose well-teams to be members of the same commensal extended families.

Jat women not only work in the house caring for children and cooking for the family, but they work in the fields irrigating the patches of garden. They also harvest and winnow grains such as *bajra*, and vegetables such as *moth*. They cut and carry thorn bushes used for barriers. They gather foliage for fuel. They cut, carry, and chop fodder for animals. They water and feed the animals as well. Jats and Minas have herds of sheep and goats. They and villagers of other castes have some cows and buffaloes. It is the children who are in charge of herding.

Joint families make possible a division of labor among the members. One wife can care for small children, while another works in the field or collects and chops fodder. It makes possible a division of labor among men, as well, either on the well—one driving the bullocks, the other emptying out the water pouch—or by some men doing agricultural work in M-K and others working outside. Older children similarly can be assigned different tasks—some in the fields, or herding, or caring for the babies, some attending school (Kolenda 1978b: 248–49; 1987: 183–85).

This Jat and Mina pattern illustrates the hypothesis of Pasternak, Ember and Ember (1976), that joint families often occur in pre-industrial societies where and when an adult has incompatible tasks to perform. The incompatibility is solved by having more than one man or more than one woman to do the tasks which would be incompatible for one man or for one woman alone to do.

Also related to the joint family as a work-team was the paucity of agricultural labour employed by the landholding Jats and Minas. Only at peak labour times, as when the sowing of the winter crop was taking place at the same time as the harvesting of the summer crop, did they employ Untouchable Balais to help them in the fields. Map 5 shows the distribution of Scheduled Castes by district in rural Rajasthan in 1961. These communities, who often serve as agrestic servants, were not heavily concentrated in the high joint family districts; of the 11 Quintile 1 districts shown on Map 4, only one, Tonk, had more than 20 per cent of its population among the Scheduled Castes. The correlation coefficient between Married Sons and Scheduled Castes was +0.22, that between Other Married Relatives and Scheduled Castes was +0.28, both low relationships. The most economical

Map 5: Proportion of Scheduled Caste People in Each District of Rajasthan (Census of India 1961)

Median 18.30 (Pali)
Minimum 4.45 (Banswara)
Maximum 30.45 (Ganganagar)

Map 6: Locations of Twenty-four Villages Surveyed by the Census of India 1961 in Rajasthan. Used for Comparative Purposes in Studying Family Structure

(See Table 3 for names of villages, their tehsils and districts)

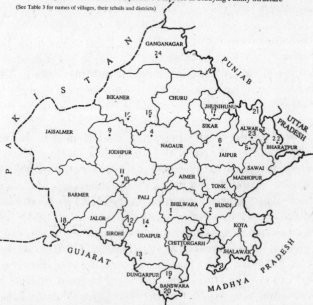

1. Bugor/2. Ramnagar/3. Kyasara/4. Bhadwasi/5. Abhaneri/6. Nagal Sooswatan/7. Sanswara/8. Gagron/9. Malar/10. Kalijal/11.Bujawa/12. Goriya/13. Panarwa/14. Kailashpuri/15. Mukam/16. Mudh/17. Bajawa/18. Janvi/19. Peepal Khoont/ 20. Khajoora/21. Hasanpur/22. Aghapur/23. Bhangarh/24. Rangmahal

way that the Jats and Minas of M-K knew of to farm was to have all work in the fields done by family members. Thus, there were only two extended families of Balais, and very few members of the five other artisan or serving castes living in the village; only 3 per cent of the population of M-K were not Jats or Minas. Among the Jats and Minas, agricultural work was done by the women and children rather than by agrestic servants of low caste. Women and children were thus vital members of the family work-team, both in the house and field.

Well-teams and, more broadly, joint families as work-teams, were also affected by the rather large proportion of men in M-K who worked outside the village in factories, foundries and services in the city of Jaipur, or on commercial farms nearby, or in public or private construction projects. Almost one-third of the adult Mina men who were not too old to work (six out of 19) worked outside the village. Among the 73 Jat adult men, 50 (68 per cent) worked on the land, 10 (14 per cent) worked outside, and 13 (18 per cent) were retired. The usual pattern was for at least one man of a joint family to work outside, contributing his cash income to the joint family pool of resources. Because of the absence of brothers who were working outside, the men who composed well-teams were sometimes more distantly related than as brothers or were unrelated (although over 90 per cent of the teams were composed of men who were both Jats) (see Kolenda 1978b: 249; 1987: 185), and hence the correlation between joint family *households* and well-teams was less than it might have been if all brothers worked in the village.

Sibling- and collateral-set marriage, young adolescent/child marriage and work-team requirements thus all supported the organisation of joint families in M-K. A fourth factor was the role of the former *jagirdar* (hereditary estate-holder) and *inamdar* (rent-free landholder), the *mahant* (head priest) of the Krishna temple in Kishanpur, in influencing household structure before the implementation of the Rajasthan Land Reforms and Resumption of Jagirs Act of 1952. Maharajapur had been a *khalsa* village (a village belonging to the Maharaja of Jaipur), while Kishanpur had been partly an inamdari and partly a jagirdari village. Most of its lands had belonged to the Krishna (locally, 'Kishan') temple. The former mahant told us that his predecessors had tried to encourage cultivation by tenants by building houses and wells for them, or else they would give tenants wood or lend them money toward the cost of building houses. But he also stated that 'during jagirdari days the cultivator's life was very unstable, because jagirdars threw cultivators off the land whenever they pleased. Therefore no cultivator could build a *pakka* [fired-brick] house' (field interview by Indira Sapru, 1 April 1968). Since building new houses was by permission of the jagirdar, inamdar, or Maharaja's official, tenants may not have built houses quite as soon as they felt they were needed for their expanding families. There is thus the possibility that more families lived in a house or shared a chulha in the past than might have chosen to do so.

That the requirement of the village landlord's permission to partition joint households may have considerable impact upon the pattern of family structure among tenants or agrestic servants is indicated by Peter Czap's study (1983) of serf households in Mishino, Russia, between 1814 and 1858. Among the serfs, 75 per cent of households were joint (Hajnal 1983: 91), and as much as 65 per cent were composed of three or more generations (Czap 1983: 133).[6] It was part of the authority of the *seigneur* to inhibit household fission (ibid.: 122, 136), possibly from a belief in the benefits of the large family system either for their members or for the estate management. The role of the jagirdar, inamdar, or royal official in Rajasthan may have included a similar inhibition.

Evidence of the unwilling persistence of some joint families in M-K is indicated by the fact that some of eldest brothers of Jat and Mina families left their joint family households in Maharajpur to build separate houses in Kishanpur or elsewhere as soon as land reform permitted it. (Kolenda 1987: 181). (Eldest sons are likely to have the largest numbers of children first in the joint family's development, and hence may feel crowded earliest.) By the Land Reform Act, Kishanpur land went to the Minas who had previously tilled it, while Maharajapur land went to the former Jat tenants of the Maharaja. After almost all the Minas had left Maharajapur to live in Kishanpur, some of the eldest sons of Jat joint families moved into the vacant houses, establishing separate chulhas there. Since so much building of new houses and moving out had taken place in the eight years since land reform (1958–1966), the proportions of joint families and the number of people in them may well have been higher in M-K prior to that time. The fact that none of the former tenants of the former jagirdar and inamdar of Kishanpur lived in Kishanpur until after land reform raises the question: did the jagirdar and inamdar forbid their tenants to live near the fields they tilled? This was possible since the Kishanpur tenants were Minas who had supported themselves as 'protectors' of the Jats of Maharajapur and thus lived in Maharajapur, until an epidemic in Kishanpur in 1928 motivated the mahant and the jagirdar to take them on as tenants. The mahant could thus insist that the Minas continue to reside in Maharajapur rather than move to Kishanpur.

The fieldwork conducted in M-K thus suggests four major factors contributing to the occurrence of joint families: (*i*) sibling-set and collateral-set marriage, (*ii*) young adolescent/child marriage, (*iii*) well-teams composed of

---

[6] Czap (1983: 122) noted that large complex households—joint family households, in the Indian term—were also reported for Latvia and Hungary in the 18th and 19th centuries.

members of the same joint family, and (iv) the need, in the past, for permission from inamdars, jagirdars or other officials in order to build houses. Sibling-set and collateral-set marriages serve to strengthen the joint family by bringing together as daughters-in-law, women who are sisters or cousin-sisters; hence quarrels between co-daughters-in-law are less likely to be serious enough to lead to demands on their part for dissolution of their common joint family. The need to economise in wedding expenses, along with Hindu teachings on the desirability of marrying daughters before puberty, encourages these sibling- and collateral-set marriages, as do multiple weddings and a very young age of marriage for brides and grooms—a crucial factor which will be taken up again later. The well-team/work-team formed by the joint family serves as a functional cause for the persistence of the joint family. Finally, the former requirement that tenants get permission from their landlords to build new living quarters is an oppressive cause of joint family households: people shared house and chulha because of a shortage of living space. Since land was allotted to the former tenants in the 1950s, a landlord's permission is no longer necessary in M-K, but the cost of building a new house or even adding on to an existing house may still be prohibitive enough for some joint families to continue to live together despite their preference for division into separate households.

Family Structure in the 1961 Census Village Surveys of Rajasthan

As part of the 1961 Census, representative villages were surveyed for every state and territory of India. For Rajasthan, 36 village surveys were done, of which 24 were obtained for this study.[7] These are listed in the bibliography. Map 6 shows the location of the 24 villages. In the surveys, four types of families were tabulated: simple, intermediate, joint, and other. Two of the Census ethnographers, Gupta and Pendharker, define these as follows:

A simple family consists of husband, his wife and unmarried children; an intermediate one consists of a married couple and un-married brother, sister or one of the parents; whereas the joint family consists of a married couple with married sons/daughters, or with married brothers/sisters. The types of families not covered by any of the above have been classified as 'others' (1969: 27).

Given these definitions, it is reasonable to equate the Census categories of

[7] At the beginning of each village survey report, the titles of all 36 done in Rajasthan are listed. Unfortunately, despite all the efforts of the inter-library loan librarian, I was unable to acquire 12 of these.

simple, intermediate and joint with those of nuclear, supplemented nuclear
and joint as I have defined them in my earlier work (Kolenda 1967: 346–47;
1987: 11–13). Table 3 shows the proportions for the four types of families in
the 24 village surveys, as well as quintile rank on proportion of married
females aged 10–14 and married males aged 10–14.

Table 3
Figures on Joint Families from 24 Village Studies in Rajasthan
(Census of India 1961)

(**Key**: S = Simple, I = Intermediate, Jt = Joint, O = Other.
Hyphenated pair of numbers at the end of lines, 1-1, 2-1, etc., refer to the quintile rank on
proportion of females 10-14 who are married and quintile rank on proportion of males 10-14
who are married.)

1. Bagor		Mandal Tehsil		Bhilwara District	1–1
(p. 26)	43 S (81%)	3 I (6%)	7 Jt	(13%)	
2. Ramnagar	Kanjar Colony	Bundi Tehsil		Bundi District	1–1
(p. 30)	168 S (93%)	12 I (7%)	0 Jt		
3. Kyasara		Dag Tehsil		Jhalawar District	1–1
(p. 39)	31 S (33%)	20 I (21%)	37 Jt	(39%) 6 O (6%)	
4. Bhadwasi		Nagaur Tehsil		Nagaur District	1–1
(p. 27)	35 S (61%)	1 I (2%)	21 Jt	(37%)	
5. Abhaneri		Baswa Tehsil		Jaipur District	1–2
(p. 30)	66 S (41%)	50 I (31%)	41 Jt	(27%) 1 O (1%)	
6. Nangal Sooswatan		Amber Tehsil		Jaipur District	1–2
7. Sanwara		Shahbad Tehsil		Kota District	1–2
(p. 31)	24 S (55%)	5 I (11%)	15 Jt	(34%)	
8. Gagron		Kanwas Tehsil		Kota District	1–2
(p. 26)	23 S (40%)	7 I (12%)	19 Jt	(33)% 8 O (14%)	
9. Malar		Palodi Tehsil		Jodhpur District	2–1
(p. 35)	77 S (55%)	25 I (18%)	39 Jt	(28%)	
10. Kalijal		Jodhpur Tehsil		Jodhpur District	2–1
(p. 28)	55 S (48%)	23 I (20%)	36 Jt	(31%) 1 O (1%)	
11. Bujawa		Jodhpur Tehsil		Jodhpur District	2–1
(p. 36)	16 S (44%)	9 I (25%)	11 Jt	(31%)	
12. Goriya		Bali Tehsil		Pali District	2–1
(p. 33)	94 S (69%)	8 I (6%)	35 Jt	(25%)	
13. Panarwa		Phalasia Tehsil		Udaipur District	2–1
(p. 32)	18 S (58%)	1 I (3%)	9 Jt	(29%) 3 O (10%)	
14. Kailashpur		Nokha Tehsil		Udaipur District	2–1
(p. 25)	119 S (66%)	21 I (12%)	27 Jt	(15%) 13 O (7%)	
15. Mukam		Nokha Tehsil		Bikaner District	2–2
(p. 32)	41 S (63%)	14 I (22%)	10 Jt	(15%)	
16. Mudh		Kolayat Tehsil		Bikaner District	2–2
(p. 41)	38 S (49%)	0 I	39 Jt	(51%)	

17. Bajawa (p. 31)		Udaipurwati Tehsil		Jhunjhunu District			2–3
	16 S (59%)	1 I (4%)	8 Jt	(30%)	2 O (7%)		
18. Janvi (p. 58)		Sanchore Tehsil		Jalor District			3–2
	72 S (53%)	23 I (17%)	39 Jt	(29%)	1 O (1%)		
19. Peepal Khoont (p. 49)		Ghatol Tehsil		Banswara District			3–2
	129 S (77%)	17 I (10%)	17 Jt	(10%)	5 O (3%)		
20. Khajoora (p. 31)		Kushalgarh Tehsil		Banswara District			3–2
	18 S (51%)	5 I (14%)	8 Jt	(23%)	4 O (12%)		
21. Hasanpur (p. 25)		Tijara Tehsil		Alwar District			3–2
	68 S (80%)	9 I (11%)	8 Jt	(9%)			
22. Aghapur (p. 33)		Bharatpur Tehsil		Bharatpur District			3–2
	64 S (54%)	27 I (23%)	25 Jt	(21%)	3 O (2%)		
23. Bhangarh (p. 34)		Rajgarh Tehsil		Alwar District			3–2
	33 S (55%)	10 I (16%)	16 Jt	(26%)	2 O (3%)		
24. Rangmahal (p. 33)		Suratgarh Tehsil		Ganganagar District			4–3
	63 S (76%)	10 I (12%)	9 Jt	(11%)	1 O (1%)		

In my 1968 comparative study of the Indian joint family, based on a comparison of 26 studies from 14 different states of India, I developed a principle of what constitutes high, medium and low proportions of joint family households in India. A proportion of 30 per cent or more is high, 20 to 29 per cent is medium, and 19 per cent or less is low (Kolenda 1968: 375; 1987: 57). By this principle, nine (38 per cent) of the Rajasthan villages considered here were high (with Mudh, Bikaner district, a largely Scheduled Caste village consisting mostly of Meghwals, the highest, at 51 per cent), eight were medium, and seven were low. Thus, 17 villages out of 24 (70 per cent) showed medium and high proportions of joint families, confirming the district statistics for Rajasthan presented earlier and showing that the state has a higher than average proportion of joint family households.

Two of the 'low' villages, Ramnagar Kanjar Colony (Bundi district) and Bagor (Bhilwara district), were composed almost entirely of Kanjars, an erstwhile nomadic criminal tribe which the government had tried to sedentarise. The ethnographers of Ramnagar Kanjar Colony, Sharma and Gupta, explained the absence of joint families as customary:

The reason is that it is customary among the Kanjars for a boy who is about to be married to receive a separate piece of land, a residential house and other necessary articles for his maintenance from his parents. After the marriage the newly married couple lives in a new house, and not with the parents (1967a: 30; see also p. 12).

According to them, the age of marriage among the Scheduled Caste seden-
tarised Kanjars of Ramnagar Kanjar Colony was 20–29 for males and 15–24
for females. While they did not specify the connection between the couple
setting up their own house immediately upon marriage and the older age of
marriage among these Kanjars as compared to other Rajasthani communities, it
would appear to be much easier for a couple to run a household if they are
older.

Concerning the Kanjars and Sansis (another former nomadic criminal
tribe) who composed Bagor village, Bhargava and Pendharker write:

> The preference for simple type of family is a natural consequence of
> the settlement of the communities on land. Separate families were
> allotted separate holdings and it was advantageous for the settlers to
> claim to belong to separate rather than joint family type (1968: 26).

According to this explanation, the low proportion of joint family households
in Bagor was not due to either custom or older age of marriage, but to the
recent redistribution of land under the Land Reform Act, as a result of
which the Kanjars and Sansis found it advantageous to maximise the number of
families among them in order to qualify for the most land possible. In fact it
is clear that at the time of the survey young adolescent marriage for girls
prevailed in Bagor. According to Bhargava and Pendharker, there were no
unmarried females over the age of 14 among the Kanjars (1968: 24), and the
usual age of marriage was 15–16 for boys and 12–13 for girls (ibid.: 12).

The influence of land redistribution on family composition, encouraging
the maximisation of nuclear families, may well have taken place in the low
joint family village of Kailashpuri (Udaipur district) as well, where Bhil
cultivators had recently been allotted former Eklingji temple lands.

The village with the lowest proportion of joint family households (9 per
cent) was Hasanpur (Alwar district), where almost two-thirds of the population (63 per cent) were Muslim Meos. The explanation offered by Sharma
and Pendharker was that 'The large number of families of the simple type is
due to the fact that landholdings are small and they cannot bear the burden
of joint families' (1969: 25). This explanation is questionable, because as will
be seen later in Table 10 showing types of families among *landless* Chamars,
those represented in the Rajasthan villages surveyed had high proportions of
joint families. Since some proportion of Hasanpur's population had departed
for Pakistan at the time of Partition in 1947 (Sharma and Pendharker 1969:
23), it is more likely that joint families had been fragmented by out-
migration of one or more of their nuclear family components. Out-migration
may also have been important in the low joint family village of Mukam
(Bikaner district), a pilgrimage centre for Jambheswarji (the founder of the

Bishnoi sect), composed only of Bishnois and their Meghwal servants. Mukam had little agricultural land, so that some Bishnoi cultivators tilled land in nearby villages, and many other Bishnois had migrated out.

In the cases of both Hasanpur and Mukam, it is likely that entire nuclear families migrated out, not just male members. It is a common pattern in many rural areas of India for men to work outside the village for months or years at a time, leaving their wives and children on the land or in the house owned there, sometimes in the care of the remaining men of their joint families, the man returning to live with his family upon his retirement from his work outside. (For an example of such a pattern, see Dandekar 1986 for a village in Maharashtra.) While such out-migration may have occurred in Hasanpur and Mukam, it also seems likely that entire nuclear families or components of joint families migrated out permanently.

Rangmahal (Ganganagar district) and Peepal Khoont (Banswara district), two other villages low in joint families, were in districts ranked in either the fourth or fifth quintile on 'married sons' and 'other married relatives'. Their low (12 per cent and 10 per cent) joint family households were consistent with their districts' low quintile ratings on measures of joint family living (to be discussed later).

Thus, alongside the factors *encouraging* joint family living (sibling- and collateral-set marriage, young adolescent/child marriage, well-teams/work-teams, and need for official permission to build new homes), there are two factors (land reform and permanent out-migration) that tend to *fragment* joint families and reduce their proportion in a village. Of the villages low in joint family households, two were in districts of Rajasthan with below average quintiles on joint family measures, but three seemed to have a low proportion of joint families because of government land redistribution, and two seemed to have been disrupted by departure, permanent out-migration. In only one was there clear evidence that the custom was for marriage to be at an older age, with the couple occupying their own new house immediately after marriage.

Caste or Tribal Preference for Joint Family Living

A popular hypothesis concerning joint family living is the ethnic one—that joint families are preferred by certain communities (in Rajasthan, by Rajputs and Jats) and rejected by others (in Rajasthan, by Bhils and other tribals). The ethnographic material in the 1961 Census village surveys provides an opportunity to test this hypothesis. Though a few of the 24 villages were populated by a single ethnic community (nos. 2 and 17) or by two (no. 15), most were multi-caste communities. (See Table 4 for caste composition of the 24 villages.)

Table 4
Castes in 24 Villages of Rajasthan
(Census of India 1961)

---

1. Bagor   Mandal Tehsil   Bhilwara District
   Castes: Sansi 32; Kanjar 21 (Nomadic criminal tribes)

2. Ramnagar   Kanjar Colony   Bundi Tehsil   Bundi District
   Castes: Kanjar 180 (a scheduled caste, formerly nomadic, dacoits and prostitutes)

3. Kyasara   Dag Tehsil   Jhalawar District
   Castes: Rajput 46; Nath 18; Chamar 12; Brahman 4; Suthar 3; Teli 1; Nai 2; Balai 2; Darzi 2; Dholi 2; Bania 1; Kumhar 1

4. Bhadwasi   Nagaur Tehsil   Nagaur District
   Castes: Mali 23; Rajput 10; Jat 10; Nayak 7; Bhambi 4; Muslim 3

5. Abhaneri   Baswa Tehsil   Jaipur District
   Castes: Brahman 69; Gujar 35; Kumhar 16; Mali 11; Chamar 8; Mahajan 4; Nai 4; Rajput 3; Koli 3; Jain 2; Khati 2; Mina 2; Bhangi 2; N = 161

6. Nangal Sooswatan   Amber Tehsil   Jaipur District
   Castes: Mina 87; Balai 13; Mali 6; Khati 5; Brahmbhat 7; Brahman 4; Mahajan 1; Dholi (Rana) 2; Jogi 1; N = 126

7. Sanwara   Shahbad Tehsil   Kota District
   Castes: Sahairya 32; Ahir 10; Brahman 1; Muslim 1; N = 44

8. Gagron   Kanwas Tehsil   Kota District
   Castes: Muslim Rajput 25; Rajput 5; Brahman 2; Bhil 6; Mali 7; Chamar 7; Moghia 3; Bhangi 2; N = 57

9. Malar   Palodi Tehsil   Jodhpur District
   Castes: Pushkarna Brahman 121; Sewak Brahman 3; Darzi 5; Suthar 1; Nai 3; Bhil 3; Bawari 2; Bhambi 3

10. Kalijal   Jodhpur Tehsil   Jodhpur District
    Castes: Jat 51; Rajput 33; Rebari 10; Bhil 8; Bhambi 7; Suthar 3; Sadh 1; Daroga 1; Bhangi 1

11. Bujawa   Jodhpur Tehsil   Jodhpur District
    Castes: Rajput 21; Raika 4; Bhambi 4; Sadh 3; Suthar 2; Darzi 1; Nai 1

12. Goriya   Bali Tehsil   Pali District
    Castes: Girasias 104 (a scheduled tribe); Bhil 28; Lohar 2; Kumhar 1; Hargada 1; Muslim 1

13. Panarwa   Phalasia Tehsil   Udaipur District
    Castes: Bhil 13; Rajput 7; Daroga 6; Girasias 5

14. Kailashpur   Nokha Tehsil   Udaipur District
    Castes: Bhil 96; Brahman 55; Mali 18; Darzi 2; Rajput 3; Muslim 1; Nai 2; Jogi 1; Manihar 1; Jat 1

15. Mukam   Nokha Tehsil   Bikaner District
    Castes: Bishnois 58; Meghwals 7

16. Mudh   Kolayat Tehsil   Bikaner District
    Castes: Meghwal 21 (scheduled caste); Darzi 15; Kumhar 11; Nayak 10; Sadh 6; Nai 2; Lohar 4; Dholi 1; Khati 2; Muslim 1; Paliwal 1; Sunar 1; Rajput 1; Pushkarna Brahman 1; N = 77

17. Bajawa   Udaipurwati Tehsil   Jhunjhunu District
    Castes: Chowkidari Mina; 27

18. Janvi Sanchore Tehsil Jalor District
   Castes: Bishnoi 2; Rajput 23; Kalbi 16; Daroga 12; Bhambi 9; Rebari 7; Brahman 4; Bhil
   5; Mahajan 3; Garuda 3; Ghanchi 3; Suthar 2; Koli 3; Swami 3; Mirasi 2; Jat 2; Sadh 1;
   Honi 1; N = 135
19. Peepal Khoont Ghatol Tehsil Banswara District
   Castes: Bhil 131 = 92% population. Remainder are Bhoi, Jogi, Chamar
20. Khajoora Kushalgarh Tehsil Banswara District
   Castes: Bhil 34; Gasa 1
21. Hasanpur Tijara Tehsil Alwar District
   Castes: Meo 53; Chamar 23; Sindhi 4; Bhangi 3; Faqir 1; Mahajan 1
22. Aghapur Bharatpur Tehsil Bharatpur District
   Castes: Gujar 43; Kachhi 19; Jat 15; Banjara 15; Brahman 10; Sikh 6; Kumhar 3; Nai 3;
   Lodha 2; Gadariyia 1; Kadera 1; Bhangi 1; N = 119
23. Bhangarh Rajgarh Tehsil Alwar District
   Castes: Jogis 10 (Kanphata); Kolis 24; Brahman 10; Chamars 5; Mina 4; Khati 1; Nai 1;
   Banjara 6; N = 61
24. Rangmahal Suratgarh Tehsil Ganganagar District
   Castes: Nayak 27; Jat 18; Meghwal 18; Baori 10; Jogi 5; Kumhar 4; Brahman 1.
   Nayaks, Meghwals and Baoris are Untouchables.

The villages surveyed included 65 different caste and tribal communities. The fragmentation of the caste system is such that only seven out of these 65 had members in as many as six different villages. Jats, Chamars and Kumhars appeared in six, Nais in eight, Bhils in nine, Rajputs in 10, and Brahmans in 12. The possibility of comparison of members of the same caste or tribal community living in different places is thus limited. Such comparison is further limited by the absence, in some of the surveys, of reports or tables showing the breakdown of household types by caste and tribal community. Comparison for Nais and Kumhars are precluded by the very small number of families of each in any one village. It has been claimed that Rajputs prefer to live in joint families. The data from the village surveys can be examined to test this, as Rajputs were to be found in 10 of the villages, ranging from one family (in Mudh, Bikaner district) to 23 (in Janvi, Jalor district). Unfortunately, the breakdown of family types by caste is not provided for three of the villages (nos. 10, 14, 16). But for the other seven villages, the proportion of Rajput families which were joint ranged from 0 to 100 per cent (see Table 5).

Applying the principle that if the proportion of joint families is 30 per cent or more in an Indian village it probably means that about half the people live in joint families, we see that in five out of the seven villages, most Rajputs lived in joint families, but that in two villages (Gagron in Kota district and Janvi in Jalor district) they did not.[8] The figures for Janvi,

[8] We are dealing here only with Hindu Rajputs; Gagron also had a large population of Muslim Rajputs (see Table 4).

Table 5
Rajputs' Family Types in Seven Rajasthan Villages

Village	No. of Families	Simple	Inter	Joint	Other
3 Kyasara, Jhal.	46	10 (22%)	15 (33%)	18 (39%)	3 (6%)
4 Bhadwasi, Nagaur	10	5 (50%)	1 (10%)	4 (40%)	
5 Abhaneri, Jaipur	3	0	0	3 (100%)	
8 Gagron, Kota	5	2 (40%)	2 (40%)	1 (20%)	
11 Bujawa, Jodhpur	21	6 (29%)	7 (33%)	8 (38%)	
13 Panarwa, Udaipur	7	3 (43%)	0	3 (43%)	1 (14%)
18 Janvi, Jalor	23	20 (87%)	3(13%)	0	

showing that none of the 23 Rajput families there was joint, are puzzling, as the proportion for total number of families in the village (135) was 29 per cent joint. Janvi included 18 different ethnic communities. The largest caste, the Bishnois, had 50 per cent joint families (18 out of 36 families), as did the Brahmans, Kalbis and Suthars. Why, then, were there no joint families at all among the Rajputs, the second largest ethnic group of Janvi?

The answer once again seems to be the effect of land reform. The *bhumichara jagirdari* (jointly held estate) land owned by the Rajputs in the past had recently been redistributed. Sixty per cent of the land had gone to Bishnois (the former tenants of the Rajputs) and members of other castes, and 40 per cent had been subdivided among the former Rajput joint-owners. It may well have been beneficial for the Rajputs to maximise the numbers of their families when it came to this redistribution of land. In addition, a number of the Rajput young men of Janvi had become sufficiently educated to become office workers in the town of Sanchore, and some Rajput men had gone into business. Thus, it seems plausible that the breaking up and partial loss of the jagirdari previously shared by the Rajputs of Janvi removed the support that had existed for joint family living among them (Singh and Gupta 1966b: 48–49, 58, 60). Unfortunately, we do not have the distribution of household types among them before land reform, so we can only postulate that there were more joint families earlier.

A further characteristic of the Rajputs of Janvi that militated against joint families was the late age of marriage reported for them—18–20 for boys and 14–18 for girls. These were much higher ages than those for Bishnoi and Kalbi children, who were reported to marry boys as young as 5 and girls as young as 3 (Singh and Gupta 1966b: 32). This factor of child marriage will be taken up in greater detail later.

The other village lacking a high proportion of joint family households among Rajputs (Gagron, Kota district) had a medium proportion of 20 per cent—one out of five families. The number of persons in each category of family was not given in the Gagron survey report, so it is not possible to say what proportion of the 29 Rajput individuals in the village belonged to the one joint family. This, of course, is also a small population with a small number of families.

Table 6
Numbers and Proportions of Permanently Unmarried Persons (Bachelors, Widows and Widowers) in 24 Rajasthan Villages

Village	No. of Unmarried Males	No. of Widowers	No. of Widows	Pop. Size	Total Unmarried	% Unmarried
1 Bagor (Bhil.)	2	5	4	229	11	5%
2 Ramnagar (Bu.)	many	7	20	655	27	?
3 Kyasara (Jha)	3	12	41	514	56	11%
4 Bhadwasi	4	4	3	363	11	3%
5 Abhaneri (Jai)	26	34	31	1005	91	9%
6 Nangal S (Jai)	3	9	36	708	48	7%
7 Sanwara (Kota)	1	2	5	222	8	4%
8 Gagron (Kota)	3	15	11	282	29	10%
9 Malar (Jodh)	15	17	41	648	73	11%
10 Kalijal (Jod)	5	14	35	689	53	8%
11 Bujawa (Jod)	6	5	17	229	28	12%
12 Goriya (Pali)	1	7	8	782	16	2%
13 Panarwa (Uda)	0	1	3	146	4	3%
14 Kailashpuri (Udaipur)	3	8	33	664	44	7%
15 Mukam (Bik)	8	13	12	298	33	11%
16 Mudh (Bik)	1	11	20	298	33	11%
17 Bujawa (Jhu)	3	2	7	149	12	8%
18 Janvi (Jal)	1	11	23	695	35	5%
19 Peepal Kh. (Banswara)	3	14	35	830	52	6%
20 Khajoora (Ba)	4	3	7	206	14	7%
21 Hasanpur (Al)	1	5	9	356	15	4%
22 Aghapur (Bha)	34	20	19	599	73	12%
23 Bhangarh (Al)	3	13	12	341	28	8%
24 Rangamahal (Ganganagar)	6	8	9	355	23	6%

Before land reform, 30 to 100 per cent of the land in five of the seven villages (nos. 3, 4, 8, 11, 18) had been controlled by the Rajputs. The Rajputs in the other two villages (nos. 5 and 13) were few in number, living in villages controlled by other dominant castes. Here again is the suggestion that large landholdings encourage a joint family structure.

A feature of Rajput life that is important in terms of family structure is that, along with **Brahmans**, Mahajans (Hindu merchants and bureaucrats) and Bishnois, they forbid the remarriage of widows. This tends to create a category of dependent women to be cared for by some family. Rajputs also tend to have especially distorted sex ratios (see Table 11)[9] which leads to some adult men remaining bachelors throughout life, another category of dependents to be cared for by some family; it does not seem to be a common Rajasthani custom to permit a single person to live alone, or more precisely, to eat from her or his own kitchen. The two factors, prohibition of widow remarriage and the greater number of males than females, may result in a sizeable number of permanently unmarried people of both sexes to be included in 'intermediate' or 'joint' families. The latter are equivalent to my terms, supplemented nuclear, and lineal- , collateral- , and lineal-collateral joint families. Of course, the addition of a single adult to a family cannot make it a joint family, since, by definition, a joint family consists of two or more related married couples. Thus, by definition, the addition of a permanently unmarried adult to a joint family can only 'supplement' it and increase its size—but such an addition does convert a nuclear family into a supplemented nuclear family/'intermediate' family.

When the 24 village surveys are compared on the proportions of their populations which fall into the categories of unmarried males over the age of 25, widowers, and widows (see Table 6), we find high proportions (10 to 20 per cent) in seven villages. Three of these were dominated by Rajputs—two by Hindu Rajputs (nos. 3 and 11) and one by Muslim Rajputs (no. 8). Two were dominated by Hindu religious specialists—one by Brahmans (no. 9) and one by Bishnois (no. 15). The other village with a high proportion of unmarried adults (Aghapur, Bharatpur district) was predominantly Gujar and Jat. According to its ethnographers, Agarwal and Gupta,

> The presence of 19 unmarried males in the age group 25–29 and the age group 30–34 is perhaps due to the fact that the economic position of the households is not strong enough to pay the high bride price demanded by the parents of the girl (1969: 32).

Aghapur's high proportion of single adults seems to have been composed largely of unmarried adult males (34 out of 73), rather than by the widows so characteristic of villages with large Rajput or other high caste populations.

The village with the lowest proportion of its population in these permanently unmarried categories was Goriya, in Pali district, in which three-

---

[9] The issue of the unbalanced sex ratios in India as a whole and in the districts of Rajasthan more specifically is one I do not have the space to discuss. The reader may wish to refer to Miller (1981) on this topic. That measures of joint family do not correlate highly with district sex ratios or child sex ratios in Rajasthan is shown in the last section of this paper.

quarters of the population were members of the Scheduled Tribe of Girasias. The sex ratio was also less unequal (52 per cent male, 48 per cent female) than in half the other villages. Among the Girasias, the common form of marriage is elopement, after which the bridegroom pays some brideprice; exchange is also allowed, requiring neither brideprice nor dowry; both widows and widowers are allowed to remarry, and extramarital relationships are not 'much looked down upon' (Gulati and Gupta 1966: 32, 16). These Girasia tribal norms seemed to result in few adults remaining unmated, hence a lower proportion of permanently unmarried adults and fewer intermediate families. Conversely, the high proportions of permanently unmarried adults among Rajputs and other high castes help account for the high proportions of 'intermediate' families among them.

What about the other major castes and tribes in the villages surveyed—the Jats, Brahmans, Bhils and Chamars? Tables 7, 8, 9 and 10 show the distribution of family types in the villages in which each community was to be found. A perusal of these tables indicates that there was no consistent pattern for Jats, Brahmans or Bhils. There were both high and low proportions of joint families among each of these ethnic groups. Clearly, therefore, Jats and Brahmans do not have consistently high proportions of joint families, nor do Bhils have consistently low proportions. Thus, the popular idea that Jats and high castes have high proportions of joint families, and that tribals do not, is not sustained by these village surveys.

Table 7
Jats' Family Types in Four Rajasthan Villages

Village	No. of Families	Simple	Inter.	Joint	Other
4 Bhadwasi, Nagaur	10	7 (70%)	0	3 (30%)	
18 Janvi, Jalor	2	2 (100%)			
22 Aghapur, Bharatpur	15	8 (53%)	1 (7%)	5 (33%)	1 (7%)
24 Rangmahal, Ganga.	18	12 (67%)	5 (28%)	0	1 (5%)

Any suggestion that joint family living is most characteristic of high castes is belied not only by the figures for Bhils in Table 9, but also by the figures in Table 10 for the low caste Untouchable Chamars. Consistently, Chamars had high proportions of joint families, as high as 88 per cent (Abhaneri, Jaipur district) and 80 per cent (Bhangarh, Alwar district). The number of Chamar families in each village was small, however, between five and 12 families. Moreover, it should be noted that both Abhaneri and Bhangarh are well-watered villages on the Sanwar river, and that the Chamars there were agricultural labourers living in one-room houses (Agarwal and Pendharker

Table 8
Brahman Family Types in Eleven Rajasthan Villages

Village	No. of Families	Simple	Inter.	Joint	Other
3 Kyasara, Jhal.	4	3 (75%)	0	1 (25%)	0
5 Abhaneri, Jaipur	69	40 (58%)	25 (36%)	5 (7%)	
6 Nangal Soos., Jai.	4	0	1 (25%)	3 (75%)	
7 Sanwara, Kota	1	0	1 (100%)	0	
8 Gagron, Kota	2	0	0	1 (50%)	
9 Malar, Jodhpur	124	69 (56%)	23 (33%)	32 (26%)	
14 Kailashpuri, Udai	55	35 (64%)	6 (10%)	7 (13%)	7 (13%)
18 Janvi, Jalor	4	0	2 (50%)	2 (50%)	
22 Aghapur,	10	2 (20%)	4 (40%)	4 (40%)	
23 Bhangarh, Alwar	10	4 (40%)	1 (10%)	3 (30%)	2 (20%)
24 Rangmahal, Ganga.	1	1 (100%)	0	0	

Table 9
Bhils' Family Types in Eight Rajasthan Villages

Village	No. of Families	Simple	Inter.	Joint	Other
8 Gagron, Kota	46	10 (22%)	15 (33%)	18 (39%)	3 (6%)
9 Malar, Jodhpur	3	2 (67%)	0	1 (33%)	
12 Goriya, Pali	28	20 (71%)	0	8 (29%)	
13 Panarwa, Udai.	13	8 (62%)	0	4 (31%)	1 (7%)
14 Kailashpuri, Udai.	96	65 (68%)	10 (10%)	15 (16%)	6 (6%)
18 Janvi, Jalor	23	20 (87%)	3 (13%)	0	
19 Peepal Khoont, B.	155	120 (77%)	15 (10%)	15 (10%)	5 (3%)
20 Khajoora, Ban.	34	18 (53%)	5 (15%)	7 (20%)	4 (12%)

Table 10
Chamar Family Types in Five Rajasthan Villages

Village	No. of Families	Simple	Inter.	Joint	Other
3 Kyasara, Jhal.	12	5 (42%)	1 (8%)	4 (33%)	2 (17%)
5 Abhaneri, Jaipur	8	0	0	7 (88%)	1 (12%)
8 Gagron, Kota	7	0	1 (14%)	4 (57%)	2 (29%)
9 Peepal Khoont, Ban.	7	3 (43%)	0	3 (43%)	1 (14%)
23 Bhangarh, Alwar	5	1 (20%)	0	4 (80%)	

Table 11
Sex Ratios for 24 Villages Studies Done in Rajasthan
(Census of India 1961)

1. Bagor		Mandal Tehsil	Bhilwara District	1–1
Sex ratio:	124 M (58%)	105 F (42%)	(p. 2) total: 229	
2. Ramnagar	Kanjar Colony	Bundi Tehsil	Bundi District	1–1
Sex ratio:	380 M (58%)	275 F (42%)	(p. 27) total: 655	
3. Kyasara		Dag Tehsil	Jhalawar District	1–1
Sex ratio:	264 M (51%)	250 F (49%)	total: 514	
4. Bhadwasi		Nagaur Tehsil	Nagaur District	1–1
Sex ratio:	201 M ((55%)	162 F (45%)	total: 363	
5. Abhaneri		Bawa Tehsil	Jaipur District	1–2
Sex ratio:	546 M (54%)	459 F (46%)	total: 1005	
6. Nangal Sooswatan		Amber Tehsil	Jaipur District	1–2
Sex ratio:	369 M (52%)	339 F (48%)	total: 708	
7. Sanwara		Shahbad Tehsil	Kota District	1–2
Sex ratio:	106 M (48%)	116 F (52%)	total: 222	
8. Gagron		Kanwas Tehsil	Kota District	1–2
Sex ratio:	161 M (57%)	121 F (43%)	total: 282	
9. Malar		Palodi Tehsil	Jodhpur District	2–1
Sex ratio:	352 M (54%)	296 F (46%)	total: 648	
10. Kalijal		Jodhpur Tehsil	Jodhpur District	2–1
Sex ratio:	372 M (54%)	317 F (46%)	total: 689	
11. Bujawa		Jodhpur Tehsil	Jodhpur District	2–1
Sex ratio:	128 M (56%)	101 F (44%)	total: 229	
12. Goriya		Bali Tehsil	Pali District	2–1
Sex ratio:	406 M (52%)	376 F (48%)	total: 782	
13. Panwara		Phalasia Tehsil	Udaipur District	2–1
Sex ratio:	79 M (54%)	67 F (46%)	total: 146	
14. Kailashpuri		Girwa Tehsil	Udaipur District	2–1
Sex ratio:	348 M (52%)	316 F (48%)	(p.2) total: 664	
15. Mukam		Nokha Tehsil	Bikaner District	2–2
Sex ratio:	p. 1: 167 M (56%)	131 F (44%)	total: 298	
16. Mudh		Kolayat Tehsil	Bikaner District	2–2
Sex ratio:	p. 4: 213 M (51%)	206 F (49%)	total: 419	
17. Bujawa	Udaipurwati Tehsil	Jhunjhunu	(Shekhawati)	2–3
Sex ratio:	p. 28: 70 M (47%)	79 F (53%)	total: 149	
Chowkidari Minas	102 M (54%)	88 F (46%)		
18. Janvi		Sanchore Tehsil	Jalor District	3–2
Sex ratio:	p. 4: 343 M (50%)	342 F (50%)	total: 685	
19. Peepal Khoont		Ghatol Tehsil	Banswara District	3–2
Sex ratio:	p. 46: 430 M (52%)	400 F (48%)	total: 830	
20. Khajoora		Kushalgarh Tehsil	Banswara District	3–2
Sex ratio:	p. 1: 103 M (50%)	103 F (50%)	total: 206	

Table 11 contd.

21. Hasanpur		Tijara Tehsil	Alwar District	3–2
Sex ratio:	p. 6: 192 M (54%)	164 F (46%)	total: 356	
22. Aghapur		Bharatpur Tehsil	Bharatpur District	3–2
Sex ratio:	p. 7: 345 M (58%)	254 F (42%)	total: 599	
23. Bhangarh		Rajgarh Tehsil	Alwar District	3–2
Sex ratio:	p. 3: 185 M (54%)	156 F (46%)	total: 341	
24. Rangmahal		Suratgarh Tehsil	Ganganagar District	4–3
Sex ratio:	194 M (55%)	161 F (45%)	total: 355	

1965: 3, 9, 20; Gulati and Pendharker 1965c: 11, 21). Possibly, then, the Chamars' high proportion of joint families was not entirely the result of choice, but also of lack of resources to build more housing. Thomas Rosin has pointed out to me (personal communication) that possibly the Chamar joint household may also be a work-team when it pursues the Chamars' traditional leather craft. He writes: 'The jointness of leather worker's families also has struck me, but their structure seems consistent with their elaborate activities in hauling, flailing, tanning, and crafting leather.' The importance of the joint family as a work-team was mentioned for Maharajapur-Kishanpur earlier, and will be discussed in greater detail for Rajasthan as a whole later.

Comparison of a caste's family structure in different Rajasthani villages thus suggests variation within the caste. In the village surveys examined here, only the Scheduled Caste Chamars showed consistently high proportions of joint family living, followed by the high caste Rajputs. While the high proportions for Rajputs may have been the result of large landholdings in the past, those for Chamars may have been due to crowded housing. The common beliefs about the relationships between ethnicity and family structure in Rajasthan are sustained by these Census village survey data only with respect to Rajputs, not with respect to Jats or Bhils.

Early Adolescent Marriage and the 'Protective Joint Family'

In the late 1960s and early 1970s, Lorraine Haddon, a graduate student at the University of Houston, calculated measures of over 60 variables in the 1961 Census. These measures fell into three groups: variables related to family, variables taken to be indices of modernisation, and other social-cultural variables such as religion, occupation, and caste or tribe membership. Only a few of these variables were found to have strong (positive or negative) correlations of +/−0.60 or better with the indices of joint family living discussed above (Married Sons and Other Married Relatives).[10] On an all-India basis, negative relationships were found between proportions of joint families and various educational variables and measures of modernisation (Kolenda and Haddon 1987: 276, 279–86). These negative relationships were not found in Rajasthan, however, probably because the districts of Rajasthan in which there were low proportions of joint families (the Gujarat border districts, Jaisalmer and Ganganagar) were not highly modernised and did not have, except possibly in some towns and in some of the more modernised parts of Ganganagar, especially good educational facilities. The largest number of schools with the maximum number of school-going children are in the districts east of the Aravallis, the very districts which are high in joint families.

The variables with which the indices of joint family were found to be most strongly related were the proportions of females and males aged 10–14 reported as married. The correlation coefficients between the proportion of Married Sons and the two measures of adolescent marriage were +0.912 for females and +0.856 for males; the same relationships for proportion of Other Married Relatives were +0.848 and +0.761. These two variables of adolescent marriage were also highly interrelated, with a correlation coefficient of +0.90.

Maps 7 and 8 show the districts in Rajasthan in Quintile 1 on proportions of married females and males aged 10–14. The nine districts shown on Map 7 ranged between 63.92 per cent (Bhilwara district) and 42.26 per cent (Jaipur district) for females aged 10–14 reported as married; 10 other districts were in the second quintile. Thus, in 19 districts of Rajasthan, the proportion of females aged 10–14 reported as married was well above all-India averages. In addition, six districts were in the third quintile and one in the fourth; none was in the fifth quintile.

Map 8 shows 11 Rajasthan districts that fell into the first quintile on proportion of married males aged 10–14, ranging from 32.48 per cent (Bhilwara district) to 13.69 per cent (Udaipur district). Moreover, with 12 districts falling into the second quintile, 23 of the districts of Rajasthan were well above average in proportion of married males 10–14. The other three districts fell in Quintile 3.

A comparison of Maps 3 and 4 with Maps 7 and 8 indicates that young adolescent marriage is more characteristic of Rajasthan than is that of joint families. That is, more districts fall above the all-India average on the two measures of adolescent marriage than on the two measures of joint family. Map 9 shows seven districts which rank in the first quintile on all four

[10] Statisticians hold that correlations from +/−0.60 to 1.00 are worth interpreting. Sometimes this criterion is relaxed to allow for interpretation of correlations as low as +/−0.40.

Map 7: Rajasthan Districts in First Quintile on Proportions of Females Aged 10-14 Reported as Married (Census of India 1961)

Map 8: Rajasthan Districts in First Quintile on Proportions of Males Aged 10-14 Reported as Married (Census of India (1961)

measures. Spatially contiguous except for Jhalawar, separated by a small section of Kota from Chitorgarh, they form a central core in which there is a high proportion of joint family households, explained to a considerable extent by the high proportions of married young adolescents.

While the proportions of married 10–14 year-olds were recorded in the 1961 Census, it was not noted whether those counted were living with their spouses or not. The meaning of the 1961 Census figures is thus questionable. Were these young adolescents married only in the sense of having had their shadis, or had their muklavas taken place already and were they living together in the husband's household? It is noteworthy that none of the Census ethnographers ever addresses this issue or the question of what is meant by a Census report of 'married' 10–14 year-old.

Here it is useful to turn to ethnographic evidence. That marriages took place at early ages in Rajasthan is supported by Rama Mehta's memoir about the Oswals (Vaishya bureaucrats) (Mehta 1982: 141) attached to the Maharana of Udaipur's court. She writes:

> . . . it must be remembered that the age of marriage in the Oswal community was between nine and twelve years prior to 1947, and the age at which a woman came to her husband's home was usually about thirteen to fourteen . . . . Among the Oswals, child marriage was widespread.
> . . . purdah becomes a means for minimalizing family disputes, allowing the child bride to function under the supervision of elders without the possibility of contradicting their commands. This was necessary, since a child bride had not been tutored to assume responsibility before she entered marriage. For the young bride, the early years of her marriage constituted a period of training and education (Mehta 1982: 146–48).

According to Mehta, the young Oswal brides were ignorant of housekeeping and were trained by their mothers-in-law as they were too young to have been properly trained before marriage. In M-K as well, new brides complained that they did not know how to do the tasks assigned them by their mothers-in-law. They were often so young that they had to be trained to do household chores by their mothers-in-law or older sisters-in-law. If a girl was the junior daughter-in-law in a joint household in which her own sister was the senior daughter-in-law, the latter might even do the work *for* her.

Young age for marriage was noted in 13 of the 1961 Census village surveys (nos. 1, 3, 4, 6, 7, 8, 9, 12, 15, 16, 18, 19, 22). In Kvasara village, Jhalawar district, for example, in which almost half the population was Rajput, another 20 per cent Nath and 10 per cent Chamar, with nine other small caste communities (Singh and Gupta 1965a: 2), three-quarters of the females aged 10–14 and one-third of the males aged 10–14 were recorded as married. According to the ethnographers, 'There is no unmarried female above the age of 14 in the village' (ibid.: 37). In only three villages were there any reports of marriage for girls normally occurring after age 14. Two reports refer to Rajputs (4, 18), and one to Kanjars (2).

That marriage ceremonies may take place at extremely young ages is suggested by the report from Kalijal village in Jodhpur district:

> Among the Jats of this village it is customary to hold the marriages of the girls of the family without consideration of their age at the time of performance of death-feast of some elderly person. The main consideration behind this custom is economy. Even girls in arms who belong to the family are married on the occasion. It is not unusual to see a small girl seated on a brass plate to be married to a boy who may be a little bigger than her. The children are lifted by the parents who go round the fire to complete the *pheras* [circumambulations of the sacred fire by the bride and groom] (Singh and Pendharker 1967: 14).

In his book on the village of Awan in Kota district, Giri Raj Gupta explains the custom of early age of marriage:

> It is a common practice for girls to marry before reaching puberty. There are several arguments advanced in favour of early marriage. The people believe early marriages tend to protect the chastity of women, ease the transfer of a girl from her father's domain to that of her husband, and make it easier for a girl to adjust to her husband and in-laws. Pre-puberty marriages are also considered to be more sacred and pure than a marriage which takes place later in a girl's life, since the girl has not been contaminated by the pollution associated with menstruation. It is also feared that a girl's approaching sexuality will lead her to relinquish her sacred status as a virgin. It is well known that the Sanskritic scriptures of the Vedic times state that a girl should be married as a virgin and before menarche.
>
> The economic consideration is also very important. A girl married before puberty becomes an economic partner in her conjugal family much earlier. This, in turn, reintegrates the economy of her natal as well as conjugal family.
>
> Traditionally, each incipient family begins with the support of an old family. The young people are responsible for bringing new people into the family, both by marriage and by birth, to replace the old members. Since marriages are expensive events, the family's economy

must be preserved by spacing marriages several years apart. The earlier the marriage is organised, the better it is for the family. Parents like to see their responsibilities fulfilled before they retire. Most marriages cost somewhat more than a year's income of the family. In some cases, as among the Rajputs, a marriage may take two to three years of the family's income. Early marriages of the children help the family to space the marriages evenly.

Another advantage of early marriages is that a person benefits immediately from any advantages he has achieved through the marital alliance.

However, on an average, the boys are usually married between the age of 12 and 16 years, while the girls are married between the age of 9 and 14 years. Analysing the caste rank and its relationship with age at marriage, it appears that there is little association between the two. One of the major inferences could be that it is not the rank of the caste, but its involvement in agricultural activities which could explain the distribution of age at *sagai* [betrothal] and marriage. For purposes of broader generalisation three perceivable trends can be delineated: (1) upper castes marry relatively late, (2) agriculturalists and artisans marry relatively early, and (3) most of the boys and girls among all the castes continue to marry earlier than the minimum ages fixed by the Hindu Marriage Act of 1955, which is 15 for girls and 18 for boys. Obviously, the legislation relating to the age at marriage has had little impact, if any, on the marital practices of the people (Gupta 1974: 65–66).

Note Gupta's statement that 'A girl married before puberty becomes an economic partner in her conjugal family much earlier.' What both Gupta and Mehta suggest is that in some communities and places in Rajasthan, the bride actually does take up residence with her husband's family before the age of 14, and possibly before first menstruation. Needless to say, among illiterate people who do not keep precise records, the exact age of a bride upon joining her husband's household may not be known, but it seems safe to say that brides have, by age 16, joined their mothers-in-law. In the case of such early marriages, the joint family functions to support very young couples not mature enough to manage a household economic enterprise alone. The Rajasthani joint family can thus be understood to be a reversal of the pre-industrial nuclear family in western Europe, a family founded by an adult male in his mid- or late twenties, trained and ready to support a wife and children, the wife also being in her twenties at marriage (Laslett 1984: 99–101; 1972: 85). Instead of postponing marriage and childbearing as the English pre-industrial family required, the Rajasthani family supports marriage for even physically immature adolescents, and childbearing for sexually mature adolescent wives, by having the family unit joint, composed of at least one adult couple and possible one or more pre-adult couples (couples under age 20).

Prakash Tandon made this contrast between British and Punjabi assumptions about the age of marriage:

> . . . . it was in accordance with father's own ideas that uncle preferred to wait for his marriage till he was settled in life. To the old way of thinking this was irrelevant. You married when you came of age and not when you began to earn. Marriage and earning were two separate things. Marriage was a social, familial and religious obligation, while earning was a matter of circumstance (Tandon 1961: 124).

This Punjabi view is quite in line with the Rajasthani view. The joint-familism of the north Indian family can be understood, at least for much of Rajasthan, as more a matter of an adult male and his wife in their thirties or forties taking the lead, with inexperienced married teenagers following their directions, than as a matter of an elderly patriarch in his fifties or sixties ordering about fully adult sons who are men in their twenties to forties.

These findings strongly suggest a kind of joint family composed of a head couple plus a young teenaged couple living together until either the members of the older couple die or the young couple mature and have so many children that they need more living space. The question would then be whether all joint families in Rajasthan, and in India as a whole, are 'protective joint families' of this type.

Of course, the strategy for establishing a couple at a young age may involve a belief that young adolescents are more malleable than older ones, that once a bride has adjusted to her husband's joint family she is less likely to be discontented that she does not have a home of her own (See Kolenda 1987: 104–05).

The Well-Team Joint Family

The high correlation between young adolescent marriage and the two measures of joint family ('Married Sons' and 'Other Married Relatives') is partly an artifact of the data, since married males aged 10–14 are included in the proportion of married sons in the household sample. Similarly, males and females aged 10–14 who are represented as married are included in the proportion of Other Married Relatives in the sample. What the high correlations between the two measures of joint family and adolescent marriage measure, then, is the correlation between the whole variable (the Married Sons or Other Married Relatives of all ages) and part of it (the Married Sons or Other Married Relatives aged 10–14). Thus, the high correlations appear to be a matter of a variable relating to part of itself. Only if the couples which included a spouse aged 10–14 lived separately in their own households separate from the Other Married Relatives would the previous statement be untrue. The ethnographic evidence, however, does not suggest that neolocal residence for such young couples occurs.

One way to find out whether there are other kinds of joint family besides the 'protective joint family' is to remove from the household samples the effects of the presence of married 10–14 year-olds. This was done,[11] and a third measure of family structure was developed, the 'Revised Family Structure'. How then does Rajasthan appear in comparison with the rest of India when joint family living is measured by Revised Family Structure?

Map 10 shows the seven districts of Rajasthan which fall in the top quintile of all the 326 districts in India on Revised Family Structure. The number, of course, is considerably less than the 15 districts in the first quintile on Married Sons (see Map 3) or the 11 districts in the first quintile on Other Married Relatives (see Map 4). We may presume that the decline in the ranking of other districts in Quintile 1 on 'Married Sons' and 'Other Married Relatives' is due to the considerable prevalence in them of 'protective joint families'. Indeed, all these districts fall in the second quintile on the Revised Family Structure measure, indicating that the frequency of joint families that are not just protecting adolescent brides and grooms is still above average for India as a whole.

How are we to understand the seven districts that are in the first quintile on joint families once the effect of adolescent brides and grooms is factored out? Here I would like to return to the village of Maharajapur-Kishanpur and the third factor contributing to the occurrence of joint families: the need for the family to function as a work-team and, more specifically, a well-team.

To help analyse this factor, I would like to introduce the mapping of Rajasthan into ecological zones by A.K. Sen of the Central Arid Zone Research Institute (CAZRI) in Jodhpur. In the *Agricultural Atlas of Rajasthan* (1972), he divided Rajasthan into four major ecological zones: the Hot Desert, the Steppe Desert, the Semi-Arid Region, and the Humid Region.

---

[11] The effects of the married among the 10–14 age group upon the indices of joint family was removed by finding in Table C–II, Age and Marital Status for each district, the number of males aged 10–14 who were reported as married, dividing this number by 5 to correspond to the 20 per cent household sample, and subtracting this dividend from the number of 'Other Married Relatives'. The same was done for the figures on females aged 10–14 who were married. The resulting remainder was then divided by the total population of the 20 per cent household sample and that proportion was the measure of Revised Family Structure.

Map 9: Seven Districts in Rajasthan in First Quintile on Four Measures: Proportion of Married Sons, Proportion of Married Relatives, Females 10-14 Married and Males 10-14 Married (Census of India 1961)

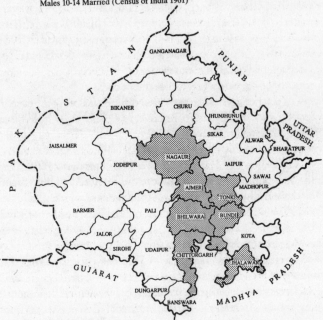

Map 10: Seven Rajasthan Districts in First Quintile on Revised Family Structure (Census of India 1961)

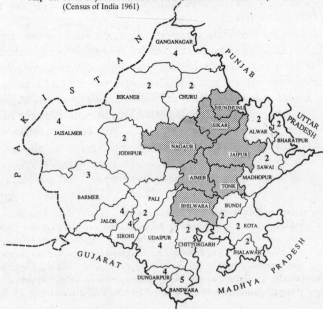

Map 11: Geographical Regions of Rajasthan (Based on Natural Regions)

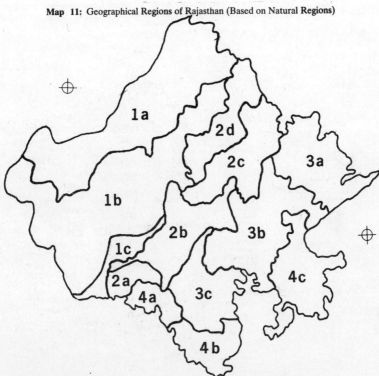

1 **Hot Desert:** *1a Ganganagar-Jaisalmer region (Raj. Canal area); 1b Jodhpur region (Dry Desert); 1c Luni region (Central & Lower Luni Basin).* 2 **Steppe Desert:** *2a Jalor region (Jawai Basin); 2b Ajmer-Pali region (Upper Luni Basin); 2c Sikar-Deedwana region (Kantli & Didwana-Sambhar Salt Basins); 2d Churu region (Dry Steppe).* 3 **Semi-Arid Region:** *3a Alwar-Bharatpur region (Sota Sahibi & Barh Basins); 3b Jaipur region (Lower Bansi & Morel Basins of the Chambal Catchment); 3c Udaipur-Chittorgarh region (Chambal-Mahi Waterparting Zone).* 4 **Humid Region:** *4a Sirohi region (Upper Sabarmati-Banas Basins); 4b Dungarpur region (Upper Mahi Basin); 4c Kota Region (Chambal Project Area)*

Source: A.K. Sen, Cartographic Laboratory, Central Arid Zone Research Institute.

With Sen's permission, an adaptation of that map is presented here (Map 11). Each of the four major zones is subdivided into three or four sub-zones, yielding a total of 13 ecological sub-zones. When the seven districts in the first quintile on Revised Family Structure are superimposed on the ecological map, they fall almost entirely into three sub-zones. Two sub-zones (2c and 2d) are in the Steppe Desert, and one (3b) is in the Semi-Arid Region. Small portions of the seven districts fall into three other sub-zones (1b, 2b and 3a). With the exception of a small portion of Nagaur district, which falls into sub-zone 1b of the Hot Desert, all seven districts fall into the Steppe Desert and Semi-Arid Region (see Map 12). What this suggests is that, in Rajasthan, the joint family is a more important adaptation in these two zones than it is in either the Hot Desert or in the Humid Region.

Map 12 shows the quintile rankings of all the districts of Rajasthan on Revised Family Structure. In the two sub-zones of southern Rajasthan and

Map 12: Seven Districts in First Quintile on Revised Family Structure by Geographical
Regions in Rajasthan (Census of India 1961)

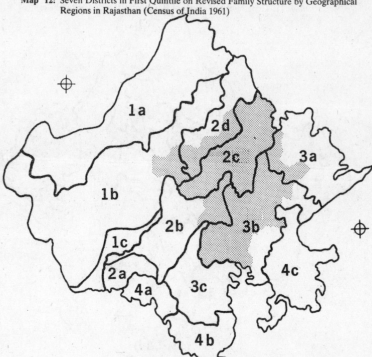

1 **Hot Desert:** *1a Ganganagar-Jaisalmer region (Raj. Canal area); 1b Jodhpur region (Dry Desert); 1c Luni region (Central &
Lower Luni Basin).* 2 **Steppe Desert:** *2a Jalor region (Jawai Basin); 2b Ajmer-Pali region (Upper ¹ ui Basin); 2c Sikar-
Deedwana region (Kantli & Didwana-Sambhar Salt Basins); 2d Churu region (Dry Steppe).* 3 Semi-Arid Region: *3a Alwar-
Bharatpur region (Sota Sahibi & Barh Basins); 3b Jaipur region (Lower Bansi & Morel Basins of the Chambal Catchment);
3c Udaipur-Chittorgarh region (Chambal-Mahi Waterparting Zone).* 4 **Humid Region:** *4a Sirohi region (Upper Sabarmati-
Banas Basins); 4b Dungarpur region (Upper Mahi Basin); 4c Kota Region (Chambal Project Area)*

Source: A.K. Sen, Cartographic Laboratory, Central Arid Zone Research Institute.

Gujarat, all four districts are well below average on Revised Family Structure, falling into either the fourth quintile (Sirohi, Udaipur and Dungarpur)
or the fifth (Banswara). The 4a and 4b sub-zones of the Humid Region are
distinguished from the 4c sub-zone (composed of Jhalawar, Kota and parts
of Bundi and Sawai Madhopur districts, see Map 11), by the considerably
greater agricultural activity in the latter, called by Misra the 'Southeastern
Agricultural Region' (1967: 176–77), due to that region's closeness to the
Chambal river waters and its flatter and better soil.

In the Hot Desert, three of the districts are average to low on Revised
Family Structure. Barmer, in the third quintile, is average in an all-India
ranking, while Jaisalmer and Ganganagar are well below average.

The strength of the joint family in the Steppe Desert and the Semi-Arid
Region suggests that the joint family is most adapted to areas where there is
water for irrigation, but not so little that agriculture is impossible (as in

Map 13: Quintiles 1 and 2 as Compared to Quintiles 4 and 5 on Revised Family Structure by Geographical Regions in Rajasthan (Census of India 1961)

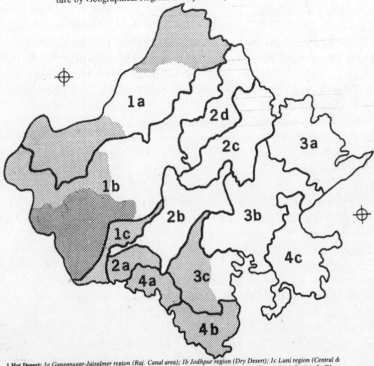

1 **Hot Desert:** *1a Ganganagar-Jaisalmer region (Raj. Canal area); 1b Jodhpur region (Dry Desert); 1c Luni region (Central & Lower Luni Basin).* 2 **Steppe Desert:** *2a Jalor region (Jawai Basin); 2b Ajmer-Pali region (Upper Luni Basin); 2c Sikar-Deedwana region (Kantli & Didwana-Sambhar Salt Basins); 2d Churu region (Dry Steppe).* 3 **Semi-Arid Region:** *3a Alwar-Bharatpur region (Sota Sahibi & Barh Basins); 3b Jaipur region (Lower Bansi & Morel Basins of the Chambal Catchment); 3c Udaipur-Chittorgarh region (Chambal-Mahi Waterparting Zone).* 4 **Humid Region:** *4a Sirohi region (Upper Sabarmati-Banas Basins); 4b Dungarpur region (Upper Mahi Basin); 4c Kota Region (Chambal Project Area)*
Source: A.K. Sen, Cartographic Laboratory, Central Arid Zone Research Institute.

Jaisalmer in the Hot Desert), or enough so that it is not a serious problem as in the Humid Region. The joint family as a well-team thus appears to be one effective strategy for coping with the irrigation problems of the Steppe Desert and Semi-Arid Region.[12]

There are, however, a number of problems with such an analysis, especially

[12] It is not claimed here that the joint family is the only organisation on which Rajasthan agriculturalists base a work-team. R. Thomas Rosin (1978: 469) describes a standard work-team for Undhyala village, Nagaur, as:

> The organization of labor crucial to the irrigation of a second crop was provided by a four-man team, each member of which was an equal partner, usually from separate families which could contribute kinsmen and affines as needed to augment the labor force at the well (see also ibid.: 475, 487 for other details of this work-team).

Rosin promises to report on a survey of irrigation work-teams in Rajasthan that he made in 1982–83 in the near future.

when Map 12 is redrawn separating districts in the first and second quintile on Revised Family Structure from those in the fourth and fifth (see Map 13). It becomes clear that above average proportions of joint families (in the second quintile and above on Revised Family Structure) occur in districts of all four ecological zones—in sub-zones 1a and 1b of the Hot Desert (Jodhpur and Bikaner) as well as in sub-zone 4c of the Humid Region (Kota, Jhalawar and Bundi).

Indeed, Map 13 suggests that Rajasthan is characterised by three Revised Family Structure zones: an 18-district zone with joint families in the first and second quintile, the third quintile zone of Barmer district, and a fourth and fifth quintile zone composed of the five districts bordering on Gujarat (Jalor, Sirohi, Udaipur, Dungarpur, Banswara) and the two Thar desert districts (Jaisalmer and Ganganagar). The problem then becomes: what are the crucial differences between the 18 high joint family districts and the seven low joint family districts?

Some leads emerge when we turn to correlations between different variables. If we take the standard that only correlations over $+/-0.608$ are suggestive of a substantial relationship between variables, then Revised Family Structure correlates only with adolescent marriage (a correlation of $+0.62$ and $+0.74$, respectively, for males and females aged 10–14 who are married). Correlations between $+/-0.40$ and $+/-0.60$, which are sometimes accepted as significant by social scientists, are found for proportion of tribals in a district's population $(+0.46)$ and for proportion of females in agriculture $(+0.511)$.

The tribal variable suggests the high proportion of Bhils along the Gujarat border, especially in the districts of Dungarpur and Banswara, where over half the population are Bhils. However, as we saw earlier in Table 8, the village surveys suggest that Bhils sometimes have low proportions of joint families and sometimes do not. The variable of females in agriculture suggests joint family work-teams or well-teams. However as shown in Map 14, the districts of Dungarpur and Banswara fall into Quintile 1 on females in agriculture but in the fourth and fifth quintile on Revised Family Structure, thus actually lowering the correlation between these two variables.

The factor that seems to be common to all seven districts in the fourth and fifth quintiles seems to be a paucity of wells. Let us first consider the districts along the Gujarat border, moving from west to east. The 1961 Census District Gazetteer for Jalor reports that only 9 per cent of the land is irrigated (Sehgal 1973a: 61). What geographer V.C. Misra calls the Aravalli Region (composed of all of Udaipur, southeast Pali, Sirohi and western Dungarpur) makes up much of the Gujarat border area. 'The area being hilly, it is only a small part of the land where irrigation is possible. In Udaipur nearly two-thirds of the land is barren and is not suitable for agricultural use' (1967: 173).

Map 14: Rajasthan Districts in First Quintile on Proportion of Females in Agriculture (Census of India 1961)

Map 15: Rajasthan Districts in First Quintile on Child/Woman Fertility (Census of India 1961)

At the east end of the Aravalli Region is Dungarpur, characterised in its District Gazetteer as 'stony hills covered with low jungle' (Sehgal 1974: 2), with its cultivated area 'confined to valleys and low ground between the hills' (ibid.: 3). Its well irrigation is by the pole-rope system (*dhenkli*) or Persian wheel (ibid.: 79), both methods requiring only one person rather than a team (Michael 1978: 198). Most of Banswara district is also hills and forest. Thus, the mountains and hills on the Gujarat border seem to prevent much well-team irrigation.

Jaisalmer district, likewise, which is almost entirely pastoral in its adaptation to the Thar desert, has 'hardly any good wells which can be the sources of irrigation' (Sehgal 1973b: 7) and extremely deep water tables. Ganganagar too, irrigated since 1927 by the Gang Canal, is characterised by 'no well irrigation nor tanks and lakes' (Sehgal 1972: 7).

This more refined analysis of well irrigation suggests that the first and second quintile districts on Revised Family Structure are districts in which, along with the practice of adolescent marriage, well-team irrigation is important, while the fourth and fifth quintile districts tend to be bereft of wells and hence irrigation methods do not require a team. Some of the Gujarat border districts are high on the variable of young adolescent marriage (all of them are in the first and second quintiles on male adolescent marriage, while on female adolescent marriage, Udaipur and Sirohi are in the second quintile, and Jalor, Dungarpur and Banswara in the third. See Maps 7 and 8). The Gujarat border districts thus seem to be districts in which more 'protective' joint families' occur than well-team joint families.

The Census figures I have examined thus suggest that the joint family structure in Rajasthan is associated with an agrarian economic-ecological adaptation which results in adult responsibilities that are incompatible if a single person has to carry them all out. My fieldwork in Maharajapur-Kishanpur likewise suggested that the joint family in Rajasthan is a work-team, associated especially with well-irrigation in semi-arid regions. While the Persian wheel, counterpoise-bucket lift or dhenkli are appropriate for water on the surface or close to the surface, and can be operated by a single person (Michael 1978: 198), the rope-and-bucket lift (*charas*) method of irrigation appropriate for deeper water requires the cooperation of at least two people. It is the charas method and deeper water that are characteristic of the wells of the Steppe Desert and Semi-Arid Regions of Rajasthan where Quintile 1 districts on Revised Family Structure are located. The charas-teams often consist of brothers, or of a father and son, and may also include a wife or unmarried daughter guiding water into the patches of crop-plants. This need for females to help in the fields in a demographic situation characterised by a general shortage of women in Rajasthan may be responded to by an eagerness to 'reserve' wives for sons by the shadi ceremony of marriage as early as possible and thus results in early marriage for females and resultant 'protective joint families'

Fertility, Sex Preference and the Joint Family in Rajasthan

A final question to be examined is whether the data for Rajasthan show any correlation between the joint family, fertility, and preference for male children. Looking first at fertility, are districts high in proportions of joint families also high in size of family, average number of children per family, and child/woman fertility rates? High correlations between measures of joint family living and these variables would suggest that joint families tend to stimulate fertility more than nuclear families.

Table 12 presents the correlation coefficients for the relationships between these measures and proportion of Married Sons, proportion of Other Married Relatives, and Revised Family Structure. For all three measures, the correlation coefficients are very small, and mostly negative in direction.

Table 12
Correlations Between Family Size, Number of Children, Child/Woman Fertility and Measures of Joint Families and Early Adolescent Marriage

	Married Sons	Married Relatives	RFS*	Married F 10–14	Married M 10–14
Family size	−0.167	0.014	0.152	−0.377	−0.433
Average number of children	−0.402	−0.245	−0.12	−0.587	−0.556
Child/woman fertility	−0.636	−0.561	−0.49	−0.720	−0.571

* Revised Family Structure

	Rajasthan			All-India		
	Mean	Median	Range	Mean	Median	Range
Family size	5.42	5.48	4.81–6.08	5.26	5.24	2.91–6.59
Average number of children	2.33	2.32	1.91–2.73	2.19	2.18	1.54–3.0
Child/woman fertility	0.795	0.797	0.675–0.949	0.739	0.743	0.0793–0.9942

Thus, no relationship between family structure and these measures appears to be of any importance. The list of means amd medians shows something else, however: that the average values on the variables of family size, number of children, and child/woman fertility ratios are higher for Rajasthan than the national averages. On all three values, Rajasthan lies in the second quintile nation-wide. Thus it seems that Rajasthani families tend to be larger and have more children than the average for the whole of India, and that a woman in her childbearing years has more children under the age of 5 than the national average.

The correlation coefficients nevertheless indicate that the higher values on these measures in Rajasthan tend not to be in districts with higher proportions of joint families (see Map 15 for districts of Rajasthan with high child/woman fertility rates). This negative relationship is suggested by the fact that the seven districts high in proportion of joint families on Revised Family Structure fall into the second, third and fourth quintiles on child/woman fertility ratios. When a bilinear analysis between measures of joint family and child/woman fertility was run, it was found that about 40 per cent of the variance in joint family values overlapped with (negative) variance in child/woman fertility. This value is much lower than the 70 per cent and higher (positive) variances for the measures of adolescent marriage. It does, nevertheless, suggest a notable negative relationship between the prevalence of joint families and fertility in women.

The hypothesis that joint families encourage high fertility is thus incorrect. A striking demonstration of this are the figures for Bhilwara district. Bhilwara was the district in Rajasthan with the highest proportion of Married Sons in the population of the household sample (8.98 per cent), the third highest proportion of Married Relatives (24.28 per cent), the highest proportion of married females aged 10–14 (63.92 per cent), and the highest proportion of married males aged 10–14 (32.48 per cent). It was also found to have the third lowest average family size (4.88 persons), the third lowest average number of children (1.91), and the lowest child/woman fertility ratio (0.67451) of all the districts in Rajasthan. Similar results could be shown for Chitorgarh district, which had the smallest average family size (4.81), the second lowest child/woman fertility ratio (0.6965), and the second lowest average number of children (1.93).

The expectation that joint families encourage high fertility may be based on various assumptions—that a general ideology of 'familism' prevails with joint families, one that encourages wives to reproduce; or that patrilineal joint families partake of a 'patriarchalism' that includes producing sons for the patriline; or that young daughters-in-laws have too little knowledge to avoid childbearing or too little capacity to refuse it. To explain the negative correlation found here between joint families and fertility, however, we may return to the theme of crowding that has come up from time to time in this discussion. When a couple has three or more children, theirs tends to be a nuclear household or supplemented nuclear household , it can be argued, either because they have broken away from the husband's brother's family as they have needed more space, or, by default, because one or both of the husband's parents are dead. One could also argue that a family in Rajasthan has two possible strategies open to it: to get the labour needed in the family economic enterprise by having as many children as possible, or by having the wives-mothers of the family work in the fields. It may be that in the high joint family districts of Rajasthan it is the latter choice that is made.

The second common hypothesis challenged by the data is that Indian joint families are biased in their preference for sons over daughters. If this were the case, joint families would be related statistically to disproportionate numbers of males over females. In fact, the three measures of joint family have an almost zero relationship to sex ratio. The Married Sons variable has a −0.087 correlation with sex ratio, Married Relatives −0.072, and Revised Family Structure −0.043. The parallel correlation coefficients between the three measures of joint family and child-sex ratio (the number of males to females in the population under age 5) are also negligible. The Married Sons variable has a correlation coefficient of −0.097, Married Relatives of −0.053, and Revised Family Structure of −0.023. This absence of correlation suggests that the joint family culture, if not sexually egalitarian, is not especially male-preferential.

·Conclusion

This paper has raised the questions: why was there a higher proportion of joint family households in Rajasthan than in other states of India. While this question cannot be said to have been conclusively answered, what this exploration of ethnographic materials and statistical data from the 1961 Census has suggested is that there are interrelated factors contributing to this high proportion of joint families in the population. Chief among these factors are the tradition of early marriage, leading to the need for the joint family to function as protector and guide of young couples, and dependence on the joint family as the work-team. In some parts of Rajasthan, particularly the semi-arid and steppe regions, this work-team is often probably also a well-team. Related to and reinforcing early marriage and the 'protective joint family' are the customs of sibling-set and collateral-set marriages, and multiple weddings on very few auspicious wedding days as a means of curtailing expenses.

Several commonly held hypotheses concerning joint family living have also been tested in the course of this study, and proven erroneous. Among them is the idea that there are clear caste or tribal preferences for joint family living, especially on the part of higher castes, as well as the belief that joint families encourage high fertility and show a marked preference for male children. Finally, data from some of the village surveys suggest that one of the effects of land reform has been to encourage landholding joint families to fragment themselves into their nuclear components.

Perhaps the most surprising finding of this study was the high proportions of joint families found among Untouchable Chamars, possibly due to their very limited housing. The most important finding, one probably important for understanding the joint family in many parts of India, is the correlation between young adolescent marriage and joint families. This suggests a model family structure quite the reverse of that found in much of pre-industrial Europe (Laslett 1984: 99–101), in which a man was required to be trained in an occupation and able to support a wife and children before he married, and the newly married couple set up its own household from the start. In the Rajasthani model of the family, young people are expected to be married and ready to reproduce when their bodies are mature enough to do so, and the adolescent husband is not expected to be able to support himself and his wife and children on his own, but rather his parents and/or older brothers expect to both support and supervise the young married couple as long as it is either necessary or desired by the couple themselves. A further contrast between the European pre-industrial family and the Rajasthani joint family is that one existed in a demographic context in which many adult men and women remained unmarried all their lives, while the other exists in a context in which virtually all females and almost all males marry.

In one of his essays, Peter Laslett raises the question of whether there is a polar family type to the Western family:

> . . . an 'Eastern' familial category, where all mothers were young when their children were born, and much younger than their husbands with whom they lived in multiple family households having no servants (Laslett 1977: 15).

A prime candidate for such a polar type 'Eastern' familial category would possibly be the joint family household of Rajasthan.

• • •

References

Twenty-four Rajasthan village surveys have been compared and drawn upon in this paper. They are indicated here with an asterisk (*) and can be found in, Census of India 1961, Volume XIV, Part VI-A.

*Agarwal, G.D. and G.R. Gupta. 1964. Malar, Palodi Tehsil, Jodhpur District.

* **Agarwal, G.D.** and **G.R. Gupta**. 1965. Nangal Sooswatan, Amber Tehsil, Jaipur District.
* ———. 1969. Aghapur, Bharatpur Tehsil, Bharatpur District.
* **Agarwal, G.D.** and **L.R. Pendharker**. 1965. Abhaneri, Baswa Tehsil, Jaipur District.
* **Bhargava, R.C.** and **G.R. Gupta**. 1965a. Mudh, Kolayat Tehsil, Bikaner District.
* ———. 1965b. Mukam, Nokha Tehsil, Bikaner District.
* ———. 1965c. Rangmahal, Suratgarh Tehsil, Ganganagar-District.
* ———. 1966. Bhadwasi, Nagaur Tehsil, Nagaur-District.
* **Bhargava, R.C.** and **L.R. Pendharker**. 1968. Bagor, Mandal Tehsil, Bhilwara.
Buhler, George (trans.). 1886. *The Laws of Manu.* Oxford: Clarendon Press.
Chauhan, Brij Raj. 1967. *A Rajasthan Village.* New Delhi: Vir Publishing House.
Czap, Peter, Jr. 1983. 'A Large Family: The Peasant's Greatest Wealth': Serf Households in Mishino, Russia, 1814–1858. *In* Richard Wall, Jean Robin and Peter Laslett (eds.), *Family Forms in Historic Europe*, pp. 105–51. New York: Cambridge University Press.
Dandekar, Hemalata C. 1986. Men to Bombay, Women at Home: Urban Influence on Sugao Village, Deccan Maharashtra, India, 1942–1982. Michigan Papers on South and Southeast Asia. Center for South and Southeast Asian Studies. The University of Michigan.
* **Gulati, B.R.** and **G.R. Gupta**. 1966. Goriya, Bali Tehsil, Pali District.
* **Gulati, B.R.** and **L.R. Pendharker**. 1965a. Sanwara, Shahbad Tehsil, Kota District.
* ———. 1965b. Panarwa, Phalasia Tehsil, Udaipur District.
* ———. 1965c. Bhangarh, Rajgarh Tehsil, Alwar District.
* **Gupta, B.R.** and **L.R. Pendharker**. 1969. Gagron, Kanwas Tehsil, Kota District.
Gupta, Giri Raj. 1974. *Marriage, Religion and Society: Patterns of Change in an Indian Village.* Delhi: Vikas.
Hajnal, J. 1983. Two Kinds of Pre-Industrial Household Formation Systems. *In* Richard Wall, Jean Robin and Peter Laslett (eds.), *Family Forms in Historic Europe*, pp. 65–104. New York: Cambridge University Press.
Johnson, Erwin. 1964. The Stem Family and Its Extension in Present Day Japan. *American Anthropologist* 66: 839–51.
Kane, P.V. 1941. *History of Dharmaśāstra.* Vol. 2, part 1. Poona: Bhandarkar Oriental Research Institute.
———. 1958. *History of Dharmaśāstra.* Vol. 5, part 1. Poona: Bhandarkar Oriental Research Institute.
Kolenda, Pauline. 1967. Regional Differences in Indian Family Structure. *In* Robert Crane, (ed.), *Regions and Regionalism in South Asian Studies*, pp. 147–225. Durham, North Carolina: Duke University Program in Comparative Studies on Southern Asia Monograph Series. Monograph No. 5. (Also in Kolenda 1987.)
———. 1968. Region, Caste, and Family Structure: A Comparative Study of the Indian 'Joint' Family. *In* Milton Singer and Bernard Cohn (eds.), *Structure and Change in Indian Society*, pp. 339–96. Chicago: Aldine Publishing Company. (Also in Kolenda 1987.)
———. 1969. Minas of Maharajpur-Kishanpur. Unpublished manuscript.
———. 1978a. Sibling-Set Marriage Alliances and the Structure of the Joint-Family among the Annana Jats of Jaipur, Rajasthan. Unpublished paper read at the 30th annual meeting of the Association for Asian Studies.
———. 1978b. Sibling-Set Marriage, Collateral-Set Marriage, and Deflected Alliance among Annana Jats of Jaipur District, Rajasthan. *In* Sylvia Vatuk (ed.), *American Studies in the Anthropology of India*, pp. 242–77. Delhi: Manohar. (Also in Kolenda 1987.)
———. 1987. *Regional Differences in Family Structure in India.* Jaipur: Rawat.
Kolenda, Pauline and **Lorraine Haddon**. 1987. Marked Regional Differences in Family Structure in India. *In* Pauline Kolenda, *Regional Differences in Family Structure in India*, pp. 214–88. Jaipur: Rawat.

Laslett, Peter. 1972. Introduction: The history of the family. *In* Peter Laslett and Richard Wall (eds.), *Household and the Family in Past Time*, pp. 2–89. London: Cambridge University Press.

———. 1977. Characteristics of the Western Family Considered over Time. *In* Peter Laslett, *Family Life and Illicit Love in Earlier Generations*, pp. 12–49. Cambridge: Cambridge University Press.

———. 1984. *The World We Have Lost Further Explored*. New York: Charles Scribner's Sons.

Lushington, C.S. 1833. On the Marriage Rites and Usages of the Jats of Bharatpur. *Journal of the Asiatic Society* 18: 273–97.

Mehta, Rama. 1982. Purdah among the Oswals of Mewar. *In* Hanna Papanek and Gail Minault (eds.), *Separate Worlds: Studies of Purdah in South Asia*, pp. 139–63. Columbia, Missouri: South Asia Books.

Michael, A.M. 1978. *Irrigation: Theory and Practice*. New Delhi: Vikas.

Miller, Barbara Diane. 1981. *The Endangered Sex*. Ithaca, New York: Cornell University Press.

Misra, V.C. 1967. *Geography of Rajasthan*. New Delhi: National Book Trust of India.

Morgan, Lewis H. 1964. *Ancient Society*. Cambridge: Belknap Press of Harvard University Press.

Nakane, Chie. 1967. *Kinship and Economic Organization in Rural Japan*. New York: Humanities Press.

Pasternak, Burton, Carol R. Ember and **Melvin Ember**. 1976. On the Conditions Favoring Extended Family Households. *Journal of Anthropological Research* 32: 109–23.

Rosin, R. Thomas. 1978. Peasant Adaptation as Process in Land Reform: A Case Study. *In* Sylvia Vatuk (ed.), *American Studies in Anthropology of India*, pp. 460–95. Delhi: Manohar.

———. 1987. Set Marriage and the Continuity of the Joint Family in Rajasthan. Paper read at Rajasthan Studies Conference, Jaipur, December 1987.

Sehgal, K. 1972. *Ganganagar*. Rajasthan District Gazetteers. Jaipur: Central Government Press.

———. 1973a. *Jalor*. Rajasthan District Gazetteers. Jaipur: Central Government Press.

———. 1973b. *Jaisalmer*. Rajasthan District Gazetteers. Jaipur: Central Government Press.

———. 1974. *Dungarpur*. Rajasthan District Gazetteers. Jaipur: Central Government Press.

Sen, A.K. 1972. *Agricultural Atlas of Rajasthan*. Jodhpur: Central Arid Zone Research Institute.

* **Sharma, B.L.** and **G.R. Gupta**. 1967a. Ramnagar Kanjar Colony, Bundi Tehsil, Bundi District.

* ———. 1967b. Kailashpuri, Girwa Tehsil, Udaipur District.

* **Sharma, B.L.** and **L.R. Pendharker**. 1969. Hasanpur, Tijara Tehsil, Alwar District.

* **Singh, Shamsher** and **G.R. Gupta**. 1964. Khajoora, Kushalgarh Tehsil, Banswara District.

* ———. 1965a. Kyasara, Dag Tehsil, Jhalawar District.

* ———. 1965b. Peepal Khoont, Ghatol Tehsil, Banswara District.

* ———. 1966a. Bujawa, Jodhpur Tehsil, Jodhpur District.

* ———. 1966b. Janvi, Sanchore Tehsil, Jalor District.

* ———. 1967. Bujawa, Udaipurwati Tehsil, Jhunjhunu District.

* **Singh, Shamsher** and **L.R. Pendharker**. 1967. Kalijal, Jodhpur Tehsil, Jodhpur District.

Tandon, Prakash. 1961. *Punjabi Century, 1857–1947*. Berkeley: University of California Press, 1968 (1st ed. 1961).

Wall, Richard. 1983. Introduction. *In* Richard Wall, Jean Robin and Peter Laslett (eds.), *Family Forms in Historic Europe*, pp. 1–63. New York: Cambridge University Press.

3

Household Form and Formation: Variability and Social Change among South Indian Muslims

Sylvia Vatuk

T HE SUBJECT of household structure in South Asia, and of the historical and cyclical patterns that affect it, have been given a great deal of attention in the anthropological and sociological literature of the past 25 years. This was particularly so in the 1960s and early 70s, when debates about the definition of the concept of household, about the prevalence of the 'joint family household' and its distribution, and about the extent to which a shift from extended to nuclear forms is occurring under the impact of social change, were central to discussions of South Asian family and kinship organisation. Fruitful though these discussions were in many respects, they seemed by the beginning of the present decade to have more or less played themselves out, despite several recent and methodologically innovative contributions by such scholars as Carter (1984) and Freed and Freed (1982, 1983). It is thus not easy to justify to oneself, let alone to one's readers, the presentation of yet another ethnographically based analysis of data on household composition within a South Asian social context, even when, as in this case, the community under study is one that has been comparatively neglected in the existing literature. On the other hand, a recent revival of interest in the household, and in the development of novel approaches to its study, outside of the South Asian region (see Sanjek 1982; Verdon 1980; Yanagisako 1979) and often through a historical perspective (see the papers collected in Laslett 1972 and Netting, Wilk and Arnould 1984, for example), helps to generate renewed enthusiasm for such an endeavour, especially in view of the role played by the conventional image of the 'Indian joint family' in recent cross-cultural comparative studies of morphological, historical, and demographic aspects of domestic organisation (see, for example, Goody 1976; Hajnal 1982).

It is not surprising, of course, that non-area specialists would tend to see the South Asian household as largely conforming to a single pattern, particularly since their purpose is to make distinctions or typologies at a high level of generality between culturally diverse regions of the world. But even among scholars of South Asia there has been, perhaps, insufficient attention paid to variability in the form of domestic groups and in patterns of their formation, that may be associated with the social, cultural, and religious heterogeneity of the South Asian population. To the degree that such diversity in domestic group structure has been examined, the major tendency has been to focus upon caste and economic variables, and upon urban-rural differences (see, for example, Kapadia 1966; Mandelbaum 1970). An important early exception is to be found in the work of Karve (1960) and, somewhat later, in that of Kolenda (1967, 1968), who has convincingly demonstrated, both through the reanalysis of micro-level data from village studies, and of aggregate data from the Census of India, that there is considerable regional variation, of a consistent and predictable kind, in the extent to which joint family residence is practised in India. She shows that differences in the prevalence of joint households are related to customary differences in the timing of household partition, which in turn are related to—among other factors—regional differences in the position of women. One of her hypotheses suggests that where women are not fully subject to the control of husband and in-laws after marriage, but retain close links with their natal families, they are likely to be more successful in pressing for early separation of their nuclear unit of husband, wife, and children from the larger family, when they see the interests of this unit as being better served by an independent domestic establishment.

Miller's 1981 work, exploring (again with aggregate data) regional differences in, and the broader demographic and human implications of, son preference and neglect of female offspring, also makes reference to the linkage between these and household formation patterns, as do Dyson and Moore (1983) in their demographic approach to South Asian family and kinship organisation. The latter posit two distinct patterns in north and south India respectively—reminiscent of, though analytically less fine-grained than, Karve's earlier categorisation of India's kinship zones. A central point of Dyson and Moore's discussion is the relationship among kinship patterns (as they define it), household form, and gender roles. All of the preceding authors would seem to agree that southern India, as compared with the north, is characterised by a less rigid patrilineal ideology, less marked segregation of a woman's natal and conjugal kindred, weaker enforcement of female seclusion and few restrictions on a woman's mobility, weaker preference for male offspring, less strict adherence to patrilocal residence rules, earlier separation of the nuclear family from the larger

household in which most couples begin their married life, and concom-
mitantly, higher proportions of nuclear households (and other 'non-joint'
household forms) than in the north.

None of these authors explores the variable of religious affiliation as it
may affect the composition of the household or the process by which it is
formed, divided, or dissolved, either directly or through the mediation of
other variables that are related to or derive from religiously sanctioned
customs, practices, or ideologies in the domain of kinship, marriage, and
family life. By implication, if not by explicit intent, their generalisations seem
to apply mainly to the dominant, Hindu, population of the core regions of
the subcontinent. Where Muslims are mentioned, it is often in the context of
calling attention to the influence of Islam upon the spread and severity of
the practice of female seclusion, one of the factors centrally implicated in the
strongly male-centred 'northern' kinship pattern.

The issue of variability in household form and formation patterns, both in
terms of region and in terms of religion, individually and as they may
intersect, is of central concern to me in the present study, because I will be
describing and analysing findings from an investigation carried out among
Muslims in southern India—findings that depart quite markedly from what
is generally reported in the literature as typical for the subcontinent. While,
as may become evident from my subsequent description, there are certain
features of this community's kinship and marriage patterns that superficially
resemble those of south Indian Hindus—at least at the level of abstraction
that would satisfy the non-culturally sensitive demographer—closer examination reveals them to be quite distinct in the details of their operation,
in their cultural meaning and significance, and almost certainly in their
origins, given the foreign ancestry of this community and their historic
maintenance of a high degree of exclusivity, not only from Hindus but from
other local Muslims, in their marriage and kinship relationships.

While, as I have indicated, the issue of regional variability has been dealt
with at some length in the literature, and a considerable body of ethnographic evidence has been accumulated on which existing hypotheses can be
tested and new ones formulated, there is unfortunately little in the literature
upon which to base strong hypotheses about how Muslim household organisation may differ from that of Hindus, even within single regions of the
subcontinent. Those anthropologists who have studied kinship organisation
among Indian Muslims have not necessarily been concerned primarily, if at
all, with questions of domestic group structure and process (for example,
Ahmad 1976; Alavi 1972; Ashraful Aziz 1979; Dube 1969; Kutty 1972;
Jeffery 1979; Mines 1972; 1976; Vreede-de Stuers 1968). On the other hand,
those who have made major contributions to the literature on the South
Asian family and household have either explicitly dealt with Hindu

communities, or have failed to discuss the issue of religious differences—
probably either because Muslims were represented in too small numbers for
generalisations on this point to be considered valid, or because they did not
in fact find religion to be a relevant variable. An article by Conklin (1976),
reporting on a study specifically designed to explore the question of Hindu-
Muslim differences in household structure, is an exception. His conclusions,
however, are that there are no systematic differences among the respondents
he interviewed that are accountable to religious affiliation.

There is, however, evidence from studies of village communities with a
mixed religious population that there are often distinct differences between
Hindus and Muslims with respect to other aspects of family and kinship
organisation (see, for example, Gaborieau 1978; Jacobson 1970). It would
not be unreasonable, therefore, to expect to find differences between the
two religious communities, under some circumstances, in the area of family
and household organisation as well, particularly when, as in the present case,
the Muslim community being studied is not descended from relatively
recent Hindu converts. Of course, given the enormous social and cultural
diversity within the Muslim community of South Asia, it is very doubtful
whether one could find consistent patterns of difference between Muslims
and Hindus as a whole, that would be generalisable for the entire subcontinent, and my purpose is not to embark upon such an obviously misguided
enterprise. However, I wish to begin to explore the possibility that by
carefully examining the relevant data from selected Muslim communities,
and by giving special attention to the question of how patterns of household
form and formation relate to features of the wider system of kinship and
marriage that are in turn distinctively Muslim in their cast or content, we
may be furthered in our general understanding of variability in patterns of
domestic group organisation in South Asia.

A broader question is posed by the situation of rapid social change in
which perforce any contemporary study of the domestic domain in South
Asia is embedded. During the period of greatest scholarly interest in the
subject of the South Asian family and household, an important theoretical
thrust was provided by the desire to demonstrate that the popular notion of
a progressive 'breakdown' of the traditional family system under modernisation and urbanisation was invalid or at least oversimplified (e.g., Collver
1963; Desai 1964; Gould 1968; Orenstein and Micklin 1966; Shah 1974;
Vatuk 1972, 1982). An alternative explanation for the relatively high proportions of nuclear family households reported from Indian village censuses
and urban surveys alike was proposed by several of these authors in terms of
the concept of a 'development cycle' characteristic of households within a
given cultural context as their members experience the universal vital events
of birth, marriage and death. According to this model, one would expect a

wide distribution of household types to be represented within a community at any given point in time, because these represent the fact that different households are at different stages of a regular developmental pattern that is in the long run cyclical in nature. One consequence of the widespread influence of the developmental approach has been, unfortunately, to direct the attention of scholars away from questions of possible secular changes in household form in South Asia—once the 'breakdown' theory had been satisfactorily debunked, and change demonstrated to be repetitive in nature, those whose imagination had been captured by these problems went on to other things. This happened despite the fact that most of the support for the developmental hypothesis was based on analyses of synchronic data, since longitudinal data on household composition in India was rarely available.

Within the past five years, however, under the impetus of a world-wide surge of activity in the fields of historical demography and micro-demography, questions of social change and the family have again begun to command the attention of South Asianists. Much of this more recent work, expectedly, emphasises the mutual cause and effect relationships between demographic shifts and household form—a theme which was already present in embryonic form in some of the early developmental cycle literature (in addition to the work of Carter and the Freeds cited earlier, see Caldwell, Reddy and Caldwell 1984). One of its important virtues over earlier work, however, is that it uses data spanning a substantial time period, whether this is obtained from historical records, from resurveys of communities studied in the late 1950s or early 60s, or from detailed interviews eliciting retrospective data on household form.

In the present paper I will examine some data on household composition and formation patterns in an urban group of south Indian Muslims, among whom I am currently engaged in a long-term ethnographic and family-historical study. One of my particular interests here is to explore the variety of factors that affect household formation, in particular the role played by cultural conceptions and values and by forces of economic and social change in the wider society of which this community is a part.

A Navayat khandan of Madras

The community with which I will be concerned here is made up of a group of related families of Urdu-speaking Muslims residing in the south Indian cities of Madras and Hyderabad. They regard themselves as members of a single khandan (Urdu 'house', 'family', or 'lineage'), which they conceive as a bounded and exclusive body of kin, sharing common descent from a man whom I will call Ghulam Mahmud, who lived and worked in Madras in the late 18th and early 19th centuries.[1] They are Sunni Muslims of the Shafa'i school of Islamic jurisprudence, and belong to a larger community known as Navayat or Naiti, which is widely dispersed in southern India. According to their own traditions, the Navayats descend from Arab traders who arrived on the west coast of India by sea in the late 8th century AD. They regard themselves as culturally and ethnically distinct from other south Indian Muslims, in part because of their Arab ancestry and their long history of residence in India, during which, according to some, they have avoided intermarriage with the indigenous population of the regions in which they have settled (see Aziz Jung 1976; D'Souza 1955).[2]

The immediate founding ancestor of this khandan was born in 1753 in the town of Arcot, present day Tamilnadu, into a family several of whose male members were in the service of the then Nawab of the Carnatic (see Kokan 1963; Iqbal 1973). Soon after his birth the Nawab and his court relocated to Madras, and the ancestor spent most of his adult life in that city, where he served the Nawab first in a religious and scholarly capacity, and later as a high-level administrative official. He had seven children, only four of whom survived to marry: two daughters and two sons. All were married within the Navayat community into families connected with the court—two, a son and a daughter, to a pair of siblings, and another daughter to a young man of Syed lineage with which Ghulam Mahmud's family had made previous marital alliances in earlier generations.[3] From these couples, and from the two subsequent marriages of his younger son, 30 offspring in turn survived to marry. With few exceptions these grandchildren of Ghulam Mahmud married either among themselves or close kinsmen of their other parent. In first marriages 13 were joined to first cousins and 11 more to first cousins once or twice removed. Additionally, five men married first cousins in second or third marriages. This pattern of close kin marriage was repeated in the next generation, and in time an almost completely endogamous descent group developed that, with few exceptions, neither gave women to, nor received them from, other Muslim families. Descendants of the older daughter, as Syeds, tended to marry either among themselves or with other

[1] This and other names used in the texts are pseudonyms, employed to protect the privacy of the living members of the khandan.

[2] The two cited works present divergent views concerning the latter point. D'Souza further-more suggests that the Navayats do not constitute a single community, but that the name is applied to at least three quite distinct groups, with independent origins. Detailed discussion of these matters is beyond the scope of this paper.

[3] Syeds are those Muslims who claim direct descent from the Prophet, through his daughter Fatima, and hence enjoy a certain precedence of rank over other Muslims. The title is transmitted in the male line. In India Syeds tend to marry endogamously, or to take women from, but avoid giving them to, non-Syed families. However, there are exceptions to this marriage pattern.

closely related Syeds, but this line of descent did not diverge entirely from those of its ancestress' three siblings, as marriages involving both the giving and taking of women have occurred from time to time over the years, and to the present day, between Syed and non-Syed descendants of the khandan founder.

In 1864, toward the end of his life, the elder son of Ghulam Mahmud, himself a leading official in the court of the last Nawab, bought a tract of land in what is now a quite central location in Madras city, and settled there with his wife and children and the family of his recently deceased younger brother. Today the largest single group of khandan families still resides in this locality. In the late 19th century several of the founder's grandsons left Madras for Hyderabad to seek employment with the Nizam. Later more followed them, and there is now a substantial, though smaller, group of families of the khandan living in that city. There the khandan is not as residentially concentrated as it is in Madras, but most of its members live in the same general area of the city, within easy reach of one another. In 1947 and 1948, with Partition and the takeover of the Nizam's dominions by the Government of India, a number of khandan men left India for Pakistan, later marrying there or taking khandan brides from India. These families have flourished, mainly in the vicinity of Karachi, and the number of households in and around that city now approaches the number in Hyderabad. More recently many young men of the khandan, some with wives and children, have begun to look farther afield for educational and employment opportunities, and today there are significant numbers of individuals and families settled, presumably permanently, in Europe, Great Britain, and North America, in addition to temporary migrants working in the Middle East and Gulf States.

The khandan has a distinguished tradition of religious scholarship, particularly in the field of Islamic jurisprudence, going back many generations before the founder himself. He and several of his descendants in the 19th and early 20th centuries were counted among the leading 'ulama' of Madras and Hyderabad. Another long tradition in the family is one of government service—either in a religious and/or judicial capacity (as qazis and muftis) or in administrative posts. Government service is still considered, as it was in the past, among the most honourable of professions (sharif kam), and the occupational patterns of men (and more recently of women as well) reflect this. Few members of the khandan in previous generations ever engaged in business or trade, an important means of livelihood for other south Indian Muslims, especially in Madras (see Mines 1972), and at the present time the khandan's educational profile continues to show a distinct preference for salaried employment in jobs that require educational training, whether religious or, as is increasingly the case, secular. The majority of employed members today are in white collar jobs: in government and private offices, in teaching (at all levels of the formal educational system as well as in Islamic institutions and as private tutors), librarianship, journalism, and in the legal, scientific and medical professions. This is generally true also of those now settled or working in Pakistan and other foreign countries. Recently some younger men in Madras have begun to go into small-scale retail trading and manufacturing, but this still represents very much a minority trend in the khandan as a whole.

In the 19th and early 20th centuries the khandan overall was relatively well-to-do, as well as being prominent and well-respected for piety and scholarship. One still has concrete evidence of the former in the large homes that were occupied at that time by khandan families, some of which are still occupied by their descendants. But in most cases these homes have since been subdivided among several generations of heirs and the living quarters of most contemporary families are small and crowded by comparison with those enjoyed by their ancestors. There are of course some individual exceptions to this.

The khandan today belongs, by and large, to India's urban middle class, in terms of occupation, income, lifestyles and aspirations. Household incomes as reported in a survey conducted in 1984 ranged between Rs. 500 and Rs. 5,000 per month.[4] Most families can adequately provide for the major necessities of life and some carefully considered luxuries, but they by no means belong to an economically privileged stratum, as did their forebears. Few have full-time servants—commonplace in the households of their ancestors—and most have no household help of any kind. Few have the complete array of modern consumer goods found in upper middle class Indian households, and they get around by bus, rickshaw and bicycle, rather than by car or motor-scooter. In part their generally modest standard of living can be explained by a prevalent abhorrence of conspicuous consumption and of modern forms of popular entertainment, which many, especially in the older generation, consider frivolous, morally unhealthy, and counter to the teachings of Islam. But, for many, financial considerations are a significant factor as well. Most, though not all, families of the khandan are highly upwardly mobile, within the framework of the contemporary Indian urban socio-economic structure. They strive hard to achieve educational, occupational and income aspirations for their children that will permit the next generation to enjoy a higher standard of living than they themselves

[4] A few individuals, mainly old men and women living alone, were reported to have incomes lower than Rs. 500. The higher figure represents, in most cases, the combined earnings of two or more household members. These income figures cannot be regarded as definitive; income from sources other than official salaries or pensions is especially likely to have been un- or under-reported in the surveys.

enjoy at present. The growing movement for overseas migration, whether on a permanent basis, or in order to earn money that can be remitted to India and used to establish a base for eventual return, is one manifestation of this.

Despite the many adaptations that members of the khandan have made to changing times and circumstances over the 165 years that have elapsed since their founder's death, they continue, as did he, to take pride in adhering to an austere Islamic orthodoxy. They consider a simple and pious lifestyle, devoid of ostentation and excessive ritualism, to be a hallmark of their khandan, and central to their identity and integrity as a group. While there is considerable variation within the khandan in terms of the extent to which this kind of religious orientation dominates in practice all aspects of their everyday life, there is general agreement that it is one of the characteristics that distinguishes them from other Muslims among whom they live, and have lived in the past, and this belief has a symbolic importance in terms of maintaining a shared sense of self and a high degree of in-group exclusivity and solidarity despite the great geographic dispersal and the economic and sub-cultural heterogeneity that has developed within the khandan during the past century.

Household Composition in the Khandan

The quantitative data presented here were obtained from surveys conducted in the spring of 1984 in Hyderabad and Madras. In each city questionnaires were administered by educated young women of the khandan, sometimes in my presence, but usually alone.[5] The selection of households to be surveyed was left to the interviewers, who were asked to cover all members of the khandan in their city of whom they had knowledge. In this way I hoped to ensure that the universe of the khandan would be defined in a way that was meaningful to the group itself (or at least to some members of the group), rather than by some arbitrary criterion, such as full-blooded descent from the founding ancestor, that I might set.

For similar motives, and because I wished especially to elicit indigenous ways of conceptualising and demarcating domestic units and domestic activities, the interviewers were left free to group individuals on the interview forms, and to group the forms into sets, as they felt appropriate. Later we discussed the individual forms and the interviewers explained features of their sorting and aspects of the organisation of domestic functions that could not easily be accommodated to the preconceived format I had provided

[5] For assistance with this survey and with other related aspects of my research on their khandan I owe special thanks to Zakira Ghouse, A.M. Shakira, Rahat Mahmouda, Rafath Yasmin and Moiz Uddin.

them. In both cities the interviewers spontaneously sorted the forms by
'house' (*ghar*) and then by what we may gloss as 'eating group' or 'commensal household' within the house. In Madras this unit was labelled the
jina; in Hyderabad the interviewer usually used the phrase 'those who eat
together' or who eat 'at one place' (*ek jagah khate hai*). Particularly in
Hyderabad, the majority of 'houses' were occupied by a single commensal
unit, but there were many cases in which a larger residence was divided
among two or more separate eating groups, sometimes closely related,
sometimes not. Examples of the former usually had resulted from the
division of a larger unit of parents and married offspring, or two married
siblings, but as a consequence of the prevailing pattern of 'diverging devotion'
(Goody 1976) of property in this khandan, it often happens that more
distantly related kinsmen have ownership rights in, and share occupancy of,
a single residential structure. This may also occur when owners of a house
rent a portion of it to another khandan family. For example, in one such
house in Hyderabad, built around the turn of the century, there are currently
three commensal households. Each has a small set of rooms, opening off a
common courtyard, for its private use. All share the courtyard, bath and
toilet, as well as a sitting room—*diwan khana*—near the front entrance, where
male guests and other outsiders are entertained. The house is now owned by
three siblings—two brothers and a sister—who inherited it from their
father. One of the brothers lives in Madras—his portion is rented out to the
sister of the other brother's wife, and her husband and children. Her mother
divides her time between her household and that of her other daughter
across the courtyard.

As the foregoing suggests, the interviewers used the criteria of co-residence
and commensality together to sort the khandan into sub-groups. But as the
survey progressed it became clear that the actual situation was more fluid
than this description of their procedure suggests. That is, there proved to be
a substantial number of individuals for whom assignment to a 'household'
by the criteria of sleeping under the same roof *and* eating together was
problematical. For example, in a number of instances individuals regularly
eat with a group that occupies one house, but sleep in another house. Others
eat some of their meals in one house and other meals in another—at
different times of day or on different days of the week. At least one family
was found not to prepare and eat meals in their own house—the members
divided themselves between two other closely related commensal households
for this purpose. Some individuals lived alone in a room which they owned
or rented, and kept a separate budget, but did not prepare their own
meals—they either ate with members of another household or were provided
with cooked food by someone else, either in return for a payment or free of
charge. Many men, and a few women, maintain two residences—one out of

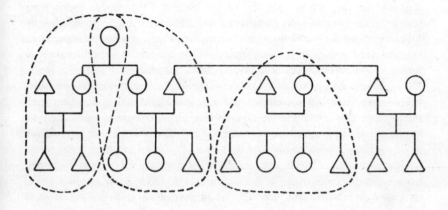

Figure 1

the city, near their place of work, and another with their immediate family. Their earnings go to support the city family and they return regularly—each week or once a month—to the household of their spouse, parent, or sibling. Some men are in a similar situation, but live and work in the Middle East, from whence they can return only once a year, or semi-annually, for a more extended visit to their wives, children, or other family members. Some married couples—whose marriages are apparently still intact—regularly sleep and/or eat in separate households (usually those of their respective parents or siblings). In a few cases such couples are divided between Madras and Hyderabad, spending lengthy vacations and special occasions together, but otherwise having what we might call a 'commuting marriage'. Such situations are not, of course, unique to this community, and are probably typical—in the South Asian context—of rapidly changing urban settings, in which rural-urban migration or overseas emigration is prevalent (see Sharma 1986). Most investigators who wish to do some kind of quantitative analysis of these kinds of data make some arbitrary decisions and then get on with it, leaving behind any further questions about the significance of the fluidity of household membership for understanding what the household is in that society. Others have placed the latter at the centre of their analysis (see Sanjek 1982). My course will lie somewhere in between. In order to proceed with some classification of households and to make computations of comparative purposes, I decided at the stage of analysis to define the household somewhat arbitrarily in terms of commensality alone. Thus individuals who regularly eat their meals together—or eat food that is prepared together by one or more persons—are considered to belong to a single household. By following this rule, it was necessary, of course, to define out of existence that co-residential group mentioned above, whose members divide themselves between two other commensal households at mealtimes.

Individuals who work or study out of town and return weekly—or more often—were counted as members of the household in which they take their meals when they are in the city. Those who return less often—including, of course, those working overseas—were not included in the survey population at all (although sometimes they had been included by their respondent family members). Those who divide their meals between two different households, including the one in which they also reside, were assigned to the latter. Single persons who normally eat by themselves in their own quarters were counted as independent householders, even if they did not prepare their own meals but received cooked food from other households. The same applies to those single men who take their meals at the mosque where cooked food is provided as a charitable act by members of the community. Individuals who alternate their residence on a regular basis between two households (usually in different cities) were counted as part of the household in which they were physically present at the time of the survey. The fact that a couple were married did not prevent their being assigned to separate households for the purpose of the quantitative analysis if they regularly eat their meals apart, even if they also sleep under the same roof and in the same bed. Arbitrary though some of these decisions may be, and counter to common sense some of the consequences, they or other equally problematic alternatives were required to facilitate the task of counting and computation. That they were made has to be kept in mind when the results of the counting are being interpreted, although it is of course only a minority of individuals for whom the issue of an appropriate assignment arises.

The resulting number of commensal households is 141: 92 in Madras and 49 in Hyderabad. In Table 1 are presented data on the composition of these households, organised according to the typology first outlined by Laslett in 1972, and later elaborated by Hammel and Laslett (1974) for use in cross-cultural and historical comparisons of domestic group organisation.[6] Table 2 presents the same data, organised from the point of view of the individual, by sex and age cohort, and in Table 3 is shown the number and percentage of khandan population in each type of household.

---

[6] Initially I had intended to present the household composition data according to the Kolenda typology (1968), which was originally designed for the classification of South Asian household data. However, that typology entails assumptions about the prevailing South Asian pattern of patrilineal descent with virilocal residence. Neither of these are characteristic of this particular population.

As the tables show, over one-half (i.e., 51.8 per cent) of all khandan households consist of what Hammel and Laslett call 'conjugal family units' (CFU), that is, a married couple (with or without children) or a single parent with offspring. Almost two-fifths of the surveyed households have a more complex structure. In 15.6 per cent of the households a single CFU is 'extended' by virtue of the presence of one or more currently maritally unattached kinsmen (usually the parent or sibling of one of the couple). 'Multiple family' households, those with two or more CFUs, constitute 22 per cent of the total. The remaining 10.6 per cent of households contain either a single person or are what Hammel and Laslett have somewhat misleadingly called 'no family' households. Most of the latter are composed of pairs or groups of never-married and/or widowed or separated siblings.

Table 1
Distribution of Household Types* in Madras and Hyderabad

	Madras		Hyderabad		Total	
	No.	%	No.	%	No.	%
1. Solitaries	**8**	**8.7**	**2**	**4.1**	**10**	**7.1**
a. Widowed	4	4.3	2	4.1	6	4.4
b. Single	2	2.2	—	—	2	1.4
c. Divorced	2	2.2	—	—	2	1.4
2. No Family	**3**	**3.3**	**2**	**4.1**	**5**	**3.5**
a. Siblings	2	2.2	2	4.1	4	2.8
b. Other	1	1.1	—	—	1	.7
3. Simple	**45**	**48.9**	**28**	**57.1**	**73**	**51.8**
a. Couple	5	5.4	6	12.2	11	7.8
b. Couple & Child/ren	33	35.9	12	24.5	45	31.9
c. One Parent & Child/ren	7	7.6	10	20.4	17	12.1
4. Extended Family	**16**	**17.4**	**6**	**12.2**	**22**	**15.6**
5. Multiple Family	**20**	**21.7**	**11**	**22.5**	**31**	**22.0**
Totals	**92**	**100.0**	**49**	**100.0**	**141**	**100.0**

* After Hammel and Laslett (1974).

With 666 persons in the 141 households, the mean size of household is 4.7. Households range in size from one to 14 persons, but only seven households out of the total contain more than eight members (see Figure 2). Generally speaking, and as one would expect, the extended and multiple family households are larger than other types, and over one-half of the population lives in commensal units of such complex structure. Most of the remainder, approximately 45 per cent, live in simple conjugal family households.

As the data have been classified, the distribution of household types within this khandan does not appear in any way remarkable.

Table 2
Khandan Population by Sex, Age and Household Type

| | Madras | | | | | | | | | Hyderabad | | | | | | | | | Total | | | | | | | | |
| | Male | | | Female | | | Total | | | Male | | | Female | | | Total | | | Male | | | Female | | | Total | | |
	A	C	T	A	C	T	A	C	T	A	C	T	A	C	T	A	C	T	A	C	T	A	C	T	A	C	T
1. Solitaries	2	—	2	6	—	6	8	—	8	2	—	2	2	—	2	4	—	4	4	—	4	6	—	6	10	—	10
2. No Family	1	—	1	6	1	7	7	1	8	2	—	2	3	—	3	5	—	5	3	—	3	9	1	10	12	1	13
3. Simple Family	53	42	95	56	40	96	109	82	190	24	23	47	40	21	61	64	44	108	77	65	142	96	61	157	173	126	299
4. Extended Family	30	11	41	33	18	51	63	29	92	7	4	11	14	8	22	21	12	33	37	15	52	47	26	73	84	41	125
5. Multiple Family	41	25	66	51	30	81	92	55	147	23	10	33	32	7	39	55	17	72	64	35	99	83	37	120	147	72	219
Totals	**127**	**78**	**205**	**152**	**89**	**241**	**279**	**167**	**446**	**58**	**37**	**95**	**89**	**36**	**125**	**147**	**73**	**220**	**85**	**115**	**300**	**241**	**125**	**366**	**426**	**240**	**666**
Sex Ratios			**85.06**									**76.00**									**81.97**						

Adult – A (18 years and over)
Child – C (0–17 years)

Figure 2: Distribution of Households by Size

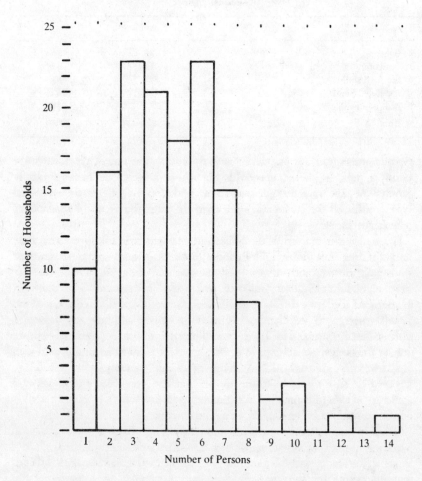

However, a careful examination of the individual compositional characteristics of the households falling within each category, particularly, of course, those of the 'no family', 'extended', and 'multiple' types, reveals some interesting features that seem to distinguish this population in terms of its domestic organisation from the more common Indian pattern.

First, although there are 31 households in the 'multiple family' category, and 22 of the 'extended' type, only one half of these (26 out of 53) conform

Table 3
Number and Percentage of Population in Each Household Type
(Combined Figures)

	No.	%
1. Solitary	10	1.5
2. No Family	13	1.9
3. Simple Family	299	44.9
4. Extended Family	125	18.8
5. Multiple Family	219	32.9
Total	**666**	**100.0**

to the pattern typically associated with the Indian patrilineal, patrilocal joint family system. In these households the two or more CFUs in the multiple family type, and/or the single individuals added to the CFU in the extended type, are kin of the husband rather than the wife: that is, the household is agnatically based.

Typical of this pattern is the household of Hamid. In addition to his wife and children, his household includes both his elderly parents. Another household of this kind is that of Rahmat Ali in Hyderabad. He and his wife have eight adult children, most of whom live in Pakistan. With them in Hyderabad are three sons, one of whom is married but still childless, and the latter's young wife. Muhammad Murtuza, a 40-year-old only son, father of two, shares his home with his widowed mother, also in Hyderabad. And in one of the largest households of this type, we find Amina Begum, a widow in her seventies, mother of five living offspring, heading a household in Hyderabad that includes three of her married sons and the wives and children of two of them. The third daughter-in-law still lives in her parent's house in Madras, where she is a college student.

Also in this category are those households in which a married son is working abroad, or elsewhere in India, but his wife (and children, if any) share a household with his parents—or in which a married son lives with his parents, while his wife and children live elsewhere. An example is the household of Abdul Aziz in Hyderabad. He and his wife are in their late seventies. In their home live their 45-year-old spinster daughter, and their 41-year-old married son. His wife and children live in Madras (in the household of her parents)—the two visit back and forth from time to time.

In addition to those households in which CFUs or extended kin are linked agnatically, there are six households with both agnatic and uterine ties among their members. One of these, for example, is the household of Zainab, a 65-year-old widow. In her household live her bachelor son, her daughter and daughter's husband, and the latter's son and son's wife. Another is a household headed by a man from outside the khandan, Masud Ali. He and

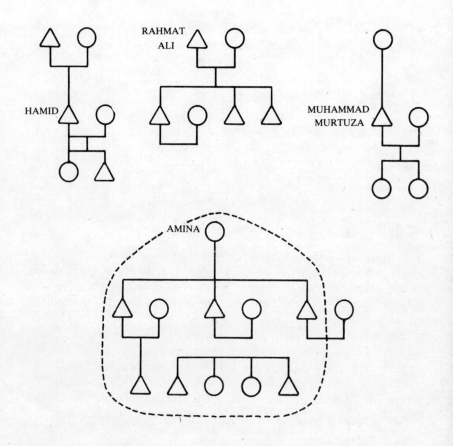

Figure 3

his khandan wife had each been previously married, their respective spouses had died, leaving them with young children. They eventually married one another (she is one of the few khandan women who has remarried after widowhood) and some time later arranged a marriage between his son and her daughter by their previous mates. The young couple now has several children, and they all live together in one household.

Finally, among these complex households there are 21 in which uterine ties alone link CFUs or extended kin to a core CFU. In the simplest kind of case, a parent (or parents) and a married daughter share a household. Thus, Aohra, a Hyderabad widow, shares a household with her daughter, her daughter's husband, and their three school-aged children. Ahmad Karim and his wife, both approaching 80, live with two married daughters and

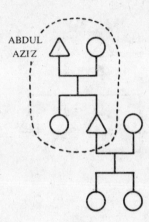

Figure 4

their husbands. One of these couples is childless—the other has several grown children, all of whom are married and living elsewhere, some overseas. In both these cases the elderly parents also have living sons, but the latter have emigrated or are working abroad temporarily and are thus not available to live with them.

However, this is certainly not the only kind of situation in which such a household is formed, for there are several cases of old people who live together with married daughters, even though they have sons living in the same city. For example, Muhammad Aftab, a widower living in Madras, has two married sons and a married daughter. His daughter and her children live with him, as do the children of another daughter, now deceased. The husband of the first daughter sleeps in the quarters of an elderly, single female relative of his, but takes his meals with his wife and father-in-law. Firoza, an 83-year-old widow also lives with a married daughter and several grandchildren. This daughter's husband works in another city and returns for occasional vacations. Firoza has a married son and his wife, and two widowed daughters-in-law, living in three separate households in the same house she occupies.

One factor that is clearly related to the formation of this kind of household is the absence of the daughter's husband, whether by death or because he is working overseas or in another city, or because he lives with other relatives of his own. Out of the 23 households in the total surveyed that include a currently married daughter (i.e., excluding daughters who are widowed or divorced), only 12 also include the son-in-law. The remaining sons-in-law return home periodically, some only once or twice a year, and often during these periods the couple joins the husband's natal family in their household.

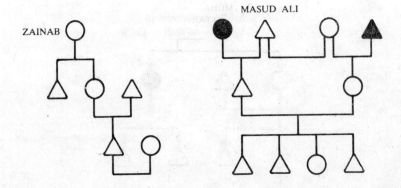

Figure 5

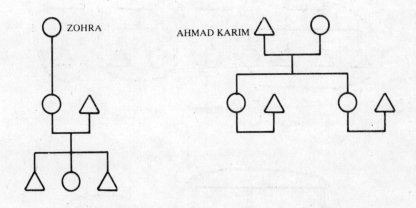

Figure 6

For example, Asima is a young married woman with a young child living in Hyderabad, whose husband has a job in another part of the state. When he returns for holidays she joins him in the household of his mother and widowed elder sister. Most of her time, however, is spent in the home of her own widowed mother, together with her mother's bachelor brother and separated sister, and the latter's teenage sons.

In other cases of this kind the arrangement is clearly a more temporary

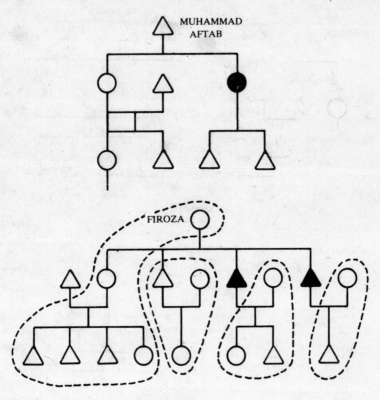

Figure 7

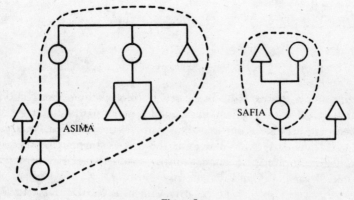

Figure 8

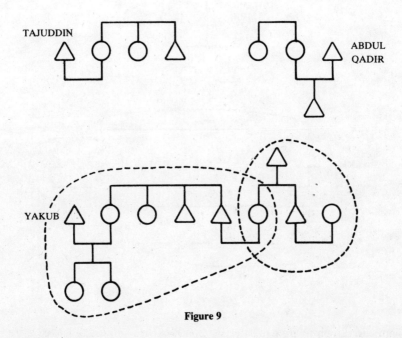

TAJUDDIN

ABDUL QADIR

YAKUB

Figure 9

one, and involves women married fairly recently. One example, that of Amina's youngest daughter-in-law, has already been mentioned. Another is Safia, married for less than a year to a young man who is completing his medical studies in Delhi. She was pregnant at the time of the survey and living with her parents. She planned to remain with them until her baby was born and her husband settled into a job before joining him permanently in his parents' household.

As shown in some of the cited examples, spinster and bachelor siblings are present in many khandan households. In addition to those households made up entirely of sets of never-married (or currently unmarried) siblings, there are nine households in which such persons are attached to a core CFU in an extended or multiple family household.

For example, the household of Tajuddin and his wife includes her 32-year-old unmarried sister and her bachelor brother, a man of 41. The spinster sister of Abdul Qadir's wife, 55 years old, is employed in a government office in the district headquarters, some four hours by train from Hyderabad. She returns to their household each weekend, and contributes to their household budget from her earnings. And, in a third example, the Madras household of Yakub, his wife, and his two young daughters, is

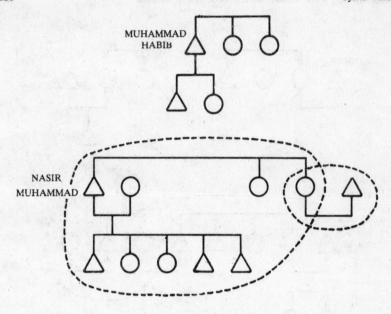

Figure 10

augmented by his wife's spinster sister and bachelor brother, as well as by her married brother, whose wife lives alternately with them and with her widowed father and married brother in Hyderabad.

Muhammad Habib's household in Madras may serve as another example. He is a recent widower in his fifties, left with two young children. In his home live his two spinster sisters, both of them a few years younger than himself. Nasir Muhammad is another man who shares his Madras household with a spinster sister. In addition, his wife and their five adult, but still unmarried, offspring and his widowed father live with him. His married, but childless, sister also spends much of her time in this household. At the time of the survey she was in Madras with her husband, and was therefore counted as a member of his household.

There are very few khandan households in which more than one married couple is co-resident (see Table 4). More than half the multiple family households consist of two incomplete CFUs, or one complete and one incomplete CFU. In only 13 of the 31 households of this type are there two married couples, and in only one are there three. Thus the incidence of 'joint family households', in the usual sense in which this term is used (see Kolenda 1967, 1968, for example), is quite low. Of these, 10 include couples in which the husbands are related as father/son or as brothers, in one the couples are linked through parent/daughter ties, and in the rest through the brother/sister relationship.

Table 4
Households by Number of Married Couples

No. of Couples	Madras		Hyderabad		Total	
	No.	%	No.	%	No.	%
None	24	26.1	17	34:7	41	29.1
One	59	64.1	27	55.1	86	61.0
Two or more	9	9.8	5	10.2	14	9.9
Total	**92**	**100.0**	**49**	**100.0**	**141**	**100.0**

A somewhat surprising observation is the number of households that contain no married couple at all—altogether 41 of the 141 households surveyed (29.1 per cent) fall into this category. These include, of course, by definition, all the single person and no family households, and those simple family households consisting of an incomplete CFU (type IIIc, Table 1). But four of the extended family, and five of the multiple family households are also without a co-resident married couple.

Interpreting the Data

The preceding summary of the results of the household survey shows a pattern which, although not markedly deviant from what has been observed elsewhere in South Asia, nevertheless clearly distinguishes this population from others in terms of domestic group structure. In order to interpret these data it is necessary to view them within the specific demographic and cultural context of the khandan, and keeping in mind the fact of rapid social and economic change in the wider nation and world in which the people of the khandan live today. In doing so, it is fairly clear that a developmental cycle model, which postulates a pattern of repetitive, cyclical alternations of household form, is not very useful.

Likewise, a normative approach, in which the form of domestic groups is seen to conform to culturally shared ideals about what groupings of persons may appropriately live together, is of little value here. Such ideals may in some cultures have considerable influence on individual choices about where to live and with whom—this is certainly true of Hindu north India (see Sharma 1986, for example), although there also normative rules are only one factor to be considered in analysing the household formation process. However, in this khandan explicit norms of household form are relatively weakly defined or articulated—the role of cultural conceptions in affecting the composition of households is not so much in the prescription of a particular form, but rather, in the specification of certain personnel requirements for the accomplishment of the central domestic activities of the household. The way in which these requirements are actually met is subject to considerable flexibility. There is some indication that this was true in the past as well, but the tendency is more marked today, probably because of the presence of stricter demographic and material constraints that would make adherence to a single pattern of domestic group difficult and maladaptive.

Demographic Constraints on Household Formation

Under the heading of 'demographic' factors affecting the formation of households in this khandan, I will limit consideration to two: those surrounding marriage and migration. A fuller treatment of this topic would require that more detailed attention be given to fertility and mortality patterns in the khandan—however, my analysis of these data has not progressed far enough to do that at this time.

Marriages in the khandan are almost invariably arranged by the parents and other senior kin of the young people involved, and the preference of most families is for marriage within the khandan, although in the past 15 years out-marriage, particularly for boys, has become increasingly acceptable and prevalent. This trend began gradually more than a generation ago, perhaps in part as a response to growing heterogeneity of education, occupation, economic level and lifestyle within the very limited marriage pool of the khandan. Although some families began to look outside the khandan for mates for their sons, it was only very recently that any khandan girls were married to outsiders. For this and other reasons we find in the khandan a relatively high incidence of spinster- and bachelorhood—in Madras and Hyderabad alone there are 14 men and 25 women over the age of 35 who have never been married. Most of these will probably never marry; this is almost certain for the seven men and 19 women who are 45 years old and over. Although in Muslim culture marriage is enjoined on both sexes, and there is no accepted social role for the unmarried woman in particular, many individuals in this khandan have not succeeded in finding a mate, and khandan household composition reflects this fact. It is an interesting fact that a large percentage of never-married adults have siblings in the same situation—in other words, some parents have (or have left) pairs or sets of never-married offspring, while most parents have managed to marry off all their children. Few have only one unmarried son or daughter.

Out of the khandan population of 666 persons, 132 men and 185 women have ever been married, and 119 men and 136 women are currently in a marital union (see Table 5). (The disparity between the sexes is accounted for by the absence of a substantial number of husbands from the Madras or

Hyderabad households of their wives.) Most of the remaining ever-married persons are widowed—divorce is extremely rare in this khandan. Most widowers are elderly, in part because men usually remarry upon the death of the wife, unless they are already quite old at the time. Furthermore, there is almost always an age differential in favour of the husband, often as much as 10 or 15 years, so fewer men than women ever experience widowerhood. Many of the 46 widows are quite young—widow remarriage is also extremely rare in this khandan (as is, incidently, polygyny, generally assumed to be prevalent among Muslims).

Table 5
Khandan Population by Marital Status and Age Cohort

No. of Couples	Madras		Hyderabad		Total	
	No.	%	No.	%	No.	%
Married, Living with Spouse	115	38.3	115	31.4	230	34.5
Married, Living Separately	4	1.3	21	5.7	25	3.7
Widowed	9	3.0	46	12.6	55	8.3
Divorced/Separated	4	1.3	3	.8	7	1.1
Never-Married, 0–34 years	154	51.3	156	42.6	310	46.5
Never-Married, 35 and over	14	4.7	25	6.8	39	5.9
Total	**300**		**366**		**666**	

The high incidence of widowhood in this khandan also has a strong impact upon household composition. Like single persons, the widowed usually join the household of a close family member if they were not already living there before the spouse's death. This is especially true for young widows—those with adolescent children or the elderly often remain in an independent household. Young widows are somewhat more likely in this khandan to join forces with natal relatives than to live with the family of their late husband—this explains many of the multiple family households that are based on uterine relationships.

Migration is another factor that weighs heavily in household formation patterns. As we can see from Table 6, there are 36 men from khandan households in Madras and Hyderabad who are currently living elsewhere—most of these are working overseas, or have emigrated abroad on a permanent basis. Thirteen of these have been accompanied by their wives—the rest are either unmarried or have left their wives at home. These figures actually underestimate the prevalence of emigration within the khandan, since it does not include persons who have emigrated with their entire family or who have left no close family members in India.

Table 6
Male Emigrants from Madras and Hyderabad, Currently Overseas, by Marital Status*

	Never-Married	Married	Total
Accompanied by Wife	—	13	13
Alone	8	15	23
Total	8	28	36

* These figures include only those persons who have migrated from the households surveyed—it is thus not complete for all khandan emigrants from these cities, since some emigration involves entire households.

Because, as in the case of young widows, young married women whose husbands are absent are not expected to live by themselves, the emigration of married men necessitates that decisions be made about their wives' living arrangements while they are away. Recently married women are most likely to stay in their natal household, particularly if they are married to a khandan man: khandan women married to outsider men, of which there are a few today in Madras and Hyderabad, are somewhat more likely to join their husband's household, a fact which may suggest some cultural differences between this khandan and other Muslims in the region. Women who already have growing children when their husbands go out of town or overseas to work often continue living independently in their own households, as widows in the same age-range typically do.

Some Material Constraints on Household Formation

Among material factors that may be shown to influence the composition of domestic groups in this khandan, the occupational roles of khandan men and women in the larger economy, and patterns of property ownership, are especially important. As I have indicated, almost all families of this khandan are dependent upon salaried employment or pensions for all or a substantial part of their income. Even those who depend upon business earnings in most cases have individually owned enterprises rather than family businesses. The only other significant source of income for some families is rental earnings from real estate—such earnings are also usually divided among individual shareholders, even when the property itself is legally in joint ownership. Thus property or income considerations rarely weigh heavily in determining co-residence or commensal arrangements. Whoever lives together or eats together is expected to make some contribution to the household expenses, if he or she has any earnings, but cash contributions can be made to one household as conveniently as to another and can be shifted from one to the other if for any reason the members decide to make a change. The only qualification to this concerns responsibilities that men or women may have for the support of non-earning relatives—it is very often the case that co-residence is dictated by the need of elderly, young, or non-employed kin for support, but in these cases more than purely financial aid is usually involved. In such situations it should be stressed that obligations for the support of close kin do not fall only or even primarily upon men, nor are they limited, from the point of view of a woman, to her husband's kin, as is effectively the case for north Indian Hindus (except when a woman's parents are totally without male offspring or other resources). Many married and unmarried women are employed, and with few exceptions use their earnings to contribute to, or sometimes solely support, the household in which they are living. In addition, earning men and women often make regular financial contributions to assist kin in other households who are in need.

Property ownership affects household composition primarily as it is related to the availability of housing. The ownership of houses or portions thereof is very widely distributed throughout the khandan. Most such property has been inherited, rather than purchased by the owners out of their own earnings. Inheritance in the khandan generally follows the Quranic rule, in which daughters receive one-half of the share of sons. Despite the fact that there is sometimes some deviation in actual inheritance practice from the strict provisions of this law, women in this khandan are not systematically denied their inheritance rights, as occurs regularly in many South Asian Muslim communities. Most adult women own title, or a share of title, in some real property, and many own substantial amounts which they have inherited from parents or received from their husband as *meher* (dower) or gifts. Since housing in the open market in both these cities is expensive to rent, the ownership of a house, or portion of a house, is an important factor determining where a family will live. Future inheritance chances also influence this: a couple may, for example, choose to live with the wife's widowed father rather than on their own, or with his parents, if she stands to inherit the quarters he occupies. The differential effect of this pattern of inheritance upon household formation, as against the male-exclusive, patrilineal inheritance pattern practised by Hindus, is clear.

Cultural Principles and Household Formation

Probably the most important cultural factor in household formation in this khandan has to do with gender and gender roles. with the sexual division of labour and notions concerning the modesty of women. In the past the sexual division of labour was quite rigid. Men were responsible for earning money and supporting the women and children of their household, as well as any close male kin who for reasons of age, infirmity, or unemployment could not support themselves. Men were also expected to handle all transactions with the world outside the home, whether on their own behalf or on that of their dependents. Some of the more routine tasks of this kind (such as shopping for groceries) were delegated to servants. Even women who owned substantial amounts of property managed it through the agency of male kinsmen. Finally, men were responsible for the protection of the women of their household and of their modesty, a task of great symbolic as well as practical significance which, if successfully accomplished, ensured not only the welfare of the women but the prestige and reputation of the responsible men. An important device in aid of this task was the practice of female seclusion. Women of the khandan rarely left the confines of their home, and when they did so moved in curtained vehicles or heavily veiled.

Within the home, women were in charge, doing some household tasks themselves and supervising servants in the rest. They were not expected to earn their own living or contribute to the support of others. When occasionally a woman was left without male support, and for some reason could not join the household of a male kinsman, she could undertake domestic production of some sort, or live on the income of property she owned, but always with male help, since to deal directly with non-khandan members would compromise her virtue.

For these reasons, the minimum requirements of a viable domestic unit were at least one adult male and one adult female.

Each man required a woman to prepare his meals and see to his other personal needs, while each woman needed a man to provide financial support (or to help her to support herself) and to be physically present in her house, at least at night, to protect her respectable status.

Today many educated women are employed; some even support non-working husbands or fathers. They no longer practise *pardah* before outsiders and move freely and unveiled in public. However, the notion that a household needs the symbolic presence of a man to perform the function of protecting women's modesty has not disappeared, either for these women or for their less educated, non-working, and pardah-observing sisters. Although, as the tables on household composition show, there are commensal households made up entirely of women, as well as a number of female 'solitaries', and several households of women with school-aged or adolescent children, few of these are in fact without a male 'guardian'. This man also, in many cases, performs other traditional male tasks involving shopping, engaging in official transactions with outsiders, and the like, on behalf of these women. Although such men do not form part of the 'household' as I have been forced to arbitrarily define it for the purpose of making tabulations, they play a necessary domestic role. Often a man will divide his time between the household of his wife and that of his sister—or maiden aunt—perhaps sleeping at the home of the latter if there is another man or men in the house he shares with his wife. In those houses that contain two or more related households, one man, attached to one of those households, may additionally perform the protective function for those that are lacking a male member. There are in fact 18 households in the khandan in which there is no adult male regularly present, and several others in which the only man is a young unmarried son of the female head—but in this community a male need not be advanced in age to adequately perform this aspect of the male role, and many older women feel comfortable moving in public with only a 10-year-old boy as chaperon, whereas they would never leave their home completely unaccompanied. Those households without a man are usually so because the husband or the married son of the senior woman is working overseas or out of the city or because the woman is a widow or divorcee, or has never been married and has no immediate male relatives. In none of them is the woman young or recently married—as I have indicated, women in this situation always join another household. Despite the significant number of women who do not have a man in their household—whether we use the criterion of commensality or co-residence—very few of them are perceived as being without a male guardian because some closely related man of another household has assumed the role of protector. The importance of this is highlighted when we note the tone of pity and concern that is evident when members of the *khandan* call attention to one of the female-headed households that does not in fact have any such male presence, even on a part-time basis. In Hyderabad, a mother and her two daughters—one never-married, the other with a husband overseas—live in a household without a man. The older woman also has a son who lives abroad, and he sends regular remittances, as does the daughter's husband. But the women are described as being 'all alone' and others wonder, with sympathy in their voices, how they manage to carry on without a man in residence.

Another cultural factor that is of great significance to household formation in this community is the open recognition of, and the legitimacy accorded to, close ties of affection and duty between parents and daughters, ties that are expected to continue with unabated force after marriage. Although a married woman is also expected to serve the needs and interests of her in-laws, she is not pressured to transfer her allegiances away from her natal family when she marries, as is the case among Hindus, particularly in northern India. Not only are a woman's natal ties expected to be emotionally strong, but they may legitimately influence her behaviour in many spheres, not least in the choice of where to live, even if this means that—as happens in a few cases—she does not share a household with her husband.

The Muslim marriage ceremony is structured in such a way that the bride
is taken on her wedding night to the groom's home—that is, normally
speaking, the home of his parents—where a room is set aside for the
consummation of their union. For some couples this is the beginning of a
period of varying duration in which they live in a common household with
the groom's immediate family. Others enter into different kinds of living
arrangements after the initial post-wedding period is over, and if we heed
the evidence of life histories it is clear that couples over the course of their
life together often live at different times with different relatives, joining and
leaving households for a variety of reasons, and not only in response to the
normal vital events within their conjugal unit. Although most people of the
khandan would probably agree that to live with the husband's family is the
more culturally 'normal' pattern, and most couples have probably lived in
such an arrangement for some period during their married life, we can see
from the figures that many other alternatives are acceptable and widely
practised. It is fairly clear that there is a strong feeling that aging parents
should not be left to live alone—an old mother should not have to cook her
own meals if there is a daughter-in-law or a daughter who could do this for
her, and in case of illness or infirmity someone should be in their home to
provide nursing care. But that does not mean that all the sons of a couple
ought to stay in their household, or that a son and his wife ought necessarily
to be the ones to do so, if a daughter and her husband can conveniently do
so instead. So 'joint' family living, when it occurs, is often a practical
response to the needs of the elderly for care and company, rather than being
motivated by an abstract desire to conform to an ideal pattern of domestic
structure.

Finally, one must remind oneself of the fact of the close kinship inter-
relatedness of all of the members of this khandan, and of the high degree of
residential concentration within each of the two cities in which the khandan
is mainly located. Furthermore, the extent to which there is continual
movement and telephonic communication between Hyderabad and Madras
must also be stressed. These characteristics of the khandan and its everyday
interactional patterns have to be kept in mind as providing a certain kind of
social framework within which the more purely domestic activities of the
household take place. Since most marriages take place between cousins or
other close relatives, there is often little sharp demarcation between the natal
and conjugal home. Kinsmen to whom a husband may have certain obligations
are often also close relatives of the wife, and the widowed mother with
whom a man's wife wishes to stay in close and regular contact may also be
his beloved mother's sister or the slightly older first cousin with whom he
grew up in the same household. The slight avoidance relationship between a
woman and her son-in-law that is recognised as sometimes making co-

residence somewhat awkward for both parties, is very often counteracted by the fact that he has been a constant visitor to, or perhaps even a member of, her household since his childhood before entering it in the capacity of daughter's husband. Furthermore, the particular ways in which an individual is attached to one household or another may lose much significance if other households to which they might alternatively be attached are right next door or across the courtyard and one may freely move among them at will, as domestic needs and activities ebb and flow. It is probably as much these circumstances of khandan society, as any particular cultural orientation on the part of khandan members, that account for the apparent high degree of flexibility, variability and changeability of household form and membership that one can observe among them.

Conclusion

The patterns of household composition and formation observed in this community of south Indian Muslims raise many questions that have only been touched upon in this paper. In terms of one of the questions initially raised in my introduction I have tried to show that there are certian features of this khandan's domestic organisation that are closely related to aspects of their culture and social organisation that are specifically Muslim—although not necessarily characterising all, or even most, Muslim communities in India. These include, in particular, their inheritance practices and their pattern of close endogamy, as well as their attitude toward uterine kinship ties and the kinship roles of women, though the relative freedom with which women are permitted to express these emotional bonds and put them into behavioural practice is not usually, in the conventional wisdom, particularly associated with Islamic cultural practice. At the same time, I have tried to stress the importance of material and demographic conditions, some of which can be seen to be by-products of cultural practices and orientations and others which are instead—or in addition—consequences of changing social circumstances largely external to this particular group, to which they can be seen to be responding as to constraints or to new opportunities. It seems clear to me that the data I have accumulated through the household survey cannot be comprehended by looking for normative rules of household formation or by attempting to discern a developmental cycle in the variety of forms of household present at this particular point in time. Living together is only one thing that family members do with one another, and decisions about what to do and with whom to do it are made by men and women, individually and in concert, within a total situational and conceptual context. A combination of practical and symbolic strategies, using cultural principles and notions about kinship obligations and rights, and taking into account new demands' created by forces of change in the wider society must all be comprehended together, in order to satisfactorily explicate the some-what artificially contrived quantitative data upon which this and other similarly motivated studies of household structure are based.

• • •

References

Ahmad, I. (ed.). 1976. *Family, Kinship and Marriage among Muslims in India*. New Delhi: South Asia Books.

Alavi, H.A. 1972. Kinship in West Punjab Villages. *Contributions to Indian Sociology* (ns) 6: 1–27.

Ashraful Aziz, K.M. 1979. *Kinship in Bangladesh*. Dacca: International Centre for Diarrhoeal Disease Research.

Aziz Jung. 1976. *Tarikh-un-Nawayat*. Hyderabad: Wala Akedemi [orig. 1904].

Caldwell, J.C., P.H. Reddy and P. Caldwell. 1984. The Determinants of Family Structure in Rural South India. *Journal of Marriage and the Family* 46: 215–29.

Carter, A.T. 1984. Household Histories. *In* R.McC.Netting et al. (eds.), *Comparative and Historical Studies of the Domestic Group*, pp. 44–83. Berkeley: University of California Press.

Collver, A. 1963. The Family Cycle in India and the United States. *American Sociological Review* 28: 89–96.

Conklin, G.H. 1976. Muslim Family Life and Secularization in Dharwar, Karnataka. *In* I. Ahmad (ed.), *Family, Kinship and Marriage among Muslims in India*, pp. 127–40. New Delhi: South Asia Books.

Desai, I.P. 1964. *Some Aspects of Family in Mahuva: A Sociological Study of Jointness in a Small Town*. New York: Asia Publishing House.

D'Souza, V.S. 1955. *The Navayats of Kanara*. Dharwar: Kannada Research Institute.

Dube, L. 1969. *Matriliny and Islam*. Delhi: National Publishing House.

Dyson, R. and M. Moore. 1983. Kinship Structure, Female Autonomy, and Demographic Behaviour in India. *Population and Development Review* 9 (1): 35–60.

Eglar, Z. 1960. *A Punjabi Village in Pakistan*. New York: Columbia University Press.

Freed, S.A. and R.S. Freed. 1982. Changing Family Types in India. *Ethnology* 21: 189–202.

———. 1983. The Domestic Cycle in India: Natural History of a Will-o'-the-Wisp. *American Ethnologist* 10: 312–27.

Gaborieau, M. 1978. Aspects of the Lineage among the Muslim Bangle-makers of Nepal. *Contributions to Indian Sociology* (ns) 12: 155–72.

Goody, J.R. 1976. *Production and Reproduction: A Comparative Study of the Domestic Domain*. Cambridge University Press.

Gould, H.A. 1968. Time Dimension and Structural Change in an Indian Kinship System: A Problem of Conceptual Refinement. *In* M. Singer and B.S. Cohn (eds.), *Structure and Change in Indian Society*, pp. 413–21. Chicago: Aldine.

Hajnal, J. 1982. Two Kinds of Preindustrial Household Formation System. *Population and Development Review* 8: 449–94.

Hammel, E.A. and P. Laslett. 1974. Comparing Household Structure Over Time and Between Cultures. *Comparative Studies in Society and History* 16: 73–109.

Iqbal, M.A. 1973. *Tazkira-i-Sayid.* Hyderabad: Sayeedia Library and Research Institute.

Jacobson, D. 1970. Hidden Faces: Hindu and Muslim Purdah in a Central Indian Village. Ph.D. dissertation, Columbia University.

Jeffery, P. 1979. *Frogs in a Well: Indian Women in Purdah.* London: Zed Books.

Kapadia, K.M. 1966. *Marriage and Family in India.* 3rd ed. Calcutta: Oxford University Press.

Karve, I. 1960. *Kinship Organisation in India.* Bombay: Asia Publishing House.

Kokan, M.Y. 1963. *Qazi Badar-ud-Daula.* Madras: Dar-ul-Tasnif.

Kolenda, P. 1967. Regional Differences in Indian Family Structure. In R.I. Crane (ed.), *Regions and Regionalism in South Asian Studies,* pp. 147–226. Durham. N.C.: Duke University Program in Comparative Studies in Southern Asia.

———. 1968. Region, Caste, and Family Structure: A Comparative Study of the Indian 'Joint' Family. *In* M.Singer and B.S. Cohn (eds.), *Structure and Change in Indian Society,* pp. 339–96. Chicago: Aldine.

Kutty, K. 1972. *Marriage and Kinship in an Island Society.* Delhi: National Publishing House.

Laslett, P. (ed.). 1972. *Household and Family in Past Time.* Cambridge: Cambridge University Press.

Mandelbaum, D.G. 1970. *Society in India.* Vol. 1. Berkeley: University of California Press.

Miller, B.D. 1981. *The Endangered Sex.* Ithaca: Cornell University Press.

Mines, M. 1972. *Muslim Merchants: The Economic Behaviour of an Indian Muslim Community.* New Delhi: Shri Ram Centre for Industrial Relations and Human Resources.

———. 1976. Urbanization, Family Structure and the Muslim Merchants of Tamilnadu. *In* I. Ahmad (ed.), *Family, Kinship and Marriage among Muslims in India,* pp. 297–317. New Delhi: South Asia Books.

Netting, R. McC., R.R. Wilk, and E.J. Arnould (eds.). 1984. *Households: Comparative and Historical Studies of the Domestic Group.* Berkeley: University of California Press.

Orenstein, H. and M. Micklin. 1966. The Hindu Joint Family: The Norms and the Numbers. *Pacific Affairs* 39: 314–25.

Sanjek, R. 1982. The Organization of Households in Adabraka: Toward a Wider Comparative Perspective. *Comparative Studies in Society and History* 24: 57–103.

Shah, A.M. 1974. *The Household Dimension of the Family in India.* Berkeley: University of California Press.

Sharma, U. 1986. *Women's Work, Class and the Urban Household.* London: Tavistock.

Vatuk, S.J. 1972. *Kinship and Urbanization: White Collar Migrants in North India.* Berkeley: University of California Press.

———. 1982. Changing Patterns of Marriage and the Family in an Urbanized Village in Delhi, India. *In* H. Safa (ed.), *Towards a Political Economy of Urbanization in Third World Countries,* pp. 119–50. New Delhi: Oxford University Press.

Verdon, M. 1980. Shaking Off the Domestic Yoke, or the Sociological Significance of Residence. *Comparative Studies in Society and History* 22: 109–32.

Vreede-de Stuers, C. 1968. *Parda: A Study of Muslim Women's Life in Northern India.* Assen: Van Gorcum.

Yanagisako, S.J. 1979. Family and Household: The Analysis of Domestic Groups. *Annual Review of Anthropology* 8: 161–205.

4

The Household in Nepal: Social and Experiential Crucible of Society

John N. Gray

Iɴ ᴛʜɪs paper I analyse that social phenomenon which Nepalese refer to by the term '*pariwar*'—which I loosely translate as 'household'—and its implications for such wider-scale social units as hamlet, village and regional caste. The analysis develops themes of an earlier paper (Gray 1983) in which I argued that the household is the fundamental structural node of the village economy. That argument consisted of two basic stages. In the first, developing Godelier's point that 'relations of kinship function as relations of production and do so internally' (1978: 764), the household's social relations were described in terms of their economic functions in labour, production and distribution activities—that is, as a domestic enterprise. The point I emphasised then, and which is maintained in this paper, is that the domestic enterprise has a character which is not totally determined by wider societal processes and principles. The second stage of the argument traced the centrifugal consequences of the domestic enterprise for the structure and economic processes of the encompassing hamlet and village. I follow a similar analytic trajectory here; but this time I do so with respect to the social principles of household relations. However, before proceeding with the analysis proper, I develop some further aspects of the approach adopted which gives 'ethnographic priority' to the household.

In Brenda Beck's ethnography (1972), Konku peasant society is conceived as a nexus of two interrelated but district series of concentric domains: a territorial and a social.[1]

---

[1] The territorial series is: region > sub-region > village > hamlet > household; and the basically parallel social series is: caste > sub-caste > clan > lineage > 'family'. While Beck did not explicitly recognise it, these two series of concentric circles involve two crucial dimensions of a social group: (*a*) a socially recognised set of individuals, (*b*) localised by, and with access to, land.

Her analysis proceeds from the widest to the narrowest domain showing how an abstract social principle (i.e., the south Indian right-left division of castes) was manifest in, and oriented the structure of, social relations in each successively smaller-scale social context. Implicit in this ethnographic strategy is the idea that each smaller-scale social unit is the sociologic sequitur to the next larger and encompassing social unit. Thus, from Beck's perspective societal principles are seen as sociologically prior to and constraining upon smaller-scale social units. However, a concentric image of society allows a converse analytic strategy—to proceed from the smallest social unit in the tradition of Alfred Schutz (1972), and Max Weber (1978). Schutz provides the basic outlines of the complementary perspective developed here in that his work seeks to reveal the experiential preconditions for the very existence of social domains of all scales in the emergence of 'intersubjectivity' between actors in the minimal societal context of the Self and the Other. Then, through a series of stages involving meaningful acts of consciousness a taken-for-granted stock of knowledge ('interpretive schemes') is constituted which actors use to interpret and structure their actions in a variety of contexts. Accordingly, while retaining Beck's concentric image of society, the approach I propose complements her analytic strategy by reversing it and giving ethnographic priority to the household. This involves the following propositions:

1. If the household is recognised as a distinct social unit, then its character cannot be analysed as totally determined by wider-scale social principles and structures. The household encompasses a particular ensemble of social actors and relations not found in other units. Any analysis of the household must incorporate and reveal that particularity which is emergent from the dynamics of these relations.
2. The household is the primary social context for everyday action and experience. Thus, it is one of the most important arenas for learning the taken-for-granted stock of knowledge that enables social relations within and beyond the household. That is, the household is a most significant context for the transformation of abstract and objective social principles into subjectively meaningful concepts.
3. Given that the household has a particularity of social relations and dynamics, it is not a neutral field for this transformation. As I attempt to show, this transformation involves situating an abstract social principle in household dyadic relations which inflect the experience that actors have of it. It is the experiential linkage of abstract social principles to a particular household dyadic relation as its structural context of appropriateness that constitutes an interpretive scheme.
4. As a primary context for the transformation and experience of basic

social principles, the household indirectly affects the structure and operation of wider-scale social units by providing some interpretive schemes for understanding and acting in them. To a certain extent, therefore, the character of wider-scale social units is explicable in terms of the particular nature of the household.[2]

In this sense, therefore, I give the Brahman-Chetri household in Nepal ethnographic primacy to complement analyses like those of Beck (1972) and Parry (1979), which, following Dumont's *Homo Hierarchicus* (1970), give ethnographic priority to hierarchy and equality as an abstract configuration of societal principles.[3] In their ethnographies the meaningful richness and social ubiquity of these principles are generated analytically by the wide variety of social groups, relations and contexts which are seen to be structured by and to manifest them. There is, however, another source of the richness and significance of hierarchy and equality which does not deny their reality as abstract societal principles. It is in the household that they are transformed and constituted in the consciousness of actors. Their meaningful richness and consequent interpretive adaptability in a wide variety of contexts are founded in the different ways they are experienced in the various dyads of household social relations. Thus my major project is to identify the core social relations of the Brahman-Chetri household and to show how hierarchy and equality are constituted in actors' experience as a result of being and acting in these relations. In this way I synthesise a configuration of the experiential meaning of these principles in social action. I end by suggesting ways in which such experience affects the structure and dynamics of wider-scale social units of Nepalese village society.

The concept and model of the household developed in this paper are derived from Chetri households of Kholagaun hamlet in Banaspati village. Banaspati is located near the southern edge of the Kathmandu Valley in an area populated largely by Hindus with close historical and cultural affinity to

---

[2] In a similar manner it must be recognised that the character of any distinct social unit is not totally determined by other social units of either larger- or smaller-scale. Each social unit has its particularity grounded internally in the specific nexus of actors, social relations, contexts of relevance, and social structure which are used to define it as a distinct social unit by the members themselves and/or by the analyst. At the same time the consequences of relations and actions in social units of larger- and smaller-scale impinge upon it. In this sense a social unit is 'a compromise . . . always imperfect, between conflicting functional imperatives, pre-existing structures, social norms and cultural standards' (Wilk and Netting 1984: 6). Perhaps the household is unique in this image of society because it is 'the next bigger thing on the social map after an individual' (Hammel 1984: 40–41).

[3] I follow Dumont (1970) here in seeing hierarchy and equality in a configuration of encompassing and encompassed. Thus one cannot experience or analyse one principle without implicating the other. It is for this reason that I link the two principles throughout the analysis.

north India (see Furer-Haimendorf 1966). Analytically Banaspati is a complex of two historically distinct forms of organisation. The most recent of
these is Banaspati as a unit of local government or *gaun panchayat*. In the
early 1960s, King Mahendra introduced panchayat democracy and politically
reorganised the Kingdom of Nepal into a pyramidal structure of 14 zones
(*anchal*), 75 districts (*jilla*) and over 3,000 villages (*gaun*), each administered
by an executive council (*panchayat*). For the purpose of electing the village
council, each village is divided into nine 'wards' as the smallest direct
electoral constituency.

This gaun panchayat political structure was imposed upon a historically
prior one. In this area of the valley the rural settlement pattern is non-
nucleated with relatively small clusters of houses scattered amongst agricultural land. These clusters of houses are locally recognised social and
residential units which I call 'hamlets'. Hamlets have no official status as
governmental units and their boundaries do not coincide with those of the
wards—some hamlets overlap the boundaries of two or more wards and
some wards incorporate all or part of several hamlets. Banaspati consists of
12 hamlets, each of which is locally acknowledged to be inhabited by a
particular social group distinguished by caste, ethnic and/or descent group
affiliation. Although hamlets consist of households of several such groups,
most are dominated numerically by one or two of them. This gives each
hamlet a particular social identity. For example, one hamlet is composed
almost entirely of Tamang households[4] internally divided into five agnatic
clans; another, curiously, is dominated by Brahman households and by
Untouchable Leatherworker (Sarki) households; members of two Mahanta
clans[5] are localised in another hamlet in which a few households of Untouchable Washermen (Dhobi) and Sweepers (Pode) also reside; and there
is one hamlet with households from a wide variety of castes and ethnic
groups, none of which numerically dominate. Kholagaun, the focus of this
paper, is one of the larger hamlets consisting of 67 households. The agnatic
descendents of Jibdar Silwal who settled the area 10 generations ago live in
57 of the hamlet's households. As Chetris they rank immediately below
Brahmans in the village caste hierarchy. Of the remaining households four
are of the Magar caste, four of the Untouchable Blacksmith (Kami) caste
and two of the Untouchable Tailor (Damai) caste.

Banaspati is 10 miles from Kathmandu where there are opportunities for
non-agricultural employment. However, until the mid-1980s, subsistence
cultivation was the major form of economic activity in the village. The

---

[4] Tamang is an ethnic group with close historical and cultural links with Tibet. They
continue to practise Tibetan Buddhism and have been incorporated into the Nepal caste
structure as a low but touchable *jat*.

[5] Mahanta is a jat of Sanyasin who historically left the celibate life.

productive relations of land-ownership, labour and distribution entailed by
subsistence cultivation are still the dominant economic links among the
village households.

The Chetri Household

In analysing the Chetri household I incorporate an analytic distinction
proposed by Carter (1984). Carter uses the term 'domestic group' for what
the Nepalese call pariwar and argues that it is composed of two dimensions:
the familial and the household. The former dimension distills the culturally
defined relations of kinship between members regardless of whether those
who are so linked live together or engage in any shared tasks. The household
dimension . . . . 'is defined by shared tasks regardless of whether its members
are linked by kinship or marriage or are co-resident' (Carter 1984: 45).[6]

To a certain extent these two dimensions are recognised by Silwals in their
conception of the pariwar. Households in South Asia go through a development cycle in which membership expands and contracts as individuals
are married, have children and die, and as joint households divide because
of social conflicts. As a result the households actually existing in Kholagaun
display wide variations in size and the kinship relations linking members.
Silwals have few problems describing the boundaries and membership of
each household in their hamlet and there is a remarkable consistency in their
descriptions. The grounds upon which Silwals base their judgements of
household boundaries and membership are kinship and overtly economic
criteria. Although all members of each Silwal household are kin of some
degree, kinship by itself—as Carter recognised—does not uniquely define a
household. Ideally the household is a patrilineal joint family whose core is a
two- to four-generation agnatic descent group (santan), their wives and
unmarried sisters and daughters. All Silwals recognise that this is an ideal
and that ultimately the joint household is an unstable group likely to divide
and to attract other kin. Interacting with this basic kinship structure are the
economic activities of the household whose central material features are
agricultural land and the hearth. These not only define the limits of kin
included in a household but are also the foci for the hostilities causing its
division or for the attraction of other kin seeking membership. Thus the
household is defined as that set of kin which has common access to and
cultivates specific plots of agricultural land and which pools and consumes
products of that land cooked on the same hearth.

6 While I maintain Carter's distinction, I use an alternate terminology: what Carter calls
'domestic group', I term 'household'; what Carter calls 'household dimension', I term 'functional dimension'; and I retain Carter's term 'kinship dimension'.

Hierarchy and equality are facets of social relations of both dimensions; and it is on these social principles that I focus my analysis. The important point is that actual household social relations appropriate both dimensions in varying degrees. Thus the meanings and experiences emergent in each dimension interpenetrate the other in the wholeness of domestic social action. This is a crucial source of the rich, multifaceted, and to some extent, ambiguous experience members have of the hierarchy-equality configuration.

Kinship Dimension

A common theme of all Brahman-Chetri kinship relations is hierarchy. However, hierarchy is not experienced as a monolithic structure. There are at least two basic forms whose intimate association in household social relations produce an ensemble of experiences of status tinged with benevolence, malevolence, conflict and cooperation. One basic hierarchical paradigm is *mannu parne* in which status is based on generation, age and gender. It incorporates notions of authority, respect and deference among humans. The other is derived from ritual practice in relations between humans and the divine in which status is based on purity. The core of ritual practice is *puja-prasad* (the reciprocity of worship and blessing) and incorporates notions of worship, adoration and humility. In the following analysis I break down the kinship dimension of the household into a basic set of dyadic relations, each of which becomes a structural context for the experience of hierarchy. By being associated with a specific social relation, these experiences coalesce into an interpretive scheme that includes a style of typical action in a social structural context.

(a) *Father-son*: This relation is the basic and minimal agnatic descent unit (santan) whose extension into future generations may result in the ideal joint family and potentially in a distinct lineage with the father as its founding ancestor.[7]

Silwals explicitly conceive of the mannu parne paradigm of hierarchy structuring interactions between father and son. They say that a father has authority over his son and is deserving of respect from his son and that a son must obey his father without question. On formal occasions the mannu parne relation between father and son is typified in a politesse known as

To become the core of a distinct household or lineage, a santan must have ownership of agricultural land and this is one reason why the inheritance of immovable property is a facet of agnation. Here we see the inextricability of Carter's kinship and household dimensions of the domestic group.

dhog:[8] the son bows his head to his father in a show of subordination and respect, and reciprocally the father touches the son's forehead with his right hand and bestows a wish for good fortune. Valeri's point about ritual is valid for dhog: ritual 'produces typical experiences from which typical results [patterns of social interaction] are likely to emerge' (1985: 344). Dhog creates a typical experience of mannu parne hierarchy—involving concepts of authority, respect, deference and obedience—through enacting a model social interaction in which the father and son actively engage. In addition, this often fleeting series of gestures links two shadings to this scheme: restraint and benevolence. These are more fully realised in everyday action in the household.

The theme of restraint in mannu parne was revealed to me on the first occasion of my giving a feast in appreciation for the Kholagaun Silwals' help in my research. Although I knew that the teenage and young married sons of the older Silwals wanted very much to attend, they refused my invitation. It was not until I offered them a separate room that they willingly accepted because otherwise they said they would feel uncomfortable drinking, smoking and joking in front of their fathers. To do so would show lack of respect. The theme of the superordinate's benevolence was made explicit when I asked a young man, who had just become engaged, what he thought of his parents arranging his marriage with a woman he did not know. He answered that his father was wiser in these matters and that, since he only had the son's welfare in mind, he would choose a girl who would be a good and faithful wife.

(b) Husband-wife: This relation is another major axis of the household. It entails a gender division to mark the relative status of the husband and wife. This context generates an interpretive scheme with different shades of meaning and experiences of hierarchy from those of the same sex but intergenerational status marking of the father-son relation. The two relations are functionally associated in the household: while the husband-wife relation lacks the generational continuity of the father-son, its purpose is to produce that continuity; or as Kondos (this volume) so aptly says, '. . . the purpose of wifehood is that the husband be born again' (in the son).[9]

---

[8] In dhog the subordinate person bows his forehead to the superordinate person; in return the latter bestows a verbal wish (*asis*) for good fortune upon the former. Dhog allows varying degrees of hierarchical distance to be marked by the part of the superordinate's body which the subordinate touches with his forehead—hand, knees or feet.

[9] In one sense the production and consumption activities characteristic of Carter's household dimension of the domestic group enable and sustain this reproductive function of the husband-wife relation. This is another way in which the two dimensions are inextricably linked. As we will see, the functional interpenetration of these two dimensions is part of the process engendering the experiential interpenetration of hierarchy-equality as produced in the two dimensions of domestic group social relations.

The husband-wife relation is also understood as a mannu parne relation incorporating the core notions of authority, respect, obedience and deference. A man's and woman's first direct experience with these in relation to the person who will be the spouse are the typical experiences produced in the marriage ritual: the bride sits on the inauspicious and inferior left side of the groom; at various times she does the most respectful form of dhog by touching her forehead to the groom's feet; and she eats food made impure by being previously eaten by the groom. These latter two rites are forms of what Harper (1964) calls 'respect pollution'. Thus, in the marriage ceremony mannu parne is typified as interpenetrated by concepts of purity and pollution. The significance of this is that purity-pollution is a metonym of the other hierarchical mode: puja-prasad. Puja-prasad is the paradigm for relations between humans and the divine in which the criterion of super-ordination is purity. As a result the stark respectful mannu parne hierarchical mode is modified by the divinity and benevolence of purity and by the danger and malevolence of the impure outsider personified by the witch (boksi). Thus the central rite of marriage is kanyadan—the gift of the virgin. Dan is a gift given during worship to the pure and divine-like Brahman. Analogously the offering of a pure virgin (kanya) in the form of a dan gift to the groom associates in experience the concept of divinity with that of the respect due the husband. At the same time, kanyadan renders the wife-giving family inferior to the wife-takers. Explicitly the inferiority of the wife and her kin is not understood in terms of purity and pollution; yet the puja-prasad context of these rites admits the possibility to do so.

This possibility is strengthened in her conjugal home where she is not only the inferior but an outsider rendering her potentially malevolent and dangerous. In village beliefs only women can be evil and malign witches (boksi); and from the point of view of household members, it is only in-marrying women—the inferior outsiders—who are considered to be potential witches. A woman is thought to learn witchcraft from her mother (herself an outsider) and it is thought that a witch's first victim is her husband himself or as reborn in her son.[10] Such evil is likened to the impurity of the ghostly spirits and lower castes.

To briefly summarise, the husband-wife relation engenders a complex experience that appropriates both modes of hierarchy. Belonging to the household by virtue of his birth, the experience of the husband's superiority and respect is tinged with purity and divinity; gaining admission to the household through marriage, the outsider wife is experienced as an inferior and dangerous being, as likely to perpetuate the household through the birth of sons and to destroy it through witchcraft.

[10] For a full account of the wife as a dangerous witch see Bennett (1983) and Gray (1983).

(c) *Brother-brother:* This relation is structured by the mannu parne mode of hierarchy but in a 'weakened' form because it lacks the clear status markers of generation or gender. Birth order is the criterion of status, elder brothers having authority over and deserving respect from younger brothers. However, being members of the same generation and having a socially equivalent relation to their father introduces the derivative idea of equality into the experience of mannu parne hierarchy. Moreover, inheritance rules explicitly typify this equivalence—and the derivative idea of equality—in legislating that each son inherits an equal share of the household estate from the father. The brother-brother relation is the prime context engendering a consciousness of hierarchy and equality as potential transformations of each other; and this in turn introduces contradiction into the relation: older brother is superordinate and equal to younger brother. It is the experience of equivalence, and derivatively of equality, as transforms of hierarchy that are the source of the cooperation and conflict that characterise social relations among brothers in the household and the interpretive scheme emergent from it.

Crudely put, cooperation among brothers is founded upon their common agnatic relation to and respect for their father as well as the generalised reciprocity with shared household resources. However, as Parry (1979) shows in detail, the conflicts which precipitate brothers to seek the division of the land and the joint household are often based on feelings that the older brother is too overbearing in exercising his authority and/or that there is an unequal distribution of labour and product from the jointly held land. Another way to state the problem is the simultaneous appearance of hierarchy and equality among brothers in the same household. Dividing the household resolves the contradiction: as heads of distinct households with their own estate, the brothers are equivalent; at the same time the hierarchical relation between them operates at the annual Dassain festival in that the eldest brother's household is the seat (*mul ghar*) of its celebration for all the brothers and members of their households. Thus there is a contextual and temporal component to the transformational relation between hierarchy and equality in the brother-brother relation.

(d) *Brother-sister:* In some respects this relation is the most complex of all in the household. It engenders an association of experiences which include major themes from all the other core relations of the household. Moreover, these themes are brought together by a social relationship which Nepalis describe as the most relaxed, open, and emotionally as well as materially supportive. While it appropriates both hierarchical paradigms it does so without the negative valences in other household relations: there is not the restraint as between father and son, the danger as between husband and wife, or the conflict as between brothers. Instead it combines hierarchical benevolence, cooperation, as well as purity and divinity. As in the relation between brothers, birth order is the criterion of mannu parne status—elder sibling having authority over and deserving respect from younger sibling. As in the husband-wife relation, cross-sex gender introduces purity and the concomitant puja-prasad but in a reverse form. Far from being the polluting and potentially dangerous outsider, a sister is a pure, divine and benevolent insider. The wife and sister typify the negative and positive forms of the supernatural, both of which are entailed in the puja-prasad paradigm.[11] Sisters are *chelibeti*—humans with a divine quality and hence deserving of worship.[12] In this sense they are more than mannu parne kin, they are *pujya*—worshipable—thus linking in consciousness a positive valence of the worship (puja-prasad) mode with the respect (mannu parne) mode of hierarchy. Unlike the husband-wife relation, where the negative aspects of the puja-prasad paradigm (impurity and danger) are overshadowed and attempted to be controlled by the mannu parne paradigm, in the brother-sister relation the divinity and benevolence of the sister tends to dominate and modify the mannu parne experience.

The analysis of the complexities of the brother-sister relation reveals a more general point about the implications of household social relations for members' experience of the hierarchy-equality configuration and the constitution of interpretive schemes. In those relations involving men (i.e., father-son and brother-brother), the mannu parne mode alone orients the experience of hierarchy, albeit with the various shadings of restraint and benevolence in the father-son relation and of equality, cooperation and conflict in the brother-brother relation. However, it is in the cross-sex relations that the supernatural-oriented puja-prasad mode becomes significant in the experience of hierarchy. A further complexity is that there is a gender specificity to that experience. For men there are two types of women in their households. Wife and sister as positions in the kinship system typify two forms of supernatural intervention in human affairs: pollution/danger and pure/divine. The supernatural beings associated with each form of intervention—ghosts and demons on the one hand and deities on the other—personify the types of action associated with inferior and superior positions in a hierarchical

[11] The explicit core referent of the puja-prasad paradigm is as a mode of interacting with deities. But more generally it provides a mode of interacting with supernaturals of all kinds. Thus exorcists and other types of specialists dealing with malign spirits also use basic puja-prasad practices to interact with demons and ghosts.

[12] The brother-sister relation is the epitome of the underlying structure which is the relation between the men of the household's agnatic santan and women born to them. For example, a daughter is a chelibeti of her father and a father's sister is a chelibeti of her brother's son. Thus, a man's chelibeti include the following: sister, daughter, father's sister, son's son's daughter, and father's father's sister, and the relationship is extended to the husbands of these women and in some circumstances, to their households (see Gray 1982).

structure. Further, a husband's mannu parne authority is threatened by pollution and the malign power of demons; conversely, a brother's mannu parne relation with his sister (whether younger or older) is overshadowed by her divinity and her being deserving of worship. For women there are two types of households—conjugal and natal—in which they may claim membership. In each there is a different experience of the relation between the mannu parne and puja-prasad modes of hierarchy. In the former, as a wife she experiences the overbearing and confining authority of her husband and her mother-in-law who attempt to control her potential danger through scrupulous adherence to mannu parne interactions. In her natal household, the strictures of mannu parne are greatly relaxed and she enjoys the adoration and trust of her brother and his wife.

The significance of this gender specificity in the experience of hierarchy in cross-sex household relations is threefold. First, from both male and female perspectives there is an ambivalence in the general concept of femaleness and its relation to hierarchy, though the ambivalence has a different character for men and women: men experience inferiority and superiority as occurring in distinct and separate female persons of different nature; women experience inferiority and superiority as dimensions of an existential being in different households such that their ambiguity is contextual. Second, as an ambivalent being woman has the character of a mediator. Third, the household contains the structural atom for understanding wider-scale social units: an agnatic descent group linked to other descent groups through women of positive or negative supernatural valence. Accordingly, the way hierarchy operates in such wider-scale social units may be partially explained in terms of the form of female mediation linking the household or other social groups whose core is an agnatic descent group on the model of the santan. I return to this point later. Now, however, I move into a discussion of those social relations entailed by the functional dimension (Carter's household dimension) of the household.

Functional Dimension

For Kholagaun Silwals agricultural land for subsistence agriculture and the common hearth are the metonymic symbols of some major activities and functions which are understood as characteristic of the household. Since it is assumed that all household members are kin, the household social relations entailed by land and hearth are discussed in terms of kinship. This interpenetration of the two dimensions will be maintained in the following analysis of household social relations engendered by land and hearth.

At the outset of this paper I claimed that a hierarchy-equality configuration would orient the analysis. Thus far the egalitarian facet has been conspicuous by its seeming absence. This is a consequence of a kinship system in which the mannu parne paradigm is dominant, and consequently, in which formally there are no equals. There is a refraction of equality among brothers, and it is significant that it emerges particularly in relation to land and hearth. Thus, one theme is to show how and why it is in household relations entailed by land and hearth that equality is a significant dimension. Another theme is that such experiences of equality are usually juxtaposed, as cause or result, to power and conflict in the household and that such conflict threatens its existence and the mannu parne hierarchy that encompasses its social relations.[13]

(a) *Land*: Household social relations co-implicated by agricultural land largely revolve around its ownership and the labour required to realise its subsistence potential. Most agricultural land in the Kathmandu Valley is under *raikar* tenure in which, except for the provision of ultimate ownership of all land by the state, individuals may buy, sell and transfer all other rights in their land. The rules and patterns surrounding transaction among people involving land largely concern the rights of various kin in the land. Together they define gradations of ownership which when associated with specific kinds of kin modify the mannu parne hierarchy among kin by introducing the theme of power into the relevant interpretive schemes.

Land is inherited patrilineally. From birth sons become coparceners in their father's landed estate. As a result a man cannot transfer the rights in that land without the consent of the other coparceners even though the land is registered solely in his name. The land may pass into the name and formal ownership of a man's wife upon his death ensuring her at least a parcel of land should the sons want partition. But whether for the whole of the estate or just a parcel, she is a temporary custodian since the land must eventually pass to her husband's sons and not to any of her natal kin or sons by another husband. A daughter generally does not actually inherit land from her father unless she remains unmarried until the age of 35. Her dowry at marriage is considered as her share of the household estate.

Rights in agricultural land are distinct sources of power in the control of those who have access to its subsistence potential and/or its monetary value. Nepali culture in general and the household in particular encompass such potential power in the mannu parne structure of kinship. To a large extent there is a mutually supportive relation between the gradation of respect in the latter and the gradations of power of the former. The agnatic santan has the strongest and most permanent rights while women connected by marriage

[13] It is perhaps not a coincidence that equality emerges in the household in precisely that realm—the economic—which Dumont claimed was the encompassed position replicating its position in the hierarchy-equality configuration of South Asian ideology.

or birth to the santan have weaker or temporary rights: a wife acts as a temporary trustee ensuring the continued association of the land with the santan, and a daughter inherits only under the socially degrading and rarely realised condition of spinsterhood. Thus, these women remain dependent on a santan throughout their lives in their right to maintenance from the land while residing with the household. The eldest male of the santan realises the most power not only because of his high position in the mannu parne hierarchy but also because of the control in the land derived from the fact that it is his name on the official land records. This power is limited by the potential rights of the sons. The ambiguous position of the wife is reflected in her rights. As an outsider she may have only temporary control, and she cannot transfer the land outside her husband's santan. However, she does realise some power over her sons because she has rights to a significant portion of the land for her own maintenance between her husband's death and her own and because she can use her custodianship to block or delay any transactions in the land until her death. Perhaps the openness and ease of the brother-sister relation is partially due to the fact that in normal circumstances they do not have rights in land which may come into competition in the transition from the unitary estate of the father to the divided estates of the sons. It is the one household relationship in which power does not seem to be a significant factor.

The other main implication of land for household social relations is the division of labour. Briefly, the wet rice agriculture practised in Banaspati involves a gender division of labour.[14] All agricultural operations are seen by Silwals as constituted by male and female tasks. However, since sisters and daughters of the household's landowning santan marry and leave at an early age, its gender division of labour devolves onto the husband-wife relation. Almost all agricultural operations are organised and supervised by the male household head or his mature sons; most of the actual labour is done by their wives. At busy seasons this female labour is supplemented by reciprocal exchange among agnatically related households in Kholagaun and/or the hiring of female labour from households in other hamlets. Only the physically heavy tasks (i.e., ploughing and threshing) or technically difficult tasks (i.e., sowing and irrigating the fields) are done by the male santan members. Together these aspects of land and kinship produce conflations of: (a) santan males (husbands), their mannu parne superiority in relation to their wives, their power deriving from superior rights to the land and their authority and supervisory role in the division of labour; and (b) females (wives), their mannu parne inferiority in relation to their husbands, their

---

[14] It also has implications for the division of labour among households in the village, but that is the theme of another section of this paper and of Gray (1983).

dependence based on their inferior and temporary rights in the household's land (cf. Sharma 1980), and their role as providing the majority of agricultural labour.

(b)Hearth: The common hearth and kitchen where the product of the land is prepared and consumed by household members is the most significant context for interactions which typify the concept of equality. In the twice-daily activity of eating together, equality is revealed as a legitimate style compared to other contexts in which it is merely an implicit and possible style of household social relations. This occurs in two senses. First, food, its preparation and consumption are together an important symbol of common kinship and equivalent purity. To share food is to replicate and contribute to the common substance (i.e., blood) and equal purity of kinsmen; the knowledge that all household members are kin is inherent in this social practice. Further, only people of equal or greater purity as the household members are permitted to enter the kitchen during cooking and eating; and only a person of equal or greater purity as household members may prepare the food. The consumption of food from the cooking vessel is an interpretive act acknowledging the equivalent purity and consequent equality of all who do so.

Second, the consumption of food from a common hearth reveals to members another dimension of equality: the equal rights each has to support from household resources. The portrayal is vivid. By representing the pooling of household members' incomes and the distribution of household resources for daily needs and major expenses such as marriage, the common pot of rice and its distribution to each of the members brings together and unifies into an intersubjective concept their disparate experiences of equality of access to household resources.

These two senses of equality engendered around eating from a common hearth are themselves a hermeneutic. The first defines all household members as equal beings in terms of purity; the second spells out the consequence of that existential equality for the equality of access to material resources; this, through the symbol of sharing food, reproduces their existential equality, thus closing the interpretive circle.

In this context of hearth activities, equality is a legitimate concept for interpreting social relations and thus it can be made socially explicit. One consequence of this contextual legitimacy is that it reveals the possibility of individual as opposed to household benefit. Thus it can be used in juxtaposition to the holism of the mannu parne paradigm to interpret social action for the benefit of one section within the household. This is one way of describing how contradiction can and does emerge in the household. It is not culturally surprising that the main locus for the manifestation of this contradiction is the conflict between brothers. This is the most fertile

ground for such conflict because in the equivalence in relation to father and
his land equality is always lurking beneath the formally hierarchical relations
between brothers. Hearth activities provide the legitimacy, issues and discursive concepts for their conflicts. Among Kholagaun Silwals, household
conflicts follow the familiar South Asian pattern. Brothers argue over what
each thinks are inequalities in the labour and income contributed to the
household pool and in the access each has to its resources.[15] The result of
this conflict is the fission of the joint household which sacrifices the brother-
brother relation to the husband-wife and father-son relations of the resultant
households. Thus, the relation where equality is most likely to emerge is
sacrificed to the dominance of hierarchy in the household.

Implications

In this analysis I sought to show how a set of interpretive schemes incorporating hierarchy and equality are constituted in the Chetri household. An
interpretive scheme consists of the conjunction of morally typified action
and a social-structural context for its efficacious performance (cf. Valeri
1985).[16] The interpretive schemes I have identified are derived from four
core dyadic relations of the household. Each of these relations serves two
functions: first, in providing a discursive name for the scheme, and second,
in constituting that scheme in everyday household practice by unifying in
consciousness (a) moral action in terms of hierarchy-equality with (b) its
legitimate context in terms of the structural characteristics of the relation.
Since human social practice is polysemous, this is not the only possible set of
schemes that could be derived from the household. I have chosen the
hierarchy-equality orientation because it is a central issue in much recent
South Asian ethnography. Moreover, as an acknowledged dimension of
social relations in a wide variety of contexts, it provides an overt path for
tracing the centrifugal implications of the household for the hamlet, village
and regional caste surrounding it.

Drawing out these implications necessitates reconceiving the nature of the
hamlet, village and regional caste. Rather than as units composed of a
lineage, castes and clans, they may also be viewed as distinct sets of households linked together in different ways. Given the nature of an interpretive
scheme as conjoining a structural context with morally typified action, if the
specific structure of the linkage *between* the households constituting such a
social unit is interpreted indigenously as a homologue or analogue of a core

[15] In order to preserve the outward picture of brotherly cooperation and harmony, this same
conflict and discourse is interpreted as occurring between their wives.
[16] Such morally typified action can have both a positive or negative social value linked to it.

dyad *in* the household, then the morally typified action conjoined with that structural context becomes a dimension of the relation between the households. I develop this point for the hamlet, household and regional caste in a suggestive rather than exhaustive manner.

The Hamlet of Kholagaun

The hamlet is a set of households headed by persons linked by agnatic kinship.[17] The structure of relations between the households is homologous to the brother-brother dyadic relation in the household. Silwals explicitly cite their written clan genealogy (*bangshawali*) as the charter for this structural homology and for interpreting hamlet social relations in terms of the brother-brother dyad. The genealogy consists of an origin story of the clan, a complete genealogy of the Kholagaun lineage and less complete genealogies of other lineages in the Kathmandu Valley. The Kholagaun lineage was founded by Jibdar Silwal who migrated with his five sons to the area now known as Kholagaun. He established the settlement by building a house and proclaiming his rights to the agricultural land. Upon his death, each of Jibdar's sons established a separate household by dividing the land to provide a separate material base, and each is now seen to be the founder of a sub-lineage (*khalak*). This story portrays the process and conditions for agnatic division: a santan and its wives, a house and the material base for its subsistence as a distinct unit.[18]

The actions of Jibdar and his sons are an ideal typical portrayal of the interpenetration of the kinship and functional dimension in household dynamics. Silwals see each household in Kholagaun as a result and replication of Jibdar's household. Based upon the principle that sons of brothers are classificatory brothers (*daju-bhai*), all Kholagaun Silwals are understood as brothers. This is an interpretation of the relation between their households and provides the basis for some important features of social life in the hamlet and the parameters for interpreting them. The hamlet has the same configuration of mannu parne hierarchy, equality, cooperation and conflict as the household. Within the household mannu parne status among brothers is determined by birth order. Formally the same principle applies to the sub-lineages: each is named and ranked according to the birth order of Jibdar's son who was its founding ancestor. Yet, as with the relation among brothers

---

[17] This process makes explicit the preconditions for a distinct social group of kin: agnatic descent group and a territory. It is only by establishing itself in a separate territory that an agnatic descent group becomes a distinct unit within the larger encompassing clan or lineage.

[18] Agnatic division may occur at any level and it involves analogous conditions: an agnatic descent group attached to a territory giving it a distinct identity.

in the household, mannu parne status is juxtaposed to equality. The focus of
the lineage is the founding ancestor who, like a household head, is the point of
both the unity and equivalence of his descendents; and just as in the household,
lineage unity has its material base in agricultural land. However, unlike the
household the lineage has no common land; instead, the unity among lineage
brothers is their cooperation in productive labour on the separate land of each.
During times in the agricultural year when the labour of the household is
insufficient, several households reciprocally pool their female labour in a system
called *parma*. Therefore, in the household and hamlet it is mostly women linked
to brothers by marriage who provide the majority of the agricultural labour.

Just as in the household, the same relation to ascendent founding ancestor
('father') that is the focus of unity and cooperation among brothers is also
the basis of their equality and conflict. I provide just one illustration of how
the conflict among lineage 'brothers' is manifest in the two factions which
canalise hamlet and village politics. The leaders of the factions are both
Kholagaun Silwals; and the issue which precipitated their conflict and
formation of their 'parties' (i.e., factions) could not be more appropriate to
their relation as brothers. The hamlet started a cooperative shop. A short
time after it began trading, the Silwal who became the leader of one faction
accused the future leader of the other faction of being involved with several
others in using the shop's money for private purposes—in other words, the
accusation was of one brother getting an unequal share from a jointly held
and cooperatively worked resource. More recently one of the faction leaders
attempted the hamlet analogue of household fission. Given the unavailability of
vacant land, he could not pursue the strategy of Jibdar Silwal. Thus he
switched to a ritual code. As brothers, lineage mates share in the pollution
caused by the death of a fellow member. As a result of this death pollution,
members of the lineage should not wash clothes, eat salt or perform rituals
for 10 days. After a death on the eve of the most important festival of the
year (Dassain), the leader of one faction argued that his sub-lineage was too
distantly related to the deceased to necessitate observance of death pollution;
accordingly he said they would celebrate Dassain. The other faction leader
and the other sub-lineages put enough pressure on members of the rebellious
sub-lineage so that they did observe the death pollution. The divisive
potency of this strategy derived from the dynamics of household fission
among brothers. The final stage of fission—after the division of the land and
building of separate residences—is when the older brother's house is no
longer considered the 'family seat' for the Dassain celebration.

The Village of Banaspati

Banaspati consists of approximately 500 households. From the perspective of any one of them, the village appears as a set of households with which it has two forms of relations. It is linked to some village households by kinship—most of these being in the same hamlet; and it is linked to the other households by non-kinship caste relations.[19] Further, as Dumont (1970) recognised, a village and its caste structure does have a material base of agricultural land in which caste defines a hierarchy of rights. Accordingly, in relation to purity and caste hierarchy, a basic village structure consists of (a) an association of purity with power derived from superior rights to land, and (b) a group of usually lineally related households with superior rights to land and the remaining households, some of which are superior and some of which are inferior, dependent on them for all or part of their subsistence. Taken together these two points provide a socio-cultural logic with the potential for interpreting other forms of social relations mediated by land (i.e., class-like agricultural labour and landlord-tenant relations) as caste relations. The social experience which generates schemes enabling this interpretive project for village social relations occurs in the household.

Biographically, an individual encounters in the household dyadic relations analogous to this basic village structure. With respect to land, a household consists of the core agnatic santan of men who are owners/coparceners and a set of dependents who have only rights of maintenance in the land. Most typically it is women linked to the santan by marriage and birth who are these dependents. Earlier we saw in the analysis of the husband-wife and brother-sister dyads that a woman introduces the puja-prasad paradigm of hierarchy and the concomitant ideas of purity, divinity, pollution and danger. Thus, in this nexus of household relations there is an analogous association of power derived from superior rights in land with purity that is a characteristic of relations between village households.

This analogy goes deeper. From the perspective of a Kholagaun Silwal household, dependent households provide labour or service in return for subsistence from the land. Some of these dependent households are pure, superior and divine Brahmins whose typified task is as priest ensuring the good fortune of the Silwal household. Other dependents are impure and of inferior castes; typically they are the labourers and tenants. From the

[19] Caste and the puja-prasad paradigm essentially concern hierarchical relations between different kind of beings. Accordingly it is a formally inappropriate scheme for interpreting relations among kin. Seemingly, then, this presents an obstacle to the argument that dyadic relations of kinship in the household can generate interpretive schemes for relations between village households organised hierarchically by caste. In the case of the Kholagaun hamlet, there is a homology of the brother-brother dyad in the household with the classificatory brother-brother relation between the households. The homology is based on the classificatory logic of the kinship terminology and on the ethnohistorical process linking Jibdar Silwal's sons with the present households. In the case of the village, there is an analogy of dyadic relations in the household with relations between village households. Analogy enables more social phenomena to be encompassed in its logic.

perspective of the santan, some dependent women (i.e., sisters) are pure and divine chelibeti who, like the Brahman, typify the benevolent intervention of the supernatural in human affairs. This is explicit in the annual Bhai Tika ritual in which sisters as divine beings bless their brothers for the continuance of their santan. Other dependent women are inferior and potentially dangerous wives who typically provide the major agricultural labour for the household.

This structural analogy of the santan-dependent women relation in the household with the landowning-dependent relation between village households suggests an explanation for why caste, purity and the puja-prasad paradigm continue to dominate the interpretation of all village social relations between households—even those which analytically are class relations based on differential relations to the means of production. There are two factors in the continuing interpretive dominance of purity, caste and the puja-prasad paradigm. First, as I argued in a previous paper (Gray 1983; also see Seddon, Blaikie and Cameron 1979), most village households engage a mixture of ownership, tenancy, labour and caste/*jajmani* relations for production. Thus, while one of these may contribute more than others to subsistence, a household does not have an unambiguous character in this respect. Second, since village households vary in the mix and material importance of these relations, there is not one type which villagers can use to characterise unambiguously the general nature of relations between village households. In the face of ambiguity and given that the superior-rights-to-land: dependency structure underlies all these relations, experience of analogous household relations contributes to the interpretive dominance of caste and the puja-prasad paradigm for understanding the hierarchical relations between village households; the ambiguity of a variety of relations with status implications is subsumed under a single interpretive scheme.

The Chetri Regional Caste

By 'Chetri regional caste' I refer to the local conception that Chetris living in the Kathmandu Valley form a distinguishable section of the Chetri caste which extends throughout Nepal. The basis for distinguishing a regional caste within the Kathmandu Valley is that it forms the usual territorial limit of marriage. Thus, as for the household and the lineage, the preconditions for the distinctive identity of a social group are a set of kin conceived to be attached to a specific territory. This provides only a partial description of the regional caste as understood by Chetris themselves. It may also be described using social concepts at three levels of kinship. The regional caste may be analysed as a set of clans among whom marriage is prescribed; as a set of localised lineages (i.e., like the Kholagaun Silwal lineage) linked by actual and potential marriage; or as a set of households linked by marriage and by potential or exogamously proscribed marriage. Whatever the level, there is a basic structure: a set of agnatic descent groups—clan, localised lineage, household santan—linked by marriage or potential marriage. These various levels of agnatic descent group are extensions in time and space of the household father-son dyad. The clan is distinguished from localised lineage and household by its lack of attachment to a recognised territory: localised lineages and households of each Chetri clan are spread throughout the Kathmandu Valley and beyond. Despite this difference, the common image for the affinal connection between agnatic descent groups is the linked dyads husband-wife/sister-brother.

The issue raised by this conception of the regional caste is that there is a different relation of hierarchy-equality among the agnatic descent groups at each level. At the clan level, all are considered of equal status enabling marriage among all the clans. However, at the household level, there is a hierarchical relation between the superior wife-taking santan and the inferior wife-giving santan. At all levels marriage binds the descent groups into a recognised unit but the status implications of marriage vary. These ethnographic facts highlight marriage as the crucial relation for the nature of the Chetri regional caste.

Experientially, marriage is first and foremost a problem for the household. Generally it is the senior man and his wife who expend a great amount of time and effort finding a suitable spouse for the unmarried men and women in their household. At this level marriage involves the linked dyads of husband-wife/sister-brother and focuses attention not on relations within the household but between households. In this sense marriage is one of the primary centrifugal social processes carrying the implications of interpretive schemes generated in household relations to inter-household relations. In the search for a spouse, they consider households of all Chetri clans—except those prohibited by rules of exogamy, i.e., father's, father's mother's, mother's father's and mother's mother's *gotras*[20]—to be of equivalent purity and status and, thus, potential affines. As we have seen previously, both the husband-wife and brother-sister dyads incorporate a notion of hierarchy based on purity and the puja-prasad paradigm. Thus, as a result of marriage, the relations between the households involved take on the hierarchical character of the dyad linking them: the wife's natal household (wife-giving) is considered inferior by the husband's household, and the sister's conjugal

---

[20] Strictly speaking rules of exogamy apply to gotras. Among the Chetris there is a complex relation between gotra affiliation, clan and localised lineage. All members of the Silwal clan are also members of the Bharaduaj gotra. However, in other Chetri clans, there may be two or three gotras, and some gotras include lineages from different clans.

household (chelibeti-taking) becomes pure, divine and superior in relation to her brother's household. Here the equality in terms of purity between households identified by clan as potential affines is transformed by marriage into hierarchy between households identified as households of actual affines.

These hierarchical consequences of marriage affect the local lineages in the same manner as lineage brothers become impure through a birth or death. This means that marriage between local lineages may be repeated only if it hierarchically replicates previously remembered or extant marriages. If a Kholagaun Silwal sister marries into a local lineage in another village, that lineage would become superior in status. Consequently, a Silwal could not marry a woman from that lineage—at least until the original marriage is 'forgotten', because it would confound the hierarchical relation already established by the previous marriage. The Kholagaun Silwal must look beyond such affinal local lineages for a spouse. Analytically he or she may marry into a different localised lineage of the same clan as an existing affinal lineage. However, Silwals do not think about it in these terms. Once the reference moves beyond existing affinal lineages, the potential marriage universe is conceived of as a set of households identified primarily in terms of their clan affiliation. At this level of thought, marriage may occur in 'both directions'; and this exchange is both the cause and effect of the nullification of any hierarchical implications of marriage for Chetri clans. Here hierarchy between households and localised lineages identified as actual affines is transformed by marriage into equality among clans identified as potential affines.

One reason why this particular moment of hierarchy-equality transformation occurs is that unlike a household or localised lineage, a clan is not attached to a specific and identifiable territory. Thus there is no easily recognisable corporate group to take on the hierarchical consequences of marriage. Being spread throughout the valley, there is no way for each household of the clan to keep up with the marriages of all the other members and to calculate the hierarchical implications for the clan as a whole. Since the concept of 'woman' generated in household social relations incorporates purity-pollution, the linkage of clans by both wives and sisters effects the status equality among all of them. Socially, marriage between households centrifugally constitutes a circulating connubium linking santan, lineage and clan agnatic descent groups and realising the transformations between hierarchy and equality. Experientially marriage constitutes in consciousness the hermeneutic relation between hierarchy and equality.

• • •

References

Beck, Brenda. 1972. *Peasant Society in Konku*. Vancouver: University of British Columbia Press.

Bennett, Lynn. 1983. *Dangerous Wives and Sacred Sisters*. New York: Columbia University Press.

Carter, Anthony T. 1984. Household Histories. *In* R.McC. Netting, R.R. Wilk and E.J. Arnould (eds.), *Households: Comparative and Historical Studies of the Domestic Group*, pp. 44–83. Berkeley: University of California Press.

Dumont, Louis. 1970. *Homo Hierarchicus*. Chicago: University of Chicago Press.

Furer-Haimendorf, C. von. 1966. *Caste and Kin in Nepal, India and Ceylon*. New York: Asia Publishing House.

Godelier, M. 1978. Infrastructures, Societies, and History. *Current Anthropology* 19 (4): 763–77.

Gray, J.N. 1982. Chetri Women in Domestic Groups and Rituals. *In* M. Allen and S. Mukherjee (eds.), *Women in India and Nepal*, pp. 211–41. Canberra: Australian National University Press.

Gray, J.N. 1983. Domestic Enterprise and Social Relations in a Nepalese Village. *Contributions to Indian Sociology* (ns): 17(2): 254–74.

Hammel, Eugene. 1984. On the *** of Studying Household Form and Function. *In* R. McC. Netting, R.R. Wilk, and E.J. Arnould (eds.), *Households: Comparative and Historical Studies of the Domestic Group*, pp. 29–43. Berkeley: University of California Press.

Harper, Edward. 1964. Ritual Pollution as an Integrator of Caste and Religion. *Journal of Asian Studies* 23 (supp.): 151–97.

Parry, Jonathan. 1979. *Caste and Kinship in Kangra*. London: Routledge and Kegan Paul.

Schutz, Alfred. 1972. *The Phenomenology of the Social World*. London: Heinemann Books.

Seddon, D., P. Blaikie and **J. Cameron**. 1979. *Peasants and Workers in Nepal*. New Delhi: Vikas.

Sharma, U. 1980. *Women, Work and Property in North-West India*. London: Tavistock Publications.

Valeri, V. 1985. *Kinship and Sacrifice: Ritual and Society in Ancient Hawaii*. Chicago: University of Chicago Press.

Weber, Max. 1978. *Economy and Society*. Berkeley: University of California Press.

Wilk, R.R. and **R.McC. Netting**. 1984. Households: Changing Forms and Functions. *In* R.McC. Netting, R.R. Wilk and E.J. Arnould (eds.), *Households: Comparative and Historical Studies of the Domestic Group*, pp. 1–28. Berkeley: University of California Press.

5

Subjection and the Domicile:
Some Problematic Issues Relating
to High Caste Nepalese Women

Vivienne Kondos

Mᵧ CONCERN is with the nature of the position of certain high caste Hindu women—a position which includes features such as the cultural constructions about self (and selves); the nature of household arrangements and the imperatives that emerge from such arrangements. In the anthropological literature dealing with the topic there has been a great deal of discussion on these issues.

Fruzzetti, adopting the symbolic interaction approach (1982: 1), argues that the position of high caste Hindu women has been misrepresented by those accounts which portray it as 'one of subjection and domination by men' (1982: 2) whereas a relationship of complementarity, she thinks, would be more apt. There is no disputing that, to some extent at least, the discipline's treatment of such women has often been cavalier, often, as she says, taking reference from Western paradigms rather than attempting to identify the particular complexities. I can also understand Fruzzetti's desire to fill out the details of the indigenous conceptions, a task she executes with great skill and perceptiveness. Yet it seems to me that this particular slant is politically dangerous and methodologically tenuous in as much as it tends to privilege the 'positive aspects' of these women's positions, and risks foreclosing any further rigourous investigation of the restrictions and disadvantages that are their lot (see also Seymour 1985: 796). And as far as the focus of this paper, the twice-born Nepalese, is concerned, there appear to be some grounds for emphasising the disadvantaged position of women. As the Nepalese government recently introduced legislative reforms to redress the traditional legal position of women, its manœuvres indicate that in its consideration there was something to be done in this area and I should add that in the view of some Nepalis, a lot remains to be done.[1] So while I would

[1] In 1987 it was reported that a further revision of the laws had been instigated.

not deny that 'complementarity' might indeed pertain in some aspects of the male/female relationship, it need not preclude the possibility of men's superordination and women's subjection. In fact it is likely that complementarity may entail just these along with any other range of possible discriminations.

In a way what also needs to be foregrounded is that 'cultural meanings' themselves incorporate a fundamental kind of subjection, in that they specify what is to constitute a persons' subjectivity, orienting how self is to be experienced and how others are to conceive it and react to it (Foucault 1982: 208–16). Without doubt, the assortment of cultural constructions of subjectivity would be applied to the men as much as to the women concerned. But if that is the case, then again it becomes methodologically necessary to consider the comparative significations in order to discern which of the categories, if any, is privileged and which disadvantaged by these cultural discriminations.

Though also utilising the symbolic interaction approach, Ortner and Whitehead (1981) problematise the issue of male 'dominance' and the control of women in their general theoretical article which attempts to 'account for sexual meanings'. But they insist on the methodological imperative of avoiding totalisation: they argue that all the women of any one society should not be regarded as constituting a homogeneous category. Rather, in their view, it is possible that distinctions may be made between consanguinal and affinal kin and that accordingly the position of the women in these categories will also vary. Specifically on this matter, the authors suggest that whichever category is relevant to the production of male prestige in the public sphere is the particular category which will be discriminated against. Concomitantly, where the kinswomen are not relevant to the production of male prestige, the position of those women in that opposed category is favourable in comparison. In the Hindu context, prestige is articulated as caste and uses the idiom of purity and pollution (ibid.: 16–19, 21–22).

Bennett, in her treatment of the high caste Nepalese, adopts Ortner and Whitehead's formulations, even though she adds her own elaborations. Her *Dangerous Wives and Sacred Sisters: Social and Symbolic Roles of High Caste Women in Nepal* (1983), is an impressive ethnography, which sets out to delineate the nature of social and symbolic roles of high caste Nepalese women. The thematic is clearly attested by the second part of the book's title, while the issues are considered in terms of the oppositional framework. Bennett claims that in the case of high caste Nepalese women (the Parbatya), gender notions articulate major categories, the affinal women (wives) and consanguinal women (sisters), where the former are defined negatively and the latter positively according to the religious symbolic system. And

correspondingly, Bennett characterises the social position of these categories
of women in oppositional terms, arguing that constraints apply to wives,
whereas daughters in contrast enjoy 'relative freedom' (ibid.: viii–ix). Thus
addressing her stated objective which is,

> to try to show how women's social roles in Hindu kinship and family
> structure are related to their symbolic roles in the ritual and mythic
> structures of Hinduism—in Geertz's (1965) terminology—the rela-
> tionships between social phenomena and ideological structures (ibid.:
> vii).

Therefore, in Bennett's portrayal of the nature of the connection, there is a
correspondence between the nature of the social circumstances (the social
role) on the one hand, and the particular symbolic role on the other, for each
type of kinswoman. And as far as the broader picture of comparison
between the sets of women's social and symbolic roles go, Bennett also
renders this according to an oppositional patterning. In her vocabulary the
sets are called 'structures'.

Bennett cites another objective. It is to show how women 'interpret these
structures' and indulge in strategic manoeuvres 'to achieve their own goals'
(1983: vi).

There are several points that I find particularly problematic. For our
purposes it is important to notice certain presumptions underlying the
methodology that articulates a binary oppositional format. First, Bennett
assumes that the thought of the Parbatya conceptualise only two categories
of kinswomen (wife and sistei or daughter). Even mother, Bennett says,
figures as an affinal, though also allegedly belonging to a 'mediation',
category. Second, Bennett imputes that the Parbatya conceptualise distinctions within an oppositional kind of vocabulary. Although the oppositional
format is not immediately discernible in the terms of the title ('dangerous
and sacred'), Bennett's elaborations definitely indicate that she means the
reader to take it as such since she proposes that it is the wives who signal
'impurity' and the daughters, 'purity'. Her discussion unfolds a string of
oppositions around this basic theme: oppositions like sexual/celibate;
reproductive woman/categoric virgin; fertility/asceticism (1983: viii–ix), and
is fully itemised in a chart which also includes the supposed mediational
notions pertaining to mother (ibid.: 310). In this case a matter of regulation
and control applies to wives while relative freedom is supposed to be
enjoyed by the sisters (ibid.: viii–ix) as mentioned before.

It is this oppositional characterisation of both the nature of 'symbolic' and
'social' roles that I think is problematic since there are grounds for suggesting
that alternative renditions are possible. It is not Bennett's ethnographic

details that provoke disquiet, for these, on the whole, constitute an important contribution to the literature on the topic. But as far as the oppositional characterisation of Hindu conceptions of the nature of the kinswoman is concerned, this could very well misrepresent the indigenous material, even though the thematic is well embedded in the literature, especially since the appearance of Dumont's classic work, *Homo Hierarchicus* (1970). Nor do I think it sound to pursue this oppositional theme in the context of the divergent social requirements, as Bennett does with her imputation that the social constraints apply primarily to affinal women while the opposite holds for the consanguinal who, instead, are meted relative freedom. Presumably this kind of portrayal derives from Ortner and Whitehead's methodological injunction to heed the possibility of varying situations (Bennett 1983: vi). Let me make it clear that I definitely take their point: any analytic attempt to reach some understanding of the complexities involved in the lives of women would of necessity have to spell out the differential circumstances applying in the assortment of positions and avoid homogenising what in all probability is a heterogeneous situation. Yet, even when working within such methodological requirements and heeding the differences, one finds some reasons to have reservations about Bennett's rendition of Parbatya social arrangements. It seems to me that there are good reasons for suggesting that both 'affinal' and 'consanguinal' Parbatya women are regulated and disadvantaged, albeit in varying ways (see Seymour 1985: 796).

That is not the only difficulty with Bennett's approach. At least as I read Ortner and Whitehead's text, there seems to be a tendency to portray the 'outside' world as the 'real' world, the world of important events and of substance, while depicting the domestic as having relevance primarily by virtue of its contribution to the men's gains acquired outside (1981: 23). I am not sure that it is wise to put one's sights on the 'outside' and use this to account for women's subordinated status. I would argue that the household itself and what it entails is also highly significant and any attempt to explicate the disadvantaged position of women *vis-à-vis* men would have to take this as a starting point.

Let me try to bring some of the major threads together. It seems fair to say that the subordination and subjection of women is a live issue for the high caste Nepalese. Furthermore, in my consideration cultural meanings may be discriminatory even if couched in terms of complementarity (cf. Fruzzetti 1982); therefore these matters warrant some attention. Accordingly, in this paper I will try to demonstrate that Parbatya women as compared to men are disadvantaged by the cultural specifications of their natures and the domestic arrangements for living. What particular historical forces have impelled women's subordination and state of subjection, I do not think we know. But one point that I do think can be made is that women's subordination and subjection affect male privilege, and if that is so, these disadvantages constitute one condition for the operation and continuity of male-privileging practices.

Rather than adopt Ortner and Whitehead's proposals which direct the focus beyond the household to the issues of the outside world (in this case, caste prestige) as the important site for a consideration of the position of women, it seems to me that it might be wiser to closely scrutinise the nature of the household arrangements themselves. This, of course, is not to deny the relevance of certain outside forces such as the state's laws, which determine differential rights with respect to important areas like inheritance of property, paternal and maternal claims over progeny, and divergent residential statuses, since these are undoubtedly highly relevant. However, if nothing else, one must recognise that such laws take a concrete shape in the daily round of conflicts in household life.

I agree that there appears to be some discontinuity between the position of 'consanguinal' and 'affinal' women as Ortner and Whitehead as well as Bennett argue, but in other respects, as I understand matters, women from both these categories are disadvantaged by the household arrangements. In certain aspects this is necessarily so, since, as I hope to show, the restrictions for one constitute a prerequisite for the other.

Furthermore, there is little doubt that it is difficult to come to grips with a mode of thinking that is different from our own and therefore one must tread gingerly: even so there are some reasons for suggesting that reports of the Hindu mode of categorising women as being oppositional in form and as being preoccupied with the theme of purity/pollution (or its variants) could misrepresent matters. This is not to deny the relevance of the concepts in some contexts but rather to protest that perhaps they have become a kind of catch-all, which, to my mind, is unwarranted. Therefore, in parts of the following discussion I shall touch on this topic. For a paper in a book focusing on the household the points can only be made sketchily and will be addressed more fully elsewhere. But it is, I think, imperative to include a few points since they directly relate to conceptions of kinswomen/kinsmen.

Speaking generally I would suggest that certain kinds of ideas about people are articulated in ontological terms rather than in qualitative terms as exemplified by the pure/impure opposition. Moreover, in my consideration the mode used for making distinctions in many contexts takes reference from a processual format, rather than an oppositional one and is of a kind which orders its universe of discourse according to three terms (Kondos 1982). This general format, as I hope to show, albeit cursorily, underpins the specific designations which define three types of kinswomen, daughter/sister, wife, and mother. Let me add immediately that none of this is meant to imply that in Hindu conceptualisations general ideas of femininity and characterisations of women's qualities are absent. Nor is it to say that the idea of a pair is irrelevant. Universes of two terms abound and find their exemplification in the sexual pair, male/female. Yet here also it seems that Hindu theorising provides an interesting approach.

There is one further objective. It is generally accepted that in any account of women's subjection, it is desirable to incorporate a scrutiny not only of the important ways in which power is exercised, but also resisted. But I also think it necessary to extend beyond this. Otherwise what could become foreclosed is an identification of the limits of possible reactions from the subordinated. It is not only the case that women can 'manipulate' affairs and 'achieve their own goals' (Bennett 1983: vii) but that their manoeuvreing of goals can indeed be thwarted. Accordingly, in parts of the following analysis I shall itemise some of the possible strategies in resisting power that are available to women. But I shall also try to indicate just how far these can go. And out of the available alternatives, I want to delineate what these actually provide by foregrounding the cost to the woman who would want to or does resort to these. In short, I am concerned with delineating the limits of resistance.

I
Three Commonplace Sayings

First of all I want to examine three everyday sayings which I think bear on the position of women and appear to be important because they are commonplace.

(a) Women as the Lustful Sex

When discussing the nature of women, Parbatya comment that one characteristic is strong sexual desire. Some, familiar with the esoteric literature, may even refer to the sacred laws, like those instituted by Manu, a text which had been used by the state judiciary until recent times and is still regarded as a source of authority. Since Manu's formulations are the most frequently cited by Parbatya (Sharma 1979: 93) they will provide an illustration of the kind of proposals made about the nature of women. Manu specifically asserts that feminine nature is 'lustful' because he, Manu, created women that way.[2] Because their nature is such, he goes on to say, it is imperative that women be constantly supervised, otherwise they are likely to

[2] See the passages in Buhler (1969: 330, IX, 15–17) where Manu asserts that certain women's dispositions including lustfulness are as they are because of his creative actions.

give vent to their sexual desires and become disloyal to their husbands with
the attendant disastrous consequences for paternity. The argument culminates
with his pronouncement of what wifehood is to constitute. According to
Manu, the essence of wifehood is the realisation of paternity for the woman's
husband, that the husband through the wife, is born again in the child
(Manu, IX 2, 7–9, 15–17 in Buhler 1969: 328–30). But when other parts are
consulted it becomes clear that what is being advocated is not simply her
producing offspring of either sex, but bearing sons (Manu, IX 81, 106–07 in
Buhler 1969: 342, 346).[3] That this is the ideal conception of womanhood
would not be disputed by Parbatya.

Several points warrant comment. The first thing to notice is that feminine
lustfulness is what might be called a 'truth-claim' about the nature of
women. Since its provenance is a sacred text it is part of that discourse
which stands as the prevailing knowledge and therefore is imputed to have
veracity. So whether or not women are inordinately passionate or more
passionate than men is precluded from becoming an issue while this general
discourse holds sway.

Second, beginning with the premise about women's passionate nature the
text builds an argument to explicitly justify surveillance so as to assure the
goal of rightful paternity.

If so, and this is the third point, the definition of women's nature and its
attendant imperative, her surveillance, is tied to the pursuit of men's objectives.

Fourth, starting with the hardly controversial observation that while
maternity is never a dubious matter, paternity is, so it would follow that
rightful paternity is dependent on a wife's fidelity. This means that the
context for such specifications about women's nature and the attendant
necessity for their patrol is one where the men are in the vulnerable position.

Fifth, if the argument asserts that the sole purpose of wifehood is that the
husband be born again by her, it is inscribing the idea that the maternal
function is nothing more than the realisation of paternal goals, that it is
simply a contingency of wifehood. In effect, the argument presents a special
kind of definition of maternity, a male-privileging definition since it does not
cede maternity as constituting a realisation in its own right.

Going further, if the argument details that wifehood constitutes reproducing the husband, it offers a further restriction. Maternity in this kind of
discourse is not being defined as reproduction per se, but reproduction of
one sex only. This constitutes point six.

Finally, such ideas about what constitutes wifehood also appear to have

[3] The *Arthasastra* put the matter in a more straightforward manner: 'women are created for
the sake of sons' (see Prabhu's discussion, 1940: 196–97).

some bearing on the construction of femininity. Since Hindu theorising maintains that womanhood is defined by the bearing of children for her husband, it is proffering a restricted definition of womanhood—here not simply of wifehood but of womanhood. If a discourse establishes reality, sets up the natural way of things, and this in particular advocates that the woman is there so that her husband can perpetuate himself in his sons, then this discourse constructs women as the reproductive instrument of men.

To condense these points: whatever else is happening, this discourse is specifying what the maternal can be and what the maternal is for. If the discourse defines maternity as the reproduction of sons only, and if it prescribes that function as instrumental to paternity, we could then say that it establishes peculiar features and limits of maternity. Similarly, at the more general level, Hindu theorising also premises a limited version of womanhood, restricting it to the special kind of maternity. As a result it leaves a space of uncertainty for those women who do not reproduce sons. Furthermore, the proposals alongside the rules associated with them are of a kind which, if followed, would effect men's advantage.

(b) Paternal Bone, Maternal Blood

The second everyday saying is about the establishment of sexual differences based on ideas about the composition of the human body. In Nepal, it is common to hear people state that 'a person gets bone from the father and blood from the mother'. Their brief commentary on the body's composition is spelt out more fully in the erudite texts, like the *Garuda Purana* to which Nepalese scholars refer. They propose that the human body is made up of two sets of components, one is derived from a person's father and the other from the mother. They explain that the two parental substances come together through sexual union, where the 'male principle' (Shiva or Purusa) activates the energy potential (Shakti or Prakrti) of the female principle (Kondos 1982: 242–43) and so the conjoined substances develop into the material body comprising components of each parent. Into this material body, the transmigrating soul' enters at the sixth month of a woman's pregnancy. The mother experiences the entry for it is the time when the body is quickened by the soul and begins to move in the mother's womb (ibid.: 253–54). The formulations then specify that the woman's womb is central in the reproductive process, defining it as the field for the location of the body and its development and that the reproductive power inheres in the female. The masculine, however, is defined as the capability which can arouse that feminine energy; that the masculine is the sex which acts upon and the feminine that which is acted upon. In this way, Hindu discourse stipulates that both the paternal and maternal are relevant though differing in their contribution to the formation of the body's components. As far as sexuality is concerned, doctrine proposes that while the masculine components come from the father and the feminine from the mother, it is the predominance of one set of body components which determines the person's sex.

Yet cultural discourse also prescribes another difference. It stipulates that the paternal and masculine components are hard and comparatively enduring parts like nails, hair and bone, whereas the soft components like flesh and blood, it claims, are feminine and are obtained from the mother. So this kind of categorisation allocates to the masculine that which endures. The idea of comparative durability is manifested in the death rites, when after the body's cremation, the bone particles, the only human remains are collected. What is of interest is that the correlation itself may be seen as political since what is defined as paternal and masculine is what lasts longer, and this is taken as highly significant for the rules which organise the sexes.

The cultural exposition not only inscribes the paternal as the locus of the enduring components, but it also uses this idea as the basis for the formulation of another definition, which is of particular social importance. Having isolated the enduring component as signifying the masculine, the discourse uses this notion as the demarcator of human continuity, for it imputes that long-term continuity can only be traced through the bone and not any feminine components. The grouping which forms as a result, is called the 'bone-line' (*harnata*). In Nepal, it is the bone-line which constitutes the locus of a person's identity and is the basic social unit. Membership for males is through birth, whereas for females it is through marriage (see Kondos 1982, 1986: 176). If the discourse defines the men as the bearers of the line, allocating women as necessary but secondary (as merely instrumental energy, the field and the source of other body components), then the constructed sexual ontology becomes the idiom for the formation of its groups. What distinguishes one group from another is membership in different bone-lines. However, while the ideas and the practices with which they are associated identify the men concerned as the reproducers of the line, the maternal involvement can hardly be denied.

While Hindu discourse does not directly challenge this incontrovertible fact, certain Hindu ideas and procedures appear to take measures to countervail its significance. But first of all, let me indicate what I mean by 'incontrovertible' maternal importance. A woman's giving birth, I think, constitutes a rare instance of a natural fact that can remain undeniable in the face of any cultural definition, for her involvement in reproduction cannot easily be disputed since the baby is seen to issue forth from the mother's body. To say otherwise, would entail the reduction of everything to a cultural determinism which I think would hold other methodological complications. Culture can of course add or subtract something, it can mute the importance of the maternal involvement, but it cannot entirely dissolve that involvement without the risk of straining credibility. So how do Hindu ideas and practices treat the birth of a child?

What the Hindu ritual of the naming ceremony performed in the advent of birth does is to focus on the paternal relation and make this the crucial issue. Should it happen, as in cases of illegitimacy, that no man presents himself as the paternal claimant, no proper naming ceremony can be performed. Therefore this ritual takes as its primary concern, the establishment of the paternal connection between the father claimant and the newborn baby. Consequent to this, the baby gains social identity, membership in the father's group, the particular bone-line in question. In this ritual, focusing on the new-born child, the mother's birth-giving act is not extolled, nor is it on any other occasion, but neither is it ignored. It is, apparently, merely rendered as of lesser consequence. The allocation of differential importance is spatially played out, with the mother sitting on the edges, while the father is situated at the centre, baby on his lap encircled by the required range of sacred objects. So the unequivocal maternal birth-giving act is, in a sense, downplayed since the paternal connection is made to supercede it and overshadow it. Furthermore, since Hindu practice establishes the paternal connection as the relevant and important one for a person's social life, this is likely to also entail the preclusion of other relations.

What is precluded? The male-centred and -centring definitions, along with the male-privileging social practices in which they are embedded also effect the possible kind of relationship between women. If Hindu thought identifies the male sex as relevant for the charting of continuity, specifying them as generators of the bone-line, this means that only men can reproduce themselves in their sons, following the precepts of this discourse. So, what is rendered possible for men is not possible for women. What Hindu thought does appear to be doing is designating females as the plastic persons necessary and of worth, but as the ones who are the unsituated energy to be affixed to and used by the husband. Parbatya appear to accept this rendition and cite a local adage to that effect: 'the daughter is the one who must go to prop up another man's wall'. It summarises the idea that a woman is instrumental for the sex which is not her own. But it also means that though a mother may produce a daughter, she does not reproduce herself in her daughter. Only men can have such a relationship with their own sex for, only men, those in the bone-line, can continue a line.

The Hindu ontological formulations about the paternal and maternal body components appear to relate to the wider social processes which regulate not only what women can and cannot do, but also what they can and cannot become. From this angle, they are comparable to the complex associated with the lust image discussed earlier; both then are parts of a mechanism which advantages the men and are tied to the regulation of women.

(c) The Son's Special Ontology

In everyday conversations reference is made to the desirability of having sons for all kinds of reasons. One reason that will invariably be foregrounded is the son's importance for the performance of the parents' death rituals. The idea acquires negative expression when sonless couples are asked rhetorically and with pity: 'but who will do your *kriya?*' Since these people would know that substitutes are available (other agnates, the Brahman priest, a daughter's son) and are used, their commentary indicates that these are merely substitutes, second best because the 'real thing' is not available. In so doing they hint at an understanding of the appropriateness of the son's nature. It is not simply a matter of recognising the necessity of executing the ritual procedure but of recognising that it be done by a particular kind of person. In that respect it is this person's ontological nature as son that seems to be pertinent. Let me spell out these points.

That Hindu doctrine allocates a special function to the filial is to be discerned in the purpose of the ritual series. The purpose of the son's (or sons') performance of kriya, immediate on the parent's death, is to make a surrogate body for the parent's disembodied soul so as to move that soul away from the precincts of the living on its transmigratory journey; further, the purpose of the subsequent *sraddhas* of the first year is to promote desirable after-death conditions for that soul, while the annual sraddhas after that, have as their ultimate goal, the soul's rebirth in human form (see Basu, 1974: 128–29, 141–43; Stevenson 1921).

As far as eligibility is concerned, doctrine decrees that the most appropriate person is the initiated son, rendered twice-born through the ritual action of the guru. Doctrine then identifies two aspects of masculinity as ontologically relevant. First, it isolates the son who, as we know, is defined as the bearer of the bone. Second, since the twice-born initiation is a prerequisite and is an initiation for men only, one which renders males mindborn of men, doctrine again situates eligibility in a special kind of masculine ontology. In instances where there is no son, eligibility nevertheless remains with men, for the rules stipulate that another twice-born agnate, if available, must perform the rite. Otherwise, it can be an adopted son or a Brahman. In such instances when ideal conditions do not prevail, all those who are acceptable are men who have undertaken the twice-born initiation executed by the guru. So doctrine isolates three factors as relevant for the performance of death rituals since it specifies that it must be a male, who is spiritually reborn and that the most desirable is the one who partakes of the same bone as the dead, his or her immediate progeny. Given that the death ritual is prescribed as a male, and where possible, a filial enterprise, how does doctrine delineate the nature of that enterprise?

The cultural specifications are of a kind which provide an avenue for nothing less than the son's involvement in cyclic existence. Hindu discourse posits that there are three planes of existence pertaining to *samsara*, the cycle of transmigration, and a special fourth, reaching the absolute state, after a person becomes released from the cycle and merges with the Absolute. So while existing in the world of time and change, a person moves through the three planes. One is that of the here and now where a person exists in the embodied form with this particular historicity; the second is the plane where the dead souls go; while the third is that of existence in the womb.

What this appears to mean is that Hindu theorising locates both son and mother as capable of operating in the existential circuit. Where it stipulates that the mother's function is to provide the energy for development, the maternal components of the material body for the transmigrating soul and the place of the location for both in her womb, it also stipulates that it is the son's function to deal with the soul in its transmigratory journey in the plane of existence after death. Both mother and son then are depicted as involved in different aspects of the soul's migratory movements.

While this suggests that culture ascribes a generative function to the son in the cycle of the soul's existence, it cannot be said that this is to be understood as constituting the son's appropriation of the maternal function, either as described in the West, or as defined by Hindu doctrine, because the son's actions are deemed to operate on a different plane. But it does, however, indicate that the son's ritual actions are culturally assigned a kind of generative role in the cycle of existence, as is the mother. The subtle differences and similarities are particularly clear when the esoteric version of what is happening is borne in mind, since it proposes that it is the son's ritual work which is orienting the soul's move into the material body of the womb. The matter was succinctly rendered thus by one Nepalese pundit: 'It is the son who gives rebirth to the parents, just as the mother gives birth to the child'. Others say it is some family forebear and not necessarily the son's parent. Irrespective of the question of whose soul is involved, it appears that there is a belief that the rebirth movement is directed at women of the group. So in this esoteric version doctrine defines the son as the relevant person in cycling members of the bone-line. At a more general level, however, such formulations provide a scheme which maps a route where the son's ritual activity would be intercepting the maternal processes, since he, according to doctrine, is ultimately the ritual actor who moves the soul into the embryo of some woman. What this also indicates is that women are precluded from participating in the existential plane of the soul's movements but are restricted to involvement in the creation of the material body.

Now it might be said that not all Parbatya are aware of the niceties involved. It is likely, however, that many are, since the *Garuda Purana* brings together many of the relevant topics, like the account of the soul's journey after death, details of the composition of the body, and ideas about conception. It also presents an outline of the procedure of the son's funeral work for the dead soul with a commentary on the significance of all this. It is likely that many people will sooner or later become familiar with its contents since it is customary to have this purana read aloud to the family in the event of death. But even if they are not familiar with the complexities, most adult Parbatya know three important details. They know that it should be the twice-born son who undertakes the rites for the parent's soul, and that his work relates to a particular plane of human existence, just as the mother's reproductive involvement with the child relates to a different existential plane. It is the juxtaposition of the proposals about both the mother's and son's involvement in the circuit of existence which is especially relevant for this investigation.

What is interesting here is how the discourse arranges the propositions *vis-à-vis* each other. The premise of the special filial ontology is co-present with notions about the maternal with its unambiguous reproductive capability which the discourse does indeed heed. In all of this, the woman's contribution to giving birth is not challenged, nothing as crass as that. Rather, the discourse inserts the necessity for the performance of a death ritual series, and decrees that this can only be executed by the son because of his imputed special ontological nature, while at the same time it also demarcates the series as belonging as much to the scenario of existence as does the plane of what we call current human existence.

To bring some of the threads together: given people's firm commitment to the ideas about cyclic existence and given that Hindu knowledge specifies that the son is ontologically the crucial ritual actor, the high value given to sons becomes understandable, though of course this function is not the only reason. In this existential context which holds the possibility for heralding the woman's singular capability, culture counterpoises it by inscribing the son's relevance as well. This is not the only instance where the maternal is pushed to the background, for as we saw, this occurs in the naming rite. The allocation of the ritual specially to males obviously also excludes the women from that ritual domain. In treating women as ontologically inappropriate, the definitions in this context locate them as ontological outsiders, so to speak. At this juncture I want to retrace some points raised in the discussion of the three sayings so as to foreground what I see as pertinent to the paper's objective. The sayings, from some angle or other, treat basic existential matters, like what is deemed to constitute maternity and paternity, the nature of sexuality, the nature of the sexes and their relevance and value, in certain contexts. The ideas embedded in or ramified from the sayings also appear to connect with each other, though not in all respects. The connectedness, moreover, can have the effect, I think, of shoring up the acceptability of each. But the discourse also orders these in what we might call a political way in that it slants the advantage to the male. Specifically,

1. The first saying, though it begins by specifying that women are characteristically lustful, appears to be part of a wider narrative tract which defines maternity in a qualified way: (a) that maternity is to be taken as simply a function of wifehood; and (b) that maternity entails not reproduction in itself, but the reproduction of males. Here, obviously, the *husband* is privileged. Within such a framework the reproduction of daughters is specified as not quite authentic and so sons are aggrandised. In addition, not only definitions but regulations are also involved.

2. The saying about male bone and female blood also carries both an *'interdiction and jurisdiction'*, to use Foucault's concepts, in that the set of ideas in which the saying figures, defines the maternal as the instrument of the paternal and prescribes that continuity is a male affair, that a man perpetuates himself in his sons, while a woman cannot in her daughters. Here the *paternal* is privileged.

3. The saying about the son's specialness is anchored to ideas about the specialness of twice-born men in general, for only such men can participate in the existential movements of the dead parent's soul. So one might say that though doctrine does not ignore the maternal it counterpoises it by inscribing filial involvement within this area of after-life which is so important for Hindus. In so doing, doctrine reiterates the ontological primacy of maleness in the filial generation, the inscribed bearers of the bone-line. And if only sons are inscribed as ontologically appropriate to perform the parent's death rites and the daughters are excluded, the ontological aggrandisement applies only to sons. This saying privileges *sons*.

Finally, if doctrine premises that womanhood is to constitute reproduction, particularly of sons, it would then leave those others, the sonless or childless women, in a perilous position. All the notions and the wider tracts in which they figure, in spite of the disparity of context, appear to present women as different from, and lesser to, men in some way or other. Such discriminations, moreover, are linked to regulatory processes and these take place in a particular site.

II
The Domicile: The Locals' Stronghold

Since women's lives are characteristically played out in the household, an examination of the nature of its arrangements and a consideration of how this would affect the women's situation becomes imperative if one is to address the wider theoretical issues bearing on the nature of male/female relations.

Starting with the descriptive features (see also Bennett 1983; Gray 1980; 1982), the *ghar* like many other twice-born households in the subcontinent is typically multigenerational, comprising a man, his wife, or wives if he is polygynous, their sons and daughters-in-law, grandchildren and their unmarried daughters. Authority over this group of people and control of its assets devolves on the senior man, the father, while his wife is in charge of domestic affairs. At the death of the senior man (and sometimes earlier) the sub-units split to form their own households expanding to the largest extent and then splitting again, each time around the man. The filial axis is also the traditional axis of partitioning the family estate, with each son, according to law, obtaining an equal share. The current reforms also allocate a share to the senior man's wife.

The household is not merely a domestic sphere to be assessed as of lesser consequence as compared to the public sphere (cf. Ortner and Whitehead 1981: 10, 16, 22, 25), but incorporates a number of things and processes, all of which are significant in the lives of those concerned. It is important because it is a social structure, a site where critical processes occur; it has its own existential arrangements; and is the locus for a person's identity; it is also a political unit.

1. As a structure the household contains a particular nexus of people who constitute its members, where belongingness is unquestionable, shelter and subsistence are one's automatic rights and from which place members, while members, cannot be excluded.
2. Because the household experience is everyday and perhaps mundane, there is a possibility that the significance of the processes which unfold there could be overlooked, yet it is the site for people's existence and continuity.
3. Further, given that each household contains its specific mix of people, it has its particular existential arrangements, the family customs, for its own way of living which will not be exactly identical elsewhere.
4. For Parbatya membership entails one kind of social identity, one's family (*parivar*), an identity which for them is basic and crucial.

5. Further, since the household conjoins a specific group of people with their particular arrangements and a particular territorial locus, but is, in addition a place where its members can exclude non-members, it may also be understood as a political unit *vis-à-vis* other like units. Rather than employ the conventional term 'household', I will use 'domicile' since it can incorporate these features.[4]

But there is a difference for the members: one sex constitutes the 'indigenes', the other the 'migrants'. The metaphors are not inapt, since the rules specify that only male offspring should remain therein and only outside females may enter as permanent inhabitants. That the female offspring are earmarked for eventual ejection from that place comes through in the Nepali homily about the daughter mentioned before. Since there is the expectation that the daughter will eventually leave, we might say that she stands as a kind of 'transient'. For her part, her natal home is not her ghar but her *maiti*. As far as the incoming wife is concerned she is the outsider who is behoven to assimilate to the prevailing customs of the particular family. In addition to her 'migrant' identity she will find herself with a migrant status as well, unlike the male residents. While it might be said that a woman's membership status is consolidated on reproducing a child, especially a son, and in her life's trajectory, by the time of her maturity she will eventually reign supreme in the arena of domestic relations with authority to exercise power over her daughters-in-law, that assimilation and assumption of authority is itself contingent. To reach this position she has to fulfil the requirement of producing sons. The woman who does not reproduce this sex cannot even consolidate her position in the household and her life's trajectory *vis-à-vis* the women who do is pathetic in comparison. While the sonless state also generates difficulties for a man, nonetheless his full membership status is not qualified as is his wife's. Nor is he open to the same kind of possibilities as is a woman, for sonless women find themselves situated in that kind of space which affords the possibility of being defined as a witch, treated with suspicion and circumspection (Kondos 1982: 254–57; also see Stone 1976, 1978).

In like vein, investigation of other features reveals further discrepancies for the sexes. A man's rights within the family are inalienable regardless of his particular behaviour, short of some criminal offence which would prevent his enjoyment of them. A woman's are not. Her rights can only be retained while she remains a wife. In instances of elopement, according to current legislation, all rights are rescinded, including maternal claims. The laws

[4] The dimension of social group, 'Home'; the territorial base (inhabitants of a place); the existential aspect (settling) and the political ('natives' as opposed to 'outsiders').

decree that the woman must forfeit access to the material assets like land, as well as the children, irrespective of how much effort she has expended whether in terms of reproduction and child-care, household tasks or work on the land. So both maternal and material enjoyment are foreclosed on a woman who chooses to quit the place or was forced to, in instances of the automatic dissolution of the marriage in the event of her confessing to or being proven to have committed adultery (see Bennett and Singh 1979: 61). By stipulating that previous rights are to be forfeited with the dissolution of the marriage and her habitation elsewhere, the state reveals its orientation towards women's rights—that they are neither automatic nor autonomous like the indigenous males, but are contingent on conforming to certain requirements.

Although the state now decrees that the householder's widow gains a share of the family estate, like her sons, her rights also carry a qualification. As a coparcener, the state decrees that she is to obtain an equal share, but only permits her to treat half of that share as her own and if she wants to alienate the other half she must first obtain her son's (s') permission (see Bennett and Singh 1979: 54–63). So even here the widow's rights over her possession are not outright—not full but a halved kind of autonomy which requires permission from the 'indigenous' males.

What about the daughters? Given that Parbatya daughters are privileged in many respects, are accorded a special status and treated with deference by the members of their father's domicile, their position at least at first sight might appear as somewhat anomalous to the theme I have been pursuing. Bennett situates the daughter's position as diametrically opposed to that of the wife, contrasting the subordination demanded in the wifely role with the relative freedom obtaining in the daughter's. As regards status, Bennett argues that the Parbatya perception of women breaks into two major oppositional categories, with wives in the one and sisters (and daughters) in the other (1983: 309), claiming that a string of oppositional symbols differentiate the two (ibid.: 310), e.g., the contrasts of 'purity versus pollution'; the 'sacred versus the dangerous'; 'asceticism versus eroticism' (ibid.: viii-ix; 309–11). This is not the place to offer a systematic extended argument but merely to make two major points relevant to the discussion, but which diverge from Bennett's suggestions.

The first important question is the Hindu conceptualisation of the nature of daughter as daughter. In trying to unravel the problem of the daughter's special position one might be tempted to locate it as somehow embedded in the Parbatya custom of treating pre-menstrual virginal girls as forms of Devi when certain rituals are performed to them in the same way as to the spirit in the idol. This would, I think, confound the two and misrepresent the particularities of the *chelibeti* complex. The specific ritual worship of young girls as forms of the goddess terminates after the girl reaches the age of 9, whereas the specific requirements for interacting with the daughter continue beyond menstruation, marriage and procreation, that is, for the daughter's entire life. I would argue that the Parbatya conception of the daughter's nature has its own particular context that is not reducible to Kumari worship as directed at these pre-pubescent young girls. In the case of the Kumari ritual, the rationale for worshipping them is said to lie in their pristine nature, their 'unevolved form', as one expert explained. The rationale would have to be different for the daughter who even when married and with offspring continues to be treated deferentially. So let us turn to one particular situation where there is a direct connection between the daughter's nature and that of her natal kin.

Take the menarche requirements. These are important because the reasons people give for adhering to the requirements articulate the specific terms that apply to the daughter's nature. During the menarche the customary practice is to locate the daughter in a place beyond the visibility of the natal home where her father and brothers and their wives and grandparents, if alive, reside.

All this is seen as necessary to avoid contact between them since doing otherwise would provoke negative consequences for her natal kinsmen. The negative effect that can result if the separation isn't adhered to is, as one Nepali said, the 'shortening of their life-span or falling into ill fortune'.[5] The same restrictions are to apply when the daughter gives birth and in the advent of widowhood lasting for the critical first year. For our purposes what is significant is that within the rationale for the precautionary measures is included a specification of the daughter's nature since it delineates her as capable of harming her natal kin in contexts where the daughter is undergoing some kind of change.

What this amounts to is a conceptualisation of the daughter's nature within an ontological framework, specifically as having a degenerative, destructive potential for the full members of the bone-line in particular circumstances. Now the destructive capability in Hindu theorising is one of the guna forces, specifically 'tamas'. This term has a range of significations:

[5] As Bennett's Parbatya informant elaborates: 'if they (fathers or brothers) see our face then *ill fortune will follow them*. And that is why it is only when Surya Puja has been performed and only after . . . that they can look upon our faces' (Bennett 1983: 239, emphasis added). The informant's explanation of seclusion in terms of the necessity to avoid any negative effects on the woman's kinsmen apparently is not pursued by Bennett. Instead, Bennett (ibid.: ix) seems to be arguing that the seclusion imperatives of the ritual symbolise the idea of the girl's sexual protection: that it is the daughter's sexuality that is being symbolically guarded. This is how Bennett renders the matter: 'Gupha basne is a ritual attempt to protect that purity by establishing a symbolic barrier between the girl's sexuality and her consanguinal male relatives' (ibid.: 242).

a tamas capability is one which darkens, breaks down, deteriorates, breaks
away, dissolves, terminates. It is a dark and fierce force. The other two gunas
of the scheme are the 'invigorating' force, *rajas*; and the 'sustaining' force,
sattva[6] (Kondos 1982: passim). It is I think significant that Parbatya only
identify the daughter's (and sister's) ontological nature as capable of affecting
her natal kin in this manner. Its range of applicability is both limited and
specific to these people unlike Hindu notions about menstruation. In that
context, as is indeed well-known, any menstruating Parbatya woman is
supposed to be capable of polluting any Parbatya man who touches her or
eats food that she has prepared (Kondos 1982). As for the daughter's
specifically destructive capability, the idea is elaborated in the well-known
story about Daksia's sacrifice when, after angering his daughter Devi, and
insulting her consort Shiva, all hell broke loose (also see Kramrish 1981:
314–19). And it is of relevance to mention that the required deference is also
accorded to the daughter's husband and their offspring and not only to
herself. Presumably this is because they are conceptualised as ontological
extensions of her though this admittedly is a complex matter that can hardly
be pursued here. But at least one point can be made. If the daughter's
husband and offspring are incorporated into the deference nexus then this
would, I think, query Bennett's suggestion that it is the ascetic value of
celibacy that would explain the daughter's special status (ibid.: 314–5). Nor
could this characterisation accommodate to the ideas expressed in another
ritual (Bhai Tika) which brings together the woman and her brothers. Since
the woman's ritual actions are described as essential for cancelling death's
force, it is the tamas capability which is being singled out again, though in
this context it is with positive consequences (Anderson 1971: 172). All in all
what is important for us to notice is that the person who is to be treated in
an exalted fashion is also the very one who is specified as having a *tamasi*
potency. What can get overlooked is that fierce forms are also accorded
deference.

If the suggestions carry any weight we can proceed and try to situate the
conceptions of the daughter in the more general context of the wider
universe of kinswomen. Within the guna framework the wife is conceptualised as generative (rajas), an idea signalled in everyday life by the
coloured red powder the wife wears in the parting of her hair. The mother's

[6] The three gunas constitute a basic classificatory scheme of Samkhyan metaphysical thought
and also, in my understanding, pervades much of Hindu theorising. What I find interesting is
that it is not an oppositional framework but tripartite and takes reference from process, 'rise,
growth and decay' as one Nepali put it. Second, this kind of scheme does not establish mutually
exclusive categories but rather, a continuum of sameness in that within each entity of a
threefold set, each guna is said to be present. What distinguishes one entity from the other
within that threefold set is the predominance of the guna concerned.

nature is rendered as having sustaining (sattva) powers, the one who provides the support for the child's existence in the womb and the stuff of nurturance. In contrast, the daughter is portrayed as the terminal point, having a nature capable of curtailing life-spans, and I should also add, capable of annihilating death's immediacy. The tamas force can be either positive or negative according to the circumstances.

As for the second major question: how to delineate the daughter's status, though the daughter is accorded this special exalted standing, I do not think that this precludes her from being disadvantaged in the domicile (her maiti, her father's ghar). Her place there should be as a 'transient', not a permanent inhabitant. Though she is of the bone-line, her sex disqualifies her from perpetuating that line—destined, as the homily says, to go elsewhere irrespective of her particular desires.

Moreover, the laws expect as much and her rights suffer accordingly. While her brothers' rights to a full share of the patrimony are automatic, hers are not. Should she marry she is disqualified, but even if she remains single, she has no claim until she reaches the age of 35 (Bennett and Singh 1979: 32), well past her 'prime'.

As far as the daughters' general position is concerned, in certain respects the family's treatment of her does diverge from that of its treatment of wives, yet, given that she is a 'transient' in one context and a 'migrant' in the other, she is also disadvantaged in both. Not only that but one is the prerequisite for the other. A famous Nepali folksong not only brings into relief the complexities involved but also accentuates the poignancy of it all. The daughter/wife sings:

There I cannot go back,
Here I am not wanted
What's to become of me?

To make a few summarising remarks at this stage: if so many qualifications apply to women; if the wife's assimilation to group membership of the domicile is contingent on producing sons; if a mother's enjoyment of progeny, wealth and things is dependent on her continuing residence there; and if, in the case of the single daughter, her full membership of the natal family's domicile is dependent on reaching middle age until when she has no territorial locus and no outright rights in the family's estate, then any assets available to women are entirely contingent. This is contrary to what happens to men. Though complementarity might pertain, it does not preclude women's disadvantage.

Just as important is the political nature of these women's positions. It is easy to pass over the significance of contingencies. Having contingent rights means that a person has to qualify before procuring the niceties of life. It means that a person is not an authentic member but is on trial until conditions are fulfilled; or a person's position to have rights is foreclosed when conditional requirements are breached. From this perspective it is the women who constantly have to prove themselves in some way or other, an imperative akin to that impinging on many kinds of migrants.

If no such qualifications apply to men, then within the domicile another kind of politics is at work. Rather than refer to this unit simply as a kinship grouping with a male bias, it might be wiser to depict it as the men's 'domicile', so as to foreground its nature as a male stronghold which uses the notion of maleness as its reference point and the idea of bone-line as its idiom of continuity. Since the cultural definitions and rules demarcate the residents into two distinct kinds of members with differential rights, it effects a political kind of arrangement, internally, where women are the 'migrants' or 'transients' for whom enjoyment is always contingent on the fulfilment of certain requirements.

This is not to say that only women are regulated and that the objectives are only men's objectives. That is definitely not the case. Both men and women, boys and girls, are regimented in terms of what they can do. An obvious illustration is the imposition of arranged marriages, applying to both. The goals of marriage, reproduction of sons, and family life may also be women's goals in many instances. The difference, and this is the point I want to stress, is that the cultural possibilities chart that kind of path which privileges one sex by rendering the other subordinate. The domicile in this culture is the men's territory, its indigenous population are its males; whose residence there is not hedged in by qualifications.

Such arrangements, in my understanding, privilege one sex and discriminate against the other. But if the existence and operation of the domicile are effected through women's subordination, a further comment is warranted. It also means that women's subordination is the condition of the male-privileging domicile. But then rules can often be bent, circumvented in some way or other. So let us turn to these situations.

III
The Strategies: Limited and Limiting

What about women's room to manoeuvre around and between the rules; what happens in instances of discontent, disagreement, outright defiance and deviance of any kind?

Can the woman or girl create any space for the realisation of her anti-thetical desires? One method is to indulge in 'chicanery', what I understand as a characteristic technique of going one's own way. But it would have to be admitted that it has a narrow range, hardly any margin for effecting an authentic change to her lot. Another, suicide, an uncommon but not rare manoeuvre does this. Yet given its irreversibility it is not much of an option and more an expression of the particular woman's extreme state of despair. A more directed manoeuvre is to seek refuge at home with the natal family where the daughter is customarily to be treated with every consideration. But eventually the parents will want to send her back to her husband if they adhere to the cultural specification that she belongs to her husband, that she had been irrevocably given to him in marriage in the ritual sequence, gifting of the virgin (*kanyadan*). So the woman cannot take it for granted that she will find her natal home an automatic haven. In such circumstances this avenue could merely provide a temporary break. Elopement, however, provided and provides something of a real alternative to the particulars of her situation and apparently was commonplace before the legal reforms. But while it provides an alternative to the particulars, it does not do so for her general situation since the woman ends up with the same range of wifely requirements but now with another man. Yet even that strategy has other restrictions. As mentioned before, a woman's elopement with another man automatically entails the foreclosure on her material and maternal rights since the laws decree that the children remain with the father. So maternity is not legally defined as automatically a consequence of physiological reproduction—but again contingent on her maintenance of the wifely relationship. It also means that the laws granted and grant priority to paternity.

The continuity of this paternal-privileging principle, though somewhat hidden in the other changes, appears to curtail the strategies for exit that the state now institutes as legally possible. The particular reforms in question stipulate that in the advent of separation and divorce, custody of the children beyond the age of 5 years is open to negotiation and a mother may take charge if she so desires (see Bennett and Singh 1979: 64–66, 101). In permitting either possibility, the legislation has moved from the past customary position of paternal ownership. Despite this, the past principle continues in that the laws decreed that should the divorced mother have custody and then choose to remarry, the children must be returned to the father. From this point of view it parallels the elopement situation of past times, continuing to enforce the principle that paternity is the primary relation. Since there is no reciprocal ruling that should a husband with custody remarry, that the husband is obliged to return the children to the wife, it continues the policy of differential rights, privileging men and disadvantaging women. But if she takes the risk and does gain custody, she may subsequently find herself in a situation where the options are again unsatisfactory. Should she want to remarry, she must surrender the children to their father; should she want to retain the children then she cannot remarry. Moreover, should she remarry she is obliged to forfeit her coparcenery share, obtained in the case of legal separation; or, in the case of divorce, her alimony, if it is still operative (alimony applies only for five years after remarriage) (Bennett and Singh 1979: 54, 60, 62).

Such manoeuvres, available through the law courts, obviously carry the complications of litigation, time, cost, and the problem of evidence. Some women may not even have any knowledge of their legal rights. None of these make litigation an easy option for women.

But if a woman wants to pursue the legally permitted strategies of divorce or separation by which to exit from a marriage, other pieces of the current legislation contain loopholes which work towards women's disadvantage. I shall briefly note the 'catches' since they are relevant to the theme of this section, even though the matter has been touched upon earlier.

Both possible exits of divorce and separation have their respective catch clauses: if the woman is legally allocated coparcenary shares where the marriage has been terminated as a legal separation, the women will not be able to remarry without rescinding those assets; in like vein, if the woman obtains alimony, this too has its limitations for it is only available for the duration of five years of remarriage. These might appear to be curious rulings in that they discriminate against the woman who would want to avoid the socially undesirable situation of living independently (Sharma 1979: 93). What it does underline is the lawmakers' orientation which premises that the man who is united with a woman sexually is to assume responsibility for her[7]—the idea that the masculine is the referent, provider and protector. So the legal specifications repeat and situate in the concrete idiom, the metaphysical construction that the husband is half of her, and in turn also hitch the woman's life fate to the man and the people with whom she resides. As far as the theme of this section is concerned, however, the point is simple: it appears that divorce is not a highly attractive option.

Another series of possibilities relates to avenues in the wider society which would allow a woman to quit the domicile by becoming economically independent. While prostitution provided the means for survival it often meant an alliance with some protector male strongarm. Other than that, given the lack of economic diversification, not much is available. Where many craft and service specialisations are concerned, these inhere in family units rather than as the means for individual employment. A possible position is in domestic service or servicing in the tourist hotels, but such a switch would merely place the woman in a situation of servility. And though the woman may have become economically autonomous and free of the

[7] Nepalis view co-habitation as constituting marriage.

domicile's particular constraints, given that Parbatya do not espouse a work ethic (that work is good and a mode for individual fulfilment) this and like avenues are hardly inconclusively favourable alternatives to the life possibilities in the family. What all this means is that the range of possibilities for becoming economically autonomous is limited and out of what is available none appears as an attractive alternative. Those women who are educated have an advantage in that they are eligible to work in the bureaucracy in the cities and large towns. But to say this is to pre-empt the problematic because being a woman tends to disqualify a person from obtaining an education in the first place. However, what does apply in general and compounds women's difficulties is the imperative that women should not reside alone but remain under 'surveillance', as mentioned earlier, and to do otherwise would invite extreme disparagement (Sharma 1979: 93). For those women who accept the prescription it becomes an additional curtailment of the possibility of extricating themselves from situations that they regard as undesirable.

It would seem that the major options that have been considered do not amount to much. In these contexts the results of the woman's possible strategies are either short-lived (temporary refuge with parents); of minor import (chicanery), hardly a true option (suicide), or else, they carry such penalties that the gain is accompanied only with other considerable losses or risks (elopement, divorce and separation). In turn, the possible strategies for the 'single' woman (divorced or legally separated woman who has custody of children) who would desire to change that state are also hedged in by the necessity to foreclose her maternal claim and her material assets. Engagement in the outside workplace is not automatically a viable alternative, simply exchanging one context with a possibly worse one, or placing oneself in a situation where the situation itself is at risk.

At this juncture I want to consider two specifically problematic cases—the childless and sonless woman and the spinster.

First, what options are open to the childless and sonless woman, the person who deviates from the ideal, albeit involuntarily? For the woman who has reached menopause, obviously childlessness or sonlessness are states from which there is no exit at all. In the case of other women where it is not as yet a foregone conclusion, some exits, though available, are not entirely satisfactory. One way of attempting to reproduce is to take another spouse. While this is possible for the husband since the state waives its prohibition on polygyny and in the event of a couple's childlessness permits the man to bring in a second wife, as noted before, it is not possible for the wife (Bennett and Singh, 1979: 53, 63). Living in a polyandrous household is totally unthinkable for Parbatya. The state not only waives its ruling against polygyny in the case of a man's childlessness, allowing him to take another wife, but it also decrees that in that eventuality his move constitutes grounds for divorce or separation activated by the first wife. This then would provide the first wife with some room for manoeuvre in extricating herself from the situation of co-wife. However, should she want to remarry, the woman then is free to do so. But the woman would have to find someone who would want to marry her. If she bears the stigma of childlessness or sonlessness and to boot is no longer young by Nepalese standards, such a woman is not viewed as a desirable match and her move in terminating the marriage risks being futile. Nor can she use the material benefits she might have gained as a means of enhancing her attractiveness because the state rules that the coparcenary shares (Bennett and Singh 1979: 29) are to be forfeited in cases of remarriage. So if she stays she must suffer what Parbatya insist is an undesirable situation of being the neglected co-wife. But if she resorts to the exit available, she may find herself remaining single, itself an ignominious state to be in according to the ideals of the Parbatya perspective, and would constitute a cost if she espoused those ideals.

What is available to the girls and women who do not espouse the idea that marriage is the means of a woman's fulfilment and choose to remain single? In instances where the daughter has managed to avoid marriage, a reform geared to redress the basic inequalities in the laws seems to be of a kind which ironically could also work against her. This particular legal reform stipulates that single daughters may now obtain a full share in the family estate like their brothers but only after they reach the age of 35.[8] So if she manages to defy the ideal and remains single, the state's provision does accord her some economic security, but should she want to utilise this in pursuit of her own objectives, because of the time-lag, she cannot do much, except mark time. The time qualification might be viewed as an attempt to correlate the daughter's position with that of her brothers' who do not usually obtain their share until partition, either at the father's death or, if living, with his consent, and when this happens it is generally at the brother's maturity. Nonetheless, it appears to be oriented to the expectation that she will marry and by virtue of this will obtain rights in her husband's estate. In other words, the legal ruling echoes the traditional orientation that the proper source of economic security lies with the husband. And it would seem that this ruling which specifies that only single daughters and not all daughters have rights in the family estate is a qualification that paradoxically may work against the woman who would prefer to remain single. Since it is only the single daughters who may obtain the same share as the sons, her

---

[8] It is important to note that in the predominantly agrarian society many people control land, albeit of varying amounts. This was effected through the state in its land reform legislation which distributed holdings and imposed ceilings on size, though this is not to say that inequalities do not persist. Nevertheless, according to Regmi (1976: 213—15) there is no large

remaining a spinster diminishes what's available for them. Therefore the sister's marriage, not her spinsterhood, is in their interest. Should they act accordingly they will encourage and possibly take measures to coerce their sister to marry and with time on their side. When it is also borne in mind that Hindu theorising posits that the parents gain merit (*punya*) when they offer their daughter as the virginal gift, then for those who follow this line, the daughter's spinsterhood would also go contrary to their interest.

Let me try to bring some of the threads together. As far as these two deviant types are concerned there does appear to be some room for manoeuvre, for the women concerned can take action: but at what cost? The strategic possibilities available carry corresponding catches in the specifications of what is to happen in diverging from the cultural requirements. This appears to be so with all the cases under review and not merely these two types. So not only may we discern the way that Parbatya women in general are regulated by these requirements but we may also notice the extensiveness of her regulation in the curtailments that accompany the alternatives open to them.

Therefore the important dimension is not merely the possibilities for resistance but the range of limitations on resistance. And it is, I think, significant that when rules are broken, there are further rules to cope with the consequences of breaking the rules.

IV
The Matter of Heterogeneity: Failures and Successes

If the foregoing discussion in the various sections makes a modicum of sense, it would seem that the gist of each of the sayings is not isolated from events on the ground, the customs and activities flowing from the legal prescriptions. This is not to imply that there is a one-to-one correlation between the discursive and the non-discursive or that the matter is straightforward. The previous discussion on defiance emphasises the complexities involved. Nor do I want it understood that one can break down people's orientation into a simple categorisation of those who comply with the imperatives as against those who defy them. There are no easy patternings.[9] Rather, my concern is merely to suggest that the everyday statements are not

---

[9] For example, some may accept the appropriateness of some of the regulations and others might accept other regulations. Or again, some people may resent the imperatives wherever they are imposed, whether or not they concur with its premises. People may also be inconsistent, while espousing an idea, they may at the same time act contrarily. There again, it can happen as it does with Parbatya, that many people, including men, are sympathetic towards the women's difficulties, yet do little to alter these even when they have a chance in a particular case. And of course people's orientation can change.

free-floating, so to speak, but can have a kind of concreteness in the context
of existential possibilities. While the particular sayings may specify what is to
occur, what is to become a reality, to become habitual for those involved, for
their part the customs and the legislation and even the rulings regarding the
consequences where deviance occurs, may constitute the possible actual-
isation of the gist of one or other specifications. As discussed earlier,
primacy is given to the pursuit of paternal goals with the custody laws and
the state's waiving of the prohibition of bigamy; the inscription that it is the
husband who constitutes the woman's referent is inherent in the legal
provisions regarding a woman's second marriage; the idea that the destiny of
woman is to be the state of wifehood as well as the idea that the pre-eminent
offspring is to be the son, are both inherent in the reformed laws, which,
while ceding a daughter's property rights, prohibit her from acquiring these
before she reaches the age of 35 and only if she remains a spinster. The
sociological implications of the expressions then are incorporated into the
legal regulations which bear on the possibilities of everyday living.

    Yet, in the concern to isolate the variety of inequities and constraints that
beset women, the inquiry might appear overly negative; and in my concern
to emphasise the sameness of women's subjection to the array of inequities
and constraints, though not denying their variation from context to context,
the inquiry might also appear to be implying that women's lives are to be
understood as being 'one of a piece'. Matters are not entirely negative as the
cases of women who achieve the cultural ideal may indicate. Nor would
there be an exactitude in the condition of women's lives since realising the
ideal also carries the possibility of reaping the corresponding benefits. In
other words, the varying circumstances of women's lives can, I think, be
distinguished and articulated around the idea of success and failure. The
state of failure, as one might expect, takes reference from that of success.
Then one might ask: where are the kinds of achievements that are realised
by women and which signify success according to indigenous conceptions.
Who would she be?

    The woman who has reached the ideal, and is also the idealised woman, is
one who has reached a particular stage of her life, for whom fortune has
gone her way. In cases where a woman has been lucky in producing sons and
has reached maturity with her husband still alive and stands in a position of
authority over the domestic domain, that woman in the Parbatya view has
actualised the ideals and the potentials open to her. Unlike other women,
this woman's position in the domicile is secured, perceived by others as less
a 'migrant' and more an ensconsed 'local'. By then her womanhood has been
vindicated by the mere presence of sons. As for these male offspring (and
female if there are any), they do not know of a time without her. By the time
of her maturity with her 'people' in her charge she has become solidly
situated in a position of authority through which she has some opportunity to

exercise her urge for power, if any. With her husband still alive her virtue is not at issue, no blemish regarding her adherence to wifely duties. This follows post-hoc because in Parbatya eyes a husband's long life depends on this. If she has realised the ideals she may be understood as the 'successful' woman.

But if there are successful women there are also failures. Failures, no matter how few, to my mind, constitute a central consideration, yet tend to be glossed over in accounts of the position of women where realisation of the ideal is given prominence. The 'failed' women would comprise the widows and the childless or sonless women. They are those women in the cultural space where there is a possibility of being regarded as witch, capable of harming other women's feminine powers, generative and nur-turant, by making them barren, drying up their milk, and so forth (Kondos 1982: 255). Should that happen, the women will be treated accordingly, others will shun and avoid them and take prophylatic measures against them (see also Bennett 1976: 14). Whether or not they are suspected of the witch capability, the way people treat widows and childless and sonless women does, I think, foreground a cultural location of failure.

Take the widow's failure. Her husband's death is explained in terms of a dereliction in wifely virtue. So if the woman outlives her husband her continuing life is post-hoc proof of her deviance. In addition, Parbatya refer to the widow as 'inauspicious' (*amangala*) and keep her away from cele-bration, especially weddings (Kondos 1982: 254–57). Fruzzetti raises this point about the widow's inauspiciousness. Yet, as I read her argument, she does not pursue its significance for these women, but instead uses the state of widowhood to illuminate the centrality of wifehood (1982: 129–30). While this is undoubtedly important, what also needs to be emphasised is that the state of widowhood holds gross discriminations against the possi-bility of her exiting from the situation and moving towards success as culturally defined. Given the images of her nature and the traditional ban on widow remarriage, despite the current legal reforms, the widow may still remain an undesirable partner. Widowhood then entails the possibility of the closure of life.

The other 'failed' women, those without sons or without any children at all, also suffer difficulties. Though perhaps barrenness is worse because a woman has not even become a mother, it is sonlessness that generates the major problems in a woman's life. Unless a woman gives birth to a son she has not inserted herself into the bone-line, and accordingly retains some-thing of the 'migrant' identity. The absence, moreover, affords the possi-bility of sharing wifehood. It also holds the possibility of insecurity in old age, without the social support of the multigenerational group. Perhaps worst of all there is 'no one to do her *kriya*'. Nor does the currently available legal exit of divorce and eligibility to remarry constitute an easy option. As a divorcee she would not constitute a highly appealing partner for the orthodox, a negativity compounded by the woman's 'demonstrated' lack of fecundity.

The desirability of avoiding failure and instead becoming the 'successful woman' is to be gleaned by the masses of women who perform Tij-Panchami, the annual ritual for women only, whose goals comprise long life for the husband, the bearing of many children, and especially sons (Anderson 1971: 116–20).

Failure then is to be circumvented for it carries a range of discriminations, not only those already outlined but also a further one. In Nepal the widow is culturally designated as being responsible for her own onerous fate either through wifely miscreance or as the result of sins committed in a previous life. Of interest here is the point that the cultural formulations could proffer any manner of explanation for her state of widowhood. For example, keeping within the indigenous framework, the husband's prior death could be explained as essentially arising from his own actions, his particular *karmaphala*, where the wife's behaviour is treated as irrelevant. Yet culpability for her husband's death is placed in her court. Similarly, a mature wife's childlessness could be attributed to the man's impotence, itself also predicated on his past sins. But it is not. In both cases failure is couched in terms of the woman's responsibility, somewhere, sometime. If the formulations about these failures are of a kind where the women themselves are blamed, it is obvious that they are not being treated sympathetically but accusingly. Since the explanation is not sought outside women's responsibility but located as their own, in instances of failure to achieve the ideal the difficulties of failure are in turn compounded: there is an inculcation of self-blame into her consciousness in those instances where the woman accepts the cultural explanation and simultaneously, on the other, there are the arrangements which provide no ready and easy exits from the particular situation. Such women then have to handle the triple difficulties: an onerous situation; the sense of self-culpability in failing to achieve what ought to be achieved; alongside the formidable blockages to altering their particular situation. And it is through realising the goals that these particular, pressing problems can be side-stepped.

So while the circumstances of women's lives diverge in the matter of success and failure, this is not to say that success provides a panacea but it is to highlight the extreme difficulties of failed women. It is also to indicate that success, like many features of Parbatya women's lives, take a pre-determined path. In the orthodox view, feminine success is predefined and not open to variation, for a woman cannot be successful in any other way or in any other terms except those specified by the structures (the domicile, the laws, the cultural imperatives to produce sons and to die before her husband). What is also important to bear in mind is that it is the woman's success in particular which effects men's privileges in everyday life.

References

Anderson, M.. 1971. *The Festivals of Nepal*. London: Allen and Unwin.

Basu, B.D. (ed). 1974. *The Garuda Purana*. Allahabad: Bhuvaneswaii Asram

Bennett, L. 1976. Sex and Motherhood among the Brahmins and Chetris of East-Central Nepal. *Contribution to Nepalese Studies* 3: 1–52, special issue.

———. 1983. *Dangerous Wives and Sacred Sisters: The Social and Symbolic Roles of High-Caste Women in Nepal*. New York: Columbia University Press.

Bennett, L. and **S. Singh** 1979. *Tradition and Change in the Legal Status of Nepalese Women*. Kathmandu: CEDA Tribhuvan University.

Buhler, G. (ed.). 1969. *The Laws of Manu*. New York: Dover Publications, Inc.

Dumont, L. 1970. *Homo Hierarchicus*. Chicago: University of Chicago Press.

Foucault, M. 1982. Afterword: the Subject and Power. *In* H.L. Dreyfus and P. Rabinow, *Michel Foucault: Beyond Structuralism and Hermeneutics*. Brighton: Harvester Press.

Fruzzetti, L.M. 1982. *The Gift of the Virgin*. New Brunswick: Rutgers University Press.

Gray, J.N. 1980. Hypergamy, Kinship and Caste among the Chetris of Nepal. *Contributions to Indian Sociology* (ns) 14(1).

———. 1982. Chetri Women in Domestic Groups and Rituals. *In* M.R. Allen and S.N. Mukherjee (eds.), *Women in India and Nepal*, pp. 211–41. Canberra: ANU Press.

Kondos, V. 1982. The Triple Goddess and The Processual Approach to the World. *In* M.R. Allen and S.N. Mukherjee, *Hindu Women*, pp. 242–86. Canberra: ANU Press.

———. 1986. Images of the Fierce Goddess and Portrayals of Hindu Women. *Contributions to Indian Sociology* (ns) 20 (2): 173–97.

Kramrish, S. 1981. *The Presence of Siva*. Princeton: Princeton University Press.

Ortner, S.B. and **H. Whitehead**. 1981. *Sexual Meanings: The Cultural Construction of Gender and Sexuality*. Cambridge: Cambridge University Press.

Prabhu, P.H. 1940. *Hindu Social Organization*. Bombay: Popular Book Depot.

Regmi, M.C. 1976. *Landownership in Nepal*. Berkeley: University of California Press.

Seymour, S. 1985. Review Article. *Signs* 10 (4): 794–97, special issue.

Sharma, P.R. 1979. Comments. *In* L. Bennett and S. Singh, *Tradition and Change in the Legal Status of Nepalese Women*, pp. 92–94. Kathmandu: CEDA Tribhuvan University.

Stevenson, S. 1921. *Rites of the Twice-born*. London: Oxford University Press.

Stone, L. 1976. Concepts of Illness and Curing in a Central Nepal Village. *Contribution to Nepalese Studies* 3: 55–80, special issue.

———. 1978. Cultural Repercussions of Childlessness and Low Fertility in Nepal. *Contributions to Nepalese Studies* 5(2): 7–36.

6

Households in Akkaraipattu: Dowry and Domestic Organisation Among the Matrilineal Tamils and Moors of Sri Lanka

Dennis McGilvray

I
Introduction

MY GOAL in this paper is to describe and analyse the pattern of descent, marriage and household organisation shared today by both Hindus ('Tamils') and Muslims ('Moors') in the town of Akkaraipattu in the matrilineal belt of Sri Lanka, the Tamil-speaking, eastern coastal region. Despite their formal religious differences, the Hindu Tamils and the Muslim Moors share many common values and practices in the marriage and household domain. What I hope to show is that the Tamil/Moorish household is a nexus of some familiar South Asian institutions—dowry, marriage, worship, ritual pollution, and matrilineal descent, to name a few—but that these familiar institutions are configured and enacted in some distinctive ways which serve to broaden our understanding of the field of 'ethnographic possibility' in South Asia. A Tamil or Moorish household consists of the people who live together within a 'house and compound,' *vitu valavu*, but houses and agricultural land are transferred as a wife's dowry and the matri-uxorilocal residence rule results in a clustering of daughters' dwellings. This household system thus offers an opportunity to explore some of the factors which seem to generate a relatively greater level of female autonomy and influence in comparison with the more widespread patrilineal/patrilocal household patterns in other parts of South Asia.

II
The Tamil/Moorish Household System in Outline

Geography, Settlement and Economy

The eastern coastal region of Sri Lanka, centred upon the district town of Batticaloa but extending approximately 100 miles from Valaichchenai in the north to Pottuvil in the south, is inhabited in roughly equal proportions by Tamil-speaking Sunni Muslims ('Moors') and Tamil-speaking Shaivite Hindus ('Tamils') whose system of matrilineal descent and uxorilocal marriage is distinctive in an island already well-known for the diversity of its kinship and marriage patterns (Banks 1957; Leach 1961; S.J. Tambiah 1958; Yalman 1967).[1] The economy of this region is based primarily upon irrigated rice cultivation, although some communities are also significantly reliant upon coastal and lagoon fishing, plantation crops (coconut, cashew nut), handloom textile production, and mercantile trade. Two types of settlement patterns can be seen: the majority of the population is concentrated in densely-packed towns and villages close to the seashore, while farther to the west, particularly on the inland shores of the major semi-saline lagoons, one finds a pattern of small nucleated villages and hamlets. The coastal settlements in some places have merged to form a continuous strip of habitation shaded by dense stands of coconut palms, but in fact a strict ethnic segregation of the Moorish neighbourhoods from those of the Tamils is maintained, despite the apparent visual continuity. The great majority of the Moors live along the coast, while the Tamils are found both in coastal towns as well as in inland villages.

Despite the dense, semi-urban habitation pattern along stretches of the coastal road, almost everyone is engaged in farming, or at least owns a bit of agricultural land, prompting one sociologist to classify these settlements as 'peasant towns' (Ryan 1950: 10). Men perform most of the rice cultivation tasks except for weeding, which is done by brigades of destitute women, and it is common for those engaged in agricultural work to commute daily perhaps 5–10 miles by bicycle, bullock cart, or bus from their homes to their fields. During critical periods in the agricultural cycle, however, cultivators and 'watchers' will sleep overnight in elevated wooden shelters erected in the fields.

Among the Tamils, the two dominant landowning castes are the Mukkuvars

[1] Starting in the 1950s, a large number of Sinhalese Buddhist peasants have been settled by the government on land colonisation schemes in the Dry Zone areas adjacent to the eastern coastal districts where the Tamils and Moors reside (Farmer 1957). These new Sinhalese-speaking settlers form a community geographically and ethnically distinct from the Tamil-speakers, and their household system is unrelated to that of the Tamils and Moors.

and the Vellalars, who jointly share the highest rank in the caste hierarchy with non-Brahman Viracaiva Kurukkal priests (McGilvray 1981). These highly-ranked castes are followed in descending order by Karaiyar Fishermen, Cantar Climbers, Tattar Smiths, Navitar Barbers, Vannar Washermen, and Paraiyar Drummers. The Mukkuvars held the old political chiefships (*vannimai*) in most parts of the region during the precolonial and early colonial periods (McGilvray 1982a), apparently a legacy of their role as mercenary warriors in the invading army of the Kalinga prince Magha who conquered the northern half of the island in 1215 AD. Somehow Magha, and possibly other Indian invaders of the medieval period, recruited the Mukkuvar soldiers from the Kerala coast of south India, where some of their descendents remain as Hindu fishermen (and Muslim Mappillas) even today. Thus, the matrilineal and matrilocal elements of social organisation in eastern Sri Lanka have historical roots in Kerala, but these practices are now shared by all the Tamil castes in the region, as well as by the Moors, who apparently acquired the same matrilineal system through intermarriage with local (matrilineal) Tamil women.[2]

The household data presented here were gathered primarily in the Tamil and Moorish wards of the coastal town of Akkaraipattu (population 30,000 in 1971) located in Amparai district, which served as my principal fieldwork site on three occasions (1969–71, 1975, 1978). However, some data on rural Tamil Hindu households were also collected on short visits to villages near Kokkatticcolai, in Manmunai Pattu, Batticaloa district. The households about which I have detailed information are predominantly high caste Tamil (Mukkuvar, Vellalar) households and Moorish households at the middle income level. Judging from the strong correspondences I have observed in the cultural domains of religion, ritual, and caste ideology, I have no reason to think that low caste and poor households differ fundamentally from higher caste and wealthier households in terms of the ideal cultural models of kinship, matrilineal descent, and domestic role structure. However, poverty and political subordination are certainly likely to deflect actual household behaviour patterns away from the cultural ideal in some situations. This is a process which I have documented in the domain of Untouchable religion (McGilvray 1983) but which I currently lack the data to examine in the household domain.

---

[2] Apart from a few Sinhalese outsiders (traders and bureaucrats; some Buddhist, some Catholic), the only groups lacking the matrilineal complex are relatively recent arrivals such as Kataiyar Limeburners or semi-tribal Telugu-speaking Kuravar gypsies (McGilvray 1974), as well as the Creole-speaking Roman Catholic Portuguese Burghers (McGilvray 1982c). The Moors and Tamils tell different versions of a basic legend explaining how Muslim traders once lent assistance to the Mukkuvars in their victorious war against the Timilars, a rival caste, and as their reward were given Mukkuvar brides, whose matrilineal clan membership and matrilineal property came to be enjoyed by their descendants in the manner seen today.

Wards, Compounds, and Houses

In a large coastal settlement such as Akkaraipattu, the residential ward (Tamil *kuricci*, locally rendered in English as 'division') boundaries which demarcate the jurisdictions of the lowest-level government headmen tend also to coincide with the discrete Hindu caste neighbourhoods of the Tamils. The residential divisions of the Moors, who lack caste distinctions, are more socially uniform.[3]

The local materials for house construction vary from wattle-and-daub to cement and fired brick, from plaited coconut frond thatching to terracotta roof tiles. In the innermost neighbourhoods, and more commonly among the Moors than among the Tamils, some large multi-storied houses are found, but most people live in ground-level houses built upon raised cement foundations. All houses are built on the model of a nuclear family dwelling, although it is expected that there will be a married daughter and a matrilocal son-in-law temporarily sharing the house at one stage of the family's developmental cycle. Every house (*vitu*) is situated within an enclosed yard or compound (*valavu*), usually walled with masonry or galvanised metal, or barricaded with barbed wire, thatch, and sharpened stakes, to discourage stray animals, thieves and intruders. The groundwater table tends to be quite high in this coastal region, so practically every house has its own well and bathing area within the compound.[4] Sheltering the compound will be stands of coconut, banana, mango, and arecanut, as well as ornamental plantings of hibiscus and temple flower, all of which contribute to a sense of leafy privacy and refuge. On a day-to-day basis, the gateway from the street into the compound is really the most important 'front door' to the house, the sandy shaded ground between the gateway and the house itself often serving as an open-air 'living room' to entertain visitors informally during the day. However, for serious activities such as eating, which could be threatened by lurking spirits or by an inadvertant glance of the evil-eye, as well as for many activities after dark, a time identified with ghosts and with dangerous

[3] The Tamil ancestors of the Moors, insofar as they can be inferred from shared matriclan names and customs, are principally the Mukkuvars. There are some vestiges of possible caste-related hierarchy among Moorish matriclans, but today the Moors are proud of their egalitarian religion and of their common bond as Muslims. There is, however, a small elite of Maulanas who claim patrilineal descent from the Prophet and a small, endogamous, stigmatised group of Osta barber-circumcisers who resemble a low caste. A small number of Bawas, or Sufi mystics, are set apart by their ecstatic religious practices, but they have marriage connections with ordinary Moorish families.

[4] The impact upon community interaction patterns of private household wells, as opposed to shared public wells, is noticeable in the largely Moorish town of Sammanturai. There, because of unusually dry and rocky terrain, wells are deep and extremely expensive to dig, so women must carry water daily from public wells. As a consequence, one observes a degree of daily public interaction by groups of Moorish women which would be considered immodest in the better-watered settlements.

'coolness', members of the house will move indoors and even close the shutters.

The most traditional and uniform house design is still found among the Tamils, while the Moorish houses show a greater degree of variation upon the basic pattern. According to local experts, the building site should be diagrammed to ensure that a new house is located away from dangerous lines of force (especially the NE-SW diagonal) and away from peripheral zones on the south and west ceded to malevolent supernaturals: *pey, picacu,* and *djin.* Middle income houses, especially in the towns, often have an enclosed squatting-style latrine and septic tank near the periphery of the compound, defecation being the only important activity appropriate for this demonic sector.

The prototypic east coast Sri Lankan Tamil house, whether it is constructed of mud and thatch or of brick and tile, is oriented toward the east (Figure 1). This orientation cannot always be achieved when houses must be built on urban lots which do not front the east side of a street, so compromises are made, often by constructing a formal and aesthetically appropriate doorway to the north, south or west which is seldom used in daily life. I have seen mud houses which consisted of only two rooms, but the ideal Tamil house should really have four: a secure, windowless 'inner room' (*ullutu,* lit. *ul vitu*) for storing grain and valuables and for worshipping Hindu deities; two sleeping rooms flanking the 'inner room' to the north and south; and a public reception room onto which the other three rooms open (an open thatched verandah may substitute for the reception room in poorer houses). If there is only one room used for sleeping, it will be the northern one (the *'mancutu',* from *mancam,* bed), which is, for the Tamils, the connubial chamber par excellence. Southern and western rooms are unpopular for sleeping because of their directional associations with death and decline: Yaman, the messenger of death, arrives from the south, and the western sunset has strong symbolic connotations of entropy and decline (Beck 1976). Judging from the households I know best, the family member most likely to occupy a southern bedroom is an older boy or an unmarried son. Senior members of the family will often prefer to sleep in the public reception hall rather than in a southern bedroom thus sometimes leaving this room available to rent to an undiscriminating anthropologist and his family.

Some of the recent 'modern' houses incorporate a kitchen and built-in chimney/hearth, the cooking in most Tamil houses is still done in a temporary wood and thatch shelter north or east of the main house. Unmarried children will eat their meals in or near the kitchen with their mother, while food may be eaten in a separate room by the father or in the bedroom by a newly-wed daughter and her matrilocal husband. The concrete-lined well, with its counterbalanced wellsweep and paved bathing apron, tends to be

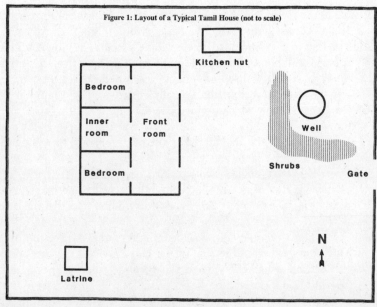

Figure 1: Layout of a Typical Tamil House (not to scale)

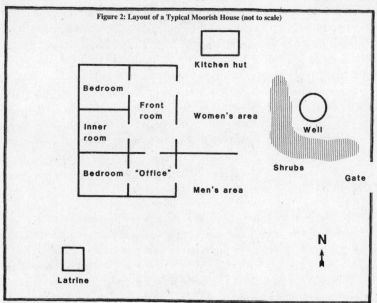

Figure 2: Layout of a Typical Moorish House (not to scale)

located east or northeast of the house, usually behind some ornamental bushes or in a partial enclosure constructed of plaited palm fronds.

Moorish houses seem to exhibit more diversity of design, but the orientation is usually toward the east, the basic layout (Figure 2) typically a variation on that of a Tamil house. There will be a secure, windowless 'inner room', as in a Tamil house, but instead of housing sacks of rice and shrines for Hindu gods, it will be used—as the northern bedroom is used by the Tamils—as the bedchamber of the sexually active married couple in the household. Because daily Muslim prayers require no specially consecrated space, the Moors choose to situate the young married couple at the very centre of the house, in the darkest and most private room. As among the Tamils, I noted a tendency for young unmarried Moorish men to occupy the southernmost bedroom, while females tend to sleep in northern bedrooms, which are usually also nearer the kitchen and the well. The other major architectural difference between Tamil and Moorish houses is that the latter houses must have some provision for female seclusion when male visitors are present. One of the simplest arrangements is to build an external free-standing wall outward from the side of the house toward the gate of the compound, behind which the women can go about their domestic tasks within earshot, but out of sight, of the male visitors who congregate in front of the doorstep. Inside the house, some sort of barrier, often a cloth curtain, will be available to block off the northern area of the house from male view. Sometimes the southern portion of the house, the area most often associated with formal dealings and male hospitality, will be made into an 'office' or reception room separated from the rest of the house by a curtain or by a masonry wall and doorway. Moorish women are expected to pull the end of their *saris* over their heads and across part of their faces (a veiling gesture called *mukkatu*) in the presence of strange men, a gesture which some women perform more fastidiously than others. In different ways, and to different degrees, the architecture of Moorish houses serves the same purpose.

Kinship, Affinity and Descent

Tamil and Moorish kinship categories reflect the same overall structure, and there are only a few lexical differences in actual kin terminology. East coast kinship conforms perfectly to the bilateral 'general structure' of Dravidian categories described by Yalman (1967) for the Kandyan Sinhalese and also fits the symmetrical paradigm of proto-Dravidian kinship categories reconstructed by Trautmann (1981: 229–37). The basic features include a terminologically coded preference for bilateral cross-cousin marriage (MB child and FZ child equally preferred), and the labelling of parallel cousins as classificatory siblings. Same sex cross-cousins exhibit an informal joking relationship which stands in striking contrast to the more formal, hierarchical behaviour toward other relatives, including an explicit avoidance relationship between son-in-law and mother-in-law. I found the incidence of marriage between biological first cross-cousins to be 17–20 per cent of sampled marriages among Moors and high caste Tamils (for data on marriage choice in other castes see McGilvray 1974). Of course, the logic of the kinship categories also defines a much larger field of classificatory cross-cousins who are eligible marriage partners, and even total strangers become reclassified as cross-cousins after they become one's spouse, or one's brother-in-law, or one's sister-in-law. The point to keep in mind here is that, unlike the Indo-Aryan marriage patterns of north India, the eastern Sri Lankan pattern of marriage conforms to the characteristically Sinhala/Dravidian preference for close marriage, frequently to a cross-cousin from either the maternal or paternal side.[5] However, the genealogical closeness of cross-cousins who marry does not imply that the bride and groom will have enjoyed an informal face-to-face relationship prior to their marriage. In early childhood this may have been true, but in late childhood and adolescence cross-cousins of the opposite sex are carefully segregated and chaperoned, so that their wedding may be the first occasion in many years for them to speak or even gaze directly at one another. Marriage between closely related cousins tends to have the effect of reducing dowry expectations (corroborated by Miller 1981: 156), while upwardly mobile families seeking alliances with strangers of high status must be prepared to offer substantially larger dowries.

Sets of dispersed exogamous matrilineal clans (called *kuti*, literally 'house, hut'),[6] linked by isogamous marriage alliance,[7] are found among both the Tamils and the Moors. Matriclan membership serves to assign a number of

[5] There is no consciously stated preference between MBD and FZD marriages, although a sample of marriages did turn up a slightly greater number of MBD marriages (McGilvray 1974).

[6] I have loosely identified the kuti as a 'matriclan' because the term is convenient and familiar, and because there seems to be no other anthropological label which would fit the ethnographic facts better. These named matrilineal descent units are dispersed throughout the region, rather than highly localised, so they might be called 'matri-sibs' (i.e., the organised memberships of these sibs in specific village clusters and urban neighbourhoods, the highest level of functional organisation and joint activity); they do have major corporate roles in the management of temple and mosque affairs, reinforced by a consistent rule of matri-uxorilocal residence, features which would seem to classify them in Murdock's scheme as 'matri-clans' (Murdock 1949: 47, 66–70). However, one crucial feature of the true Murdockian matriclan is lacking: the in-marrying matri-uxorilocal husband is *not* assimilated as a member of his wife's matrilineal descent group. According to Murdock, when the residential group is not coterminous with the descent group, the essential features of the matriclan as a 'compromise kin group' are not attained. However, until an important theoretical issue can be shown to hinge upon these taxonomic distinctions, I prefer to utilise the more generic term 'clan' and give it a distinctive Tamil/Moorish inflection.

[7] Fieldwork by Hiatt (1973) and McGilvray (1974) has found no empirical evidence of the pattern of hypergamous marriage between matriclans postulated by Yalman (1967: 325–31).

ritual privileges (*varicai*) related to kingly honours and status distinctions which are traditionally displayed at domestic life-crisis observances as well as temple and mosque festivals (Dirks 1987; McGilvray 1982a). Male matri-clan elders constitute the boards of trustees which manage the Hindu temples and Muslim mosques in the Batticaloa region, and in the precolonial polity—only vestiges of which remain today—succession to local Tamil chiefships was passed matrilineally within particular matriclans. Members of the most prestigious local matriclans often favour the perpetuation of existing marriage alliances with other prestigious matriclans, while members of smaller, more obscure, or lower ranked clans are less concerned about such matters. For everyone, however, the matriclan system is a significant con-straint upon marriage choice: kuti affiliation is one of the first questions a family will ask when a marriage is proposed, and I found violations of kuti exogamy to be extremely rare.[8]

It is interesting to note that neither the Tamil nor the Moorish wedding ceremonies show any trace of transubstantiation or ritual assimilation of the bride or the groom to their respective spouse's lineage or descent group. Furthermore, a bride remains susceptible to her parents' and siblings' death pollution after she is married. This reflects the independent non-Brahman/non-Sanskritic matrilineal tradition of the east coast region which has no concept that a bride could be assimilated (bodily, legally, or otherwise) into the husband's matrilineal bloodline, lineage, or *gotra*[9]. However, the more orthodox Brahmanical/Sanskritic/patrilineal pattern of bride transfer and 'the gift of a virgin' has been noted in Jaffna (David 1973) and is widely attested in Indian wedding rituals (Barnett 1970; 1976; Fruzzetti 1982; Fruzzetti and Ostor 1976; Inden and Nicholas 1977; Madan 1962). It is perfectly normal for a husband to hold office (e.g., as mosque trustee) in his own matriclan quite independently from the clan activities of his wife's

---

[8] The rule of kuti exogamy 'overlaps' and reinforces the Dravidian kinship rule against marrying a matrilateral parallel cousin (MZS or MZD). The Dravidian classification is actually more inclusive and exhaustive, since it also prohibits marriage with patrilateral cross-cousins, who might or might not belong to Ego's matriclan. Even so, informants indicated that matriclan membership would be the first thing marriage-minded families would investigate, before the cousin relationship. Although violations of kuti exogamy may occur, very few such cases were revealed to me. I noted only one case of a 'public' violation of the clan exogamy/Dravidian cousin rule—a Moorish schoolteacher who was determined to marry his very close classificatory sister (his MZD), also a teacher. Her family experienced classic pangs of incest horror, and her brother tried to block the marriage, but the couple went ahead and legally 'registered' their marriage. After the furor subsided, they quietly started living together, and at last report they had three or four children.

[9] The term gotra (*kottiram*) is used by members of one caste, the Viracaiva Kurukkals, as a synonym for matriclan (kuti). Gotras as mythically-chartered exogamous patrilineal descent units (Mandelbaum 1972: v. I, 145–48) are not found in eastern Sri Lanka, except presumably among a few immigrant Brahman temple priests.

family. Among the Moors, a man's formal membership in one of the several local mosque congregations is simply a matrilineal continuation of his mother's, or actually his mother's brother's, mosque affiliation—since women themselves do not attend mosque.

Marriage, Residence and Dowry

Everyone—Hindu and Muslim, high caste and low—follows the same basic pattern of marriage and residence: the daughters stay put, the sons marry out, and the parents and unmarried children periodically shift domicile. In preparation for marriage, Tamil families inaugurate their daughters into womanhood and 'eligibility' through a female puberty rite which commences with the onset of a girl's first menstrual period. Initially polluted and 'hot' because of the blood flowing from her body, the girl is gradually purified and dietarily 'cooled' during a period of seclusion. On the last day, in a highly publicised celebration conducted entirely by women, she is given a ritual bath, dressed in a red wedding sari and jewelry, and is honoured as a mock-bride as she ritually re-enters the natal house which will eventually become her matrilocal married home. Moorish families in Akkaraipattu have now discontinued what had been simpler, but basically analogous, puberty rituals for Moorish girls. (For more on female puberty rites see McGilvray 1982b).

From the standpoint of the parents, and also from the standpoint of sons and brothers, the fundamental kinship obligation is to arrange respectable and secure marriages for their daughters and sisters. Typically, the woman's side takes the initiative in marriage negotiations, while the man's side is content to entertain proposals from several quarters. While the social status, educational level, and personal qualities of the partners are important factors in any proposal of marriage, the ultimate issue to be decided is the size of the dowry (citanam) which the bride will bring to the marriage. Here in the matrilocal/matrilineal zone of Sri Lanka, virtually all the family wealth goes to the daughters as dowry, which thus functions as the main channel of premortem matrilineal inheritance (Goody and Tambiah 1973; Harrell and Dickey 1985). Sons inherit little or nothing from their parents; instead, they enjoy, cultivate, and eventually strive to augment their wives' dowry assets. The essential core of a woman's dowry is land and a house, while cash, jewelry, clothing, and utensils—the main constituents of dowry for women elsewhere in South Asia—are treated as enticing fringe benefits which may help to sweeten a marriage proposal. The absolute minimum dowry a woman must have is a house; without it, or without at least a firm pledge that it will be built, a marriage is usually impossible.

In the typical pattern, it is the mother's dowry house which becomes the eldest daughter's dowry house. Daughters are expected to marry in strict order of age, so the eldest daughters in each generation will tend to occupy the same ancestral house, while new houses must be built for each of the younger daughters. Nowadays, however, the first son-in-law may insist upon having a newer 'modern-style' house, so the more charming old ancestral home might be given to a younger daughter. One of my research assistants, a sought-after university graduate from an isolated Tamil village in the Batticaloa region, was able to demand a major decision making role from his future parents-in-law, including specification of the design and ritual inauguration of his fiancee's dowry house. Needless to say, this sort of thing becomes a major financial burden to a family with many daughters, although the scale and sumptuousness of these houses will vary significantly with the socio-economic status of the family.

In families with higher levels of social status to maintain (or achieve), the task of ensuring an adequate dowry for the daughters becomes a focal concern of both the parents and unmarried sons. In families devoted primarily to agriculture, sons will be expected to defer solicitations of marriage in order to work the family lands on behalf of their sisters, while in mercantile and professional families, sons will postpone marriage in order to divert their cash earnings into their sisters' dowry fund. Families with the necessary funds in hand, and looking for a hedge against inflation, may construct new dowry houses while their daughters are still young children and rent them to middle class bureaucrats, salesmen, or teachers. I have had the honour of being the first tenant in two such houses, the first of which had been built as a dowry for the daughter of my landlord, a Moorish shopkeeper, when she was only 3-years old.

There is no doubt that dowry is a focal concern in this society, especially among the young unmarried men who sit in the tea shops and saunter along the main road every evening. When I tried to ascertain who actually makes the crucial decisions about marriage and dowry, it became evident that kin of both sexes—husbands and wives, uncles and aunts—can have an equally significant impact upon the outcome of the negotiations. This was reflected in a widely divergent set of responses to my questions concerning who took the lead in marriage negotiations. The bride and groom also have veto power—at least technically—and senior men always do the 'official' talking at the final stages. Women frequently take the lead in planning and sending out the first informal 'feelers' which may evolve into formal negotiations, and in the course of the customary food exchanges they also carry covert messages and information between the two negotiating kin groups. Most people stress the collective 'team' aspect of marriage and dowry decision making, and it is obvious that women as well as men are deeply involved at several levels.

Because it is only through their wives' dowry that men gain access to the wealth of the previous generation, a man who fails to drive a hard bargain is considered a fool. I knew of one Tamil bridegroom who, to the absolute consternation of his mother's brother who was trying to negotiate a good dowry for him, ended up capitulating to the bride's family on every crucial issue. They first offered only a house and compound, and the groom's side responded with a demand for an additional Rs. 1,000 cash payment. This was refused, as also a modified request for Rs. 500. At that point the groom's MB advised him to look for another proposal, but the groom, evidently lusting for the bride (despite the fact that he did not know her name until two days before the wedding!), said he would settle for the original offer. Later it was learned that the bride's family had not deeded the house to their daughter as promised, claiming they could not afford the Rs. 30 stamp duty and the notary's fees. At this point, the groom's uncle stated flatly that he could not condone the marriage and that neither he nor any of the groom's kin would play any further role in the matter. Consequently, none of the customary boxes of sweets were exchanged between the families, and no one from the groom's family went to the wedding.

I attended, however, just out of curiosity, and what I saw was apparently the minimal Tamil wedding, short of elopement or clandestine nuptials.[10] The groom actually had to borrow some money from his wife's family to buy the wedding sari, and there was no *tali* (wedding necklace) at all, although the groom said he would buy one later. It even seemed that the groom, a carpenter, might end up having to build his own house on his wife's property. With the collapse of formal dowry negotiations between two kin groups, this marriage had become merely an eccentric private transaction between the groom and his wife's nuclear family. The groom's kinsmen remained on good personal terms with him, but they told me privately that they had never seen a marriage as crazy as his. I knew at least one other set of parents who were privately worried that their older sons, known for their impetuous behaviour, might similarly forfeit their best chance for wealth, status, and security by seeming too eager to marry and thus undermine their negotiating position for a good dowry. The opposite problem, excessive obstinacy or suspicion on both sides, also occurs sometimes. Despite the best efforts, negotiations can go sour, sometimes repeatedly, forcing both families to pick up the pieces each time and seek a new match.

[10] I am told that the absolute minimal acts which will make a man and woman, husband and wife are their privately feeding food to each other (*kalattil potukiratu*, putting [food] on the brass dish) or the man blockading himself inside the house with the woman (the expression is *vittukkul pukuntar*, 'he penetrated into the house'). One may note that eating food from a common plate in an inner room of the bride's house is an essential part of the standard Tamil and Moorish wedding rituals and is echoed in the direct commensal symbolism of poorer Kandyan Sinhalese marriages (Yalman 1967: 108).

Every marriage begins matrilocally, but it becomes an independent uxorilocal union over time.[11] The Moors do conduct a preliminary Islamic marriage rite (nikah) in the home of the groom, but both the Moors and the Tamils escort the groom in similarly noisy processional fashion to the home of the bride for what is the ritual core of the nuptial event, the tying of her wedding necklace (tali) and the eating of food from a common plate. Both the Tamil and the Moorish wedding rituals are marked by symbolic gestures which express the idea that the groom is being incorporated as a new high status member of his wife's household. For example, the bride's younger brother worshipfully washes the groom's feet (or, in more Westernised families, polishes his shoes) at the threshold of the bride's house, then leads him by the hand inside for the tali-tying ceremony. With the exception of a brief 'homecoming' visit by the couple to the groom's natal home approximately a week after the wedding, the bride and groom remain for a period of six months to two years as co-residents of the bride's parents' house. They are allotted one of the scarce private rooms, and in the early stages of the marriage they are treated as honoured guests: special foods are prepared for them, and the domestic workload is reduced to encourage sexual intimacy leading to an early pregnancy (McGilvray 1982b). This is a period during which the daughter is given her final training in cooking and the domestic arts, while the son-in-law demonstrates his skill in cultivating his wife's dowry lands or his reliability as a salaried employee.

When the bride and groom seem well-established and self-reliant, or when there is another nubile daughter who must be wed, the bride's parents, together with some or all of the bride's unmarried brothers and sisters, move out of the dowry house, leaving the married couple in charge of their own independent nuclear household. In effect, the married daughter 'stays put' while everyone else shifts into a newly constructed dwelling nearby which will become the dowry house for the next daughter in line for marriage. This process by which every matrilocal wedding house eventually becomes a uxorilocal dowry house is repeated until all the daughters are married and settled in their own dwellings. If the size of the original maternal compound permits, it will be subdivided and the new dowry houses for the younger daughters will be sequentially constructed adjacent to the original maternal house. If vacant lots are available and affordable, building sites may be acquired nearby to expand this clustering of sisters' houses around the maternal homestead; otherwise, cheaper land may have

---

[11] The residence pattern is matrilocal in the sense that the couple resides with the wife's parents. Given the cross-cousin marriage preference, however, it would also be quite possible to classify some of these marriages as avunculocal when the groom's father-in-law happens *also* to be his real or classificatory mother's brother. For a marvellous example of such multiple and overlapping residence classifications take a look at the Garo of Assam (Burling 1963: 93–97).

to be purchased for dowry house construction farther away from the mother's original dwelling. In fact, in areas with urban crowding and steep inflation in land prices, the ideal clustering of daughters' houses is becoming more and more difficult to attain.

Similar considerations govern the decision as to where the bride's parents will live after all their daughters have been married. In some instances, the father and mother may reside with the youngest daughter and her husband, but there is a strong underlying sentiment that elderly parents should really 'step aside' in a visible sort of way, perhaps retire to a small hut in a corner of one of their daughters' compounds, and allow the next generation to shoulder the burdens of life. This viewpoint seems to reflect an underlying concept of the ideal Tamil/Moorish life-cycle, one which assumes that the parents' active sexuality should cease when their daughters are ready for marriage and that houses are meant to accommodate only one procreating couple at a time.

In the ideal pattern of household growth and development, who then will take over the leadership role formerly played by the wife's father? Contrary to the more common South Asian pattern, it will not be his eldest son, for by this time he will have succumbed to the blandishments of an attractive marriage proposal, will have become a contributing member of his own wife's matri-uxorilocal household, and will have begun to focus his energies and earnings toward his own family of procreation as well as toward the welfare of his wife's remaining unmarried sisters. The mother's brother, so often a figure of power and authority in other matrilineal systems (e.g., Nayar and Trobriand), is here an ally and advisor to the family—and of course an interested party to all marriage decisions, since he is a potential father-in-law to his sisters' children—but he has no official role to play in the running of his sisters' households. As the father gradually discharges his obligations to his daughters, or simply as he becomes elderly and less effectual, the male leadership role falls increasingly upon the senior son-in-law, the eldest daughter's husband, who was carefully recruited for this eventual responsibility in the first place.

It is understood by everyone that the first son-in-law will increasingly play a major economic and leadership role in his wife's family, and it is in order to obtain the most qualified candidate for this position that the largest dowry will tend to go to the eldest daughter. In all dowry decisions, but especially so in this case, there is the straightforward notion that a family should seek to get the best son-in-law that a dowry can buy. Parents may also overspend on their first daughter's dowry on the unrealistic assumption that future earnings will restore the dowry assets of their younger daughters. Dowry serves multiple purposes, but it is certainly correct to identify one of

its dimensions as 'bridegroom price' (Caplan 1984; S.J. Tambiah 1973)
However, it is understood that the 'purchased' son-in-law will, in return,
reorient his kinship loyalties away from his natal kin and toward his new
wife and sisters. It is worth noting that the modern urban (Colombo and
Jaffna) practice of a new husband appropriating his wife's dowry assets and
transferring them into a dowry fund for his own unmarried sisters[12] is
strongly condemned among the east coast Tamils and Moors, who retain the
older South Asian sense of citanam (Sanskrit *stridhanam*, woman's property)
as property intended for a daughter's conjugal estate, and later, as property
for the daughter's daughters' conjugal estates (S.J. Tambiah 1973). Accordingly, land and houses are deeded solely to the daughter (or increasingly
nowadays to the daughter and son-in-law jointly), but never to the son-in-law
alone. Because dowry property is kept within the daughter's conjugal family,
and because dowry consumes most of the parents' assets long before their
death, the system functions as one of total premortem matrilineal inheritance,
thus depriving postmortem inheritance of much practical significance.[13]

Weddings, Spouses and In-laws

The initiative which the bride's family must seize in the conduct of a
marriage proposal, and the dowry which they must offer in order to obtain a
suitable son-in-law, reflect their strategic inferiority *vis-à-vis* the groom's
side. This is the same asymmetrical logic of social exchange which is
expressed in the shastric ideal of the 'gift of a virgin' (*kanyadan*, Fruzzetti
1982; Trautmann 1981: 288–315). Although no one I spoke with seemed
familiar with this particular Hindu scriptural term. In this region, the

[12] Jaffna-born residents of Akkaraipattu explained to me that dowry (*citanam*) in Jaffna is
frequently accompanied by an additional payment to the groom, referred to as *inam* (historically,
the Indo-Persian word for a royal land grant, but here meaning 'gift') or in English as
'donation.' The inam is a substantial cash payment from the bride's family which is intended
explicitly as a contribution toward the groom's sisters' dowry fund.
[13] The matrilineal inheritance law of the chiefly Mukkuvar caste (Brito 1876) governed all the
Hindu castes of the Batticaloa region until 1876 when it was deprived of legal force by the
Matrimonial Rights and Inheritance Ordinance and the prevailing Roman-Dutch law was
applied in its place (Nadaraja 1972; H.W. Tambiah 1954: 157). The Moors are legally governed
by the Shafi law of Islamic inheritance. Today neither the Tamils nor the Moors show much
concern for the technicalities of inheritance law, since very little inheritance actually takes place.
Instead, when there is residual property, it is usually assigned to a specific heir by a written deed
executed when death seems imminent. If there is a daughter still unmarried at the time of the
parent's death, she is very likely to be the designated heir. If the married children do receive
inheritance from a parent, there will be moral pressure for them to voluntarily hand over their
shares to their unmarried sister. Despite strong litigious tendencies in other domains of social
conflict, neither the Tamils nor the Moors seem to expend much time or money on legal
disputes over inheritance.

inferiority of the bride's side is real, but it does not have the enduring and strongly marked quality of north Indian affinal hierarchies (Parry 1979). It is a temporary imbalance, destined to fade as the son-in-law is incorporated into his wife's family, and in the long run it is structurally incompatible with the bilateral pattern of marriage choice. Sons and daughters marry between families in both directions, occasionally even in the same generation (i.e., in *marrukkaliyanam*, an 'exchange marriage' of two pairs of brothers and sisters), so the superiority of the 'groom's side' in one marriage will be cancelled by their inferiority as 'bride's people' in the next. What endures, and grows, is the status and authority of the husband within his own nuclear household, rather than permanent corporate inequality between families or matriclans. Marriage negotiations begin in a symbolic matrix of inequality, but they evolve toward strong expressions of isogamy, as shown even in the wedding rituals themselves.

After the first surreptitious 'feelers' from the bride's side have shown promise of success, formal delegations are sent to the groom's house bearing gifts of customary sweets (especially *palakaram*, oilcakes). As negotiations proceed, however, the groom's side must reciprocate with even larger quantities of sweets, in order to indicate their interest and good faith. The final marriage negotiations (*peccuvarttai*) are conducted by men representing both families, but not necessarily directly by the fathers of the bride and groom themselves. Often the bride's side will be anxious to cement a deal, even when the groom, for reasons of incomplete education, or lack of local employment, or fraternal obligations to his unmarried sisters, is not yet prepared to consummate the marriage and reside matrilocally. In such circumstances, the bride's side may pledge the brides's dowry in advance, in return for the groom's willingness to 'register' the marriage as a legal fact with the appropriate government registrar. Although the couple are technically man and wife, the actual wedding from a cultural point of view, the tying of the tali, may be postponed for up to a year or more, while the groom discharges his prior obligations. During this period, the bride and groom may be allowed to talk to each other, but no intimacy will be permitted. This reflects the strong value placed upon female chastity and honour in eastern Sri Lanka, as in most of South Asia.

On the day of the wedding itself, the bride's side will sometimes send her brother (actual or classificatory) bearing soap and toiletries to assist in bathing the groom, certainly an expression of solicitousness if not subordination. When the groom's procession reaches the bride's gate bearing the boxed *kurai* (wedding sari) and gold tali (necklace) for the bride, there will sometimes be a brief mock contest between the sides, with the groom's party feigning reluctance to relinquish either the groom or the *kuraipetti* (wedding sari box, nowadays often a suitcase). In some wealthier Moorish weddings, the groom's women may expect to receive a substantial cash gratuity (*kuraipetti marru kacu*, 'wedding sari box exchanging money') before they hand it over.[14] However, once past the watershed gesture of handing over the kuraipetti, the ceremonies proceed to express the equality of both sides and the cementing of an alliance between them. Among the Tamils this is most strikingly shown when the mother of the bride faces the mother of the groom at the bride's gateway in the *cantippu* ('meeting') ritual. First the mother of the bride honours and adorns her counterpart by applying perfume, sandalwood paste, and other cosmetics to her face and hair and concludes by holding up a mirror to her face. Then the ritual is reversed, the mother of the groom honouring the mother of the bride by applying cosmetics from her own tray. Sometimes this theme of reciprocity is carried over in an exchange of umbrellas, so that the groom, having marched from home under his own cloth-covered umbrella, is ushered into the wedding house under an umbrella supplied by his bride's family.

Once inside his bride's house, the groom is treated as an honoured guest. In Tamil weddings, the groom (often assisted by his married older sister) ties the tali around the bride's neck as they both stand on a cloth-wrapped wooden plank just outside the threshold of the bride's house. Then a young brother or sister of the bride will wash his feet, and conduct him to the bedroom where the final stages of the wedding ritual take place. Sometimes, as a further gesture of appreciation, a specially packaged meal (*mappillaiccoru*, 'bridegroom rice') will be carried by the bride's parents to the groom's parents' house a few days after the wedding. The newly-weds themselves are also expected to make a 'homecoming' visit for several days to the groom's natal home (*kal mari pokutal*, 'going to switch locations'), usually within a week or two of the wedding.

After this, the focus of attention is on the son-in-law himself, as he is gradually given more and more responsibility in his wife's house. Although before the marriage they may have enjoyed an informal joking relationship with him, after the marriage the wife's brothers must show him respect and deference. They should address him as *maccan* (male cross-cousin, formal), while the new brother-in-law may address his wife's brothers as *maccinan* (male cross-cousin, informal). Nowadays, in pursuit of a reciprocal and less hierarchical idiom, some of the more Westernised young men in Akkaraipattu have created a new kin term, '*bil*', which is the English acronym for 'brother-in-law'. Over time, as the sister's husband feels more and more at home with his wife's close family members, he may permit a greater degree of informality from his wife's brothers, but he is always entitled to deference even if he does not insist upon it.

[14] The amount of money reportedly handed over during the bridal sari exchange at one high status Moorish wedding in 1984 was Rs. 2,000.

What is the reason for this deference? It is not generated by any long-standing asymmetrical alliance relationship with the groom's family, nor does it appear to be the conscious enactment of scriptural ideals of kanyadan (with which, however, it coincides perfectly). Instead, informants assert it is a reflection of the fundamental responsibility which the son-in-law is expected to assume for the welfare of his wife, his wife's sisters, and ultimately his wife's parents. It also reflects the vulnerability of the wife's family to desertion by the son-in-law if he is unhappy with the state of affairs in his wife's house. The Tamils have a proverb about the unreliability of the groom until after he steps off the marriage plank,[15] but in fact, the groom could abandon the marriage at any time later on simply by walking out. Virginity in a bride is highly prized both by the Tamils and by the Moors; it is not easy for a woman to find a second husband, although both Islamic and local Hindu norms do allow it.[16] The bride and her family have a strong interest in making a marriage work, since it will be very difficult to attract a second husband the calibre of the first, at least with the same dowry. In a pinch, however, most of that original dowry would be available to use again, since the first husband could not have absconded with his wife's house or rice fields.

During the matrilocal period of adjustment following the wedding, the son-in-law enjoys extra deference from his wife's family, but he is also very politely on trial: if his conduct proves unacceptable, he can be asked to leave. Once the bride's parents have moved out, leaving the son-in-law as the head of his own nuclear household, it is more difficult to apply this kind of leverage against him. Still, he will always remain to some degree an 'outsider' residing in close proximity to his wife's parents and sisters, and this can greatly affect the tranquillity of his home. In the long-run, however, the major factor motivating a man to honour his marriage and to throw in his lot with his wife's people is that he usually has no real property of his own, his sisters having taken all the inheritance—and probably much of his own bachelor earnings—to build their dowries. Thus, there are strong incentives for stability on both sides of the marriage, and we will now see some examples of how they are manifested in household dynamics.

[15] *Palakaiyil nirkira kaliyanankuta, kalaincittu pokavillaiya?* 'Even if [the groom] is standing on the wedding plank, might he not scatter away?'

[16] Although polygyny is allowed under Muslim law, it is rare among Moors in the Batticaloa region. The matrilocal residence pattern virtually rules it out except in cases of sororal polygyny (e.g., two sisters married to one man in the same house). I found a few marriages of the latter sort among the Tamils as well as among the Moors. Leviratic and sororatic marriage is encouraged by both groups.

III
Activities Within the Household

The Daily Routine

An overview of the major sequences of the household day would begin with the preparation of tea or coffee by the adult women of the household well before dawn. Men told me that a good wife should adhere to the ideal enshrined in the Tamil aphorism: *pin tunki mun eluval* ('she will retire after and arise before [her husband]'). As the tea is being brewed and the men are rousing, the wife rakes and cleans up the sandy yard in front of the house, which may have seen visitors the night before. Although men arise from bed later than the women, no one snoozes much past dawn, since these are among the coolest and most beautiful hours of the tropical day. After a cup of tea in the pre-dawn light, the men usually retire to the latrine,[17] then go to the household well for a morning bath. If the adult men do not have to leave early for the fields or for other businesses, they will prefer to eat breakfast one or two hours later, at perhaps 8 or 9 o'clock in the morning, after what Americans might call a 'slow start'. During those seasons of the year when the men of the household are intensely engaged in rice cultivation, they will usually rise very early and depart for the fields before eating, trusting their wives or children to bring them breakfast later in the fields if the distance is not too great. Otherwise, they may grab a snack along the way and wait for the noon meal.

Men consider the morning the best time of day for hard labour in the fields, the afternoons being devoted, if possible, to eating, napping, and socialising. Men from poorer labouring families, however, spend the entire day in the fields, returning only in the late afternoon. In the poorest families the women, too, may work in the fields as members of all-female weeding brigades or as gleaners at the time of the threshing. However, such women are pitied for being forced to leave their homes—and to jeopardise their honour—to work in the fields, which are a domain of predominantly male activity. If possible, after the younger children have been set off to school, the wives and older unmarried daughters of a household will devote most of the morning to the preparation of the noon meal. If groceries or other household supplies are needed, they will be purchased by the men or children of the household, not by the women. The public food market,

---

[17] It is usual nowadays for a house in the densely populated coastal settlements to have a private latrine in a corner of the compound with its own septic tank and water-seal floor fixture. Members of poorer households sometimes designate a specific corner of the yard or go to nearby open fields or to the beach to defecate.

located next to the central bus stand, is considered a very disreputable place for a woman, and in fact the only women one finds there are some impoverished old women selling small quantities of their own manually husked rice. Tamil women are somewhat more liberal with regard to appearances in public places than Moorish women, and so several Tamil women, or a woman with her husband or brother, might occasionally go on a joint shopping expedition for household goods and textiles to the main street shops. Moorish women generally rely upon the men and children of the household to do all the necessary public errands, including bringing home samples of fabrics from the textile shops for the women to examine before buying.

The mid-day meal of rice and coconut milk-based curry marks the culmination of the entire mornings' labour for everyone in the household: for the women who cooked it, as well as for the men and school-going children who—if at all possible—return home to eat it. It is strongly felt that boiled whole rice should be the major component of this meal, as opposed to foods made with rice flour or other grains which are believed to be less nutritious although more easily digested. Afterward, everyone sleeps or rests while the hottest hours of the day slowly pass. Women, however, also use this period of male slumber to take their turn bathing at the well and to have leisurely conversations among themselves.

Around 4 o'clock, the heat begins to abate and torpid bodies begin to stir. This marks the beginning of the visitation and socialisation hours, generally called *pin neram* (the afterward time). Older people enjoy visits at home from their female neighbours, friends, and relations, while younger men in particular change into their best clothes and throng onto the main road to stroll, gossip, and sip tea for most of the remaining daylight hours. Women are absent from this public scene, and the main streets during the pin neram hours are exclusively a male domain. Hospitality at home may continue after nightfall, which at this latitude in the tropics falls very abruptly around 6 pm, but guests are expected to depart by 8 or 9 pm. A late supper, consisting of food left over from the noon meal, is then eaten, and most people go immediately to bed, having bolted the gates, doors and shutters against thieves, ghosts, and nocturnal 'coolness'.

Gender Roles and Domains of Activity

One of my first impressions of daily life in Akkaraipattu was that men and women seemed to live in separate worlds. In this respect, the local rules about gender segregation are quite typical of most parts of South Asia, but perhaps the layout of densely packed houses and walled compounds accentuates the impression of a strong separation between a female domain, the home, and a male domain, the public streets and fields. Within the residential compound and the house, there is also a tendency for the female activities, centred upon food preparation, to revolve around the northern and eastern areas, adjacent to the kitchen and well, while the male activities, especially visitation and conviviality, are located in southern and western rooms or in the yard in front of the doorstep leading from the gate of the compound. This pattern of male/female spatial segregation is more strictly enforced in Moorish homes, where additional walls, doors and curtains serve to block the glances (but not the overheard remarks) of visiting men.

Individual women will leave their residential compounds for neighbourly visits and quick trips to some of the small corner boutiques selling basic commodities such as matches, packaged biscuits, or betel leaves, but for a Tamil woman to visit the central market or the larger textile shops on the main road it would be necessary to assemble a larger female party or obtain a male escort. Respectable Moorish women would not go even on those terms. Life-crisis ceremonies, such as female puberty rites, male circumcision celebrations, weddings and the like, as well as Hindu temple festivals and Muslim saints' commemorations, offer the best opportunities most Tamil and Moorish women have to venture outside their neighbourhood or settlement, and naturally they seek to take full advantage of them. What has been said here must be understood to apply most strictly to women between puberty and menopause: younger girls and post-menopausal women enjoy much greater freedom and mobility, because the culture implicitly defines them as pre- and post-sexual beings, respectively. Men, on the other hand, go everywhere, except into other households unannounced or uninvited: there are various discreet attention-seeking gestures which men perform at the gate in order to indicate their presence without being so rude as to actually call out the name of someone inside.

It would be an exaggeration—but perhaps a useful one to begin with—to say that husbands and wives cross paths primarily at mealtimes and in bed, and even then the interaction may seem, to a Western observer, somewhat reserved. Both Tamils and Moors accept the notion that public display of affection between men and women is embarrassing and improper, and the system of arranged marriage certainly reflects a non-romantic approach toward the typical domestic union. Actually, most marriages in eastern Sri Lanka seem stable and successful, with husbands and wives becoming increasingly friendly and inter-reliant over time. Each spouse tends to occupy quite separate activity spheres, but the matri-uxorilocal household has areas and tasks which will accommodate each of them. And as a couple grow older, their degree of informal conversation and collaboration in household activities seems to increase.

Symbols of Status and Honour

Among the Tamils, the status of any household is tied up with its caste rank, which is indexed in turn by the residential neighbourhood, or headman's division, in which it is located. A reference to an address in, for example, Division 8, will give local listeners reason to presume that the household in question is that of a family belonging to the Cantar Climber caste, since Cantars are concentrated in that Division. Cantars are today widely employed in non-traditional occupations, such as the building trades, while other castes, such as the Vannar Washermen, continue to practise their hereditary laundry trade at home in full view of passers-by. Since the highest ranking castes are farmers and landlords whose work takes place in distant rice fields, the absence of any visible occupational activity in the home or compound can sometimes be taken as a further sign of high caste status. It is also a traditional privilege of the high ranking castes to give patronage to, and to receive the services of, the three local domestic servant castes: Vannar Washermen, Navitar Barbers, and Paraiyar Drummers. The collective term for these hereditary service castes is *kutimai* ('household establishment') or *kuti makkal*, ('children of the house'), and the right to command their services on ritual occasions such as weddings and funerals is still a highly prized prerogative of the highest castes, a right which is still regulated in Akkaraipattu by the Urppotiyar, the district chieftain of the Mukkuvars.

The Moorish community, on the other hand, is relatively unstratified in terms of hereditary sub-groups. A few Moorish Maulana households, known to trace descent from the Prophet Mohammed, enjoy enhanced prestige and respect, while a very small number of hereditary Osta (*ustad*) Circumciser/ Barbers suffer the stigma of markedly lower status. A third Moorish group, the Bawas (Sufi mystics), are regarded as religiously unorthodox, hence a bit marginal to the mainstream of Moorish life, although they are intermarried with ordinary Moorish families. The lower Tamil castes have also enjoyed long-standing relationships with Moorish households, although these have suffered in recent years because of Hindu/Muslim communal friction. Paraiyar Drummers are no longer employed as criers and musicians for mosque festivals, but Tamil Washermen still wash the laundry for many Moorish households.

Wealth and occupation are also fundamental components of household status, but they probably serve an even more predominant role among the Moors, who lack the intervening caste hierarchy of the Tamils. One highly visible measure of wealth is the scale and quality of the dwelling itself, with items such as terracotta tile roofs or an electrical connection highly prized as status symbols. The well-publicised dowry transactions which accompany all marriages in this region serve as primary occasions for the display of wealth, education and occupational status.

One further dimension of household rank and prestige throughout the Batticaloa region of eastern Sri Lanka is a historical residue of the precolonial political system, a cluster of regional sub-chiefdoms (conventionally conceptualised as seven in number) controlled by the Mukkuvars. It is difficult to know many details about the precolonial political history of the *Mukkuvar vannimai*, or 'chiefship of the Mukkuvars', except through those ritual institutions and practices which survive in attenuated form today. Some of my elderly informants could recall a time in their youth when, in some parts of the Batticaloa region, Moorish representatives still played a regular role in Tamil temple festivals and in the system of political honorifics enforced by the Mukkuvar chiefs; but everywhere today the Moors have severed these connections. The Hindu Tamils, particularly those in the more traditional settlements, still celebrate temple rituals which reflect and validate their vision of the Mukkuvar vannimai, rituals which dramatise the marks of honour (varicai) and participatory 'shares' (*panku*) of communal worship allotted to different castes and matriclans under the old Mukkuvar hegemony (McGilvray 1982a).

At the household level, these concepts of political honour survive in rights to domestic ritual service from the kutimai castes and in privileged displays of specified types of ceremonial lamps, specified numbers of cloths (saris, actually) draped besides doorways, and specified configurations of decorated brass pots (*vittu muti*, 'house-crowns') placed on the roof at life-crisis rituals. This is a ritual idiom in rapid decay, however, because the local caste-based Tamil political offices formerly controlled by the Mukkuvars and Vellalars can no longer marshall the sanctions necessary to enforce this system of unequal privileges. Still, many high caste Tamil families with a desire to display their hereditary marks of honour still do so, and it is not difficult to imagine with what pride and how punctiliously these matters would have been attended to only a generation or two ago. The term varicai refers to any of the various symbolic prerogatives and sumptuary privileges which, it is said, were bestowed by ancient political authority to recognise and elevate specific hereditary groups such as castes and matriclans. Regional texts and chronicles mention many such marks of honour which are nowadays extinct, but pots on the roof and cloths hung by the doorway are still in active use—each of the higher castes (or within them, each matriclan) claiming the exclusive right to display a particular number of pots and cloths. In so doing, the household is expressing its group affiliation, e.g., its matrilineal descent group membership, rather than any unique status of the household as an independent unit. It is also celebrating its 'share', or its participatory rights, in a system of rank based on a kingly or martial ideal: this is echoed in some of the matriclan names, which refer to positions of military leadership or skill (e.g., *Pataiyantakuti* 'leader of the army clan',

Racampillaikuti 'royal prince clan'). If asked upon what basis their matri-lineally inherited honours were established, Tamils will usually cite the legitimate authority of the Mukkuvar polity and a system of matrilineal law or commandment which the Mukkuvars are believed to have enforced upon the inhabitants of the Batticaloa region after their arrival sometime in the 13th century AD.

Worship, Sorcery, and Souls of the Dead

Among the Tamils, the most conspicuous religious activity occurs at nume-rous local and regional Hindu temples and at island-wide pilgrimage centres such as Kataragama (Pfaffenberger 1979), and preparations for these annual festivals are a major preoccupation of Tamil households at certain times of the year. For most Moorish families, however, the Hadj, or pilgrimage to Mecca, is too expensive to contemplate, and there are fewer opportunities for religious outings closer to home. The annual Muslim festival at the so-called 'seaside mosque' (*katarkarai palli*) near Kalmunai is a major event which Moorish women still traditionally attend, in addition to annual *kanturi* feasts held at local mosques and shrines to commemorate the death of local Muslim saints entombed there.

In addition to such public forms of religiosity, however, both Tamils and Moors conduct a number of ritual and devotional activities within the household itself, not to mention rites of passage such as birth, tonsure, puberty, and marriage (McGilvray 1982b). I will briefly discuss here three categories of ritual activity oriented toward the protection of the household: domestic forms of worship, measures against sorcery, and observances to appease souls of the dead.

Tamil Domestic Worship: Once every year, most Tamil households con-duct a domestic *puja* for a tutelary Hindu goddess who protects the house and its occupants from illness and misfortune. This ceremony of worship and propitiation is termed colloquially '*Ammalukka ceyra*,' or 'doing it for Ammal,' an honorific form of the Tamil word for 'mother', and is a generic epithet for all local Hindu goddesses. Mariyamman, the Tamil goddess of smallpox, is probably the most popularly worshipped in this regard, although some families in Akkaraipattu (including my own Tamil landlord) wor-shipped Katanacciyamman instead. These local goddesses (and others) are popularly believed to cause 'heat', drought, and eruptive skin diseases unless propitiated. Katanacciyamman is a sea-goddess (*katal*, sea; *nacci*, lady), so some households perform her annual puja on the beach. The more common pattern, however, is to perform a mid-day domestic puja on the floor of the 'inner room' for the goddess, followed by a night-time puja outside in the compound for the male guardian deity Vairavan, a fierce manifestation of Shiva who protects the perimeter of the residential compound from thieves and intrusive spirits.

I never saw a professional Hindu priest conduct these domestic rituals; the senior male in the household, or a religiously-minded neighbourhood man, usually assumes the role of officiant (*pucari*). The goddess is commonly invoked into a consecrated brass pot of water (*kumbam*) which may occasionally be accompanied by a portable metal face-image (*tirumukam*) and displayed with additional regalia (all of which are stored away in the 'inner room' during the year). She is then offered special piles of fruit and flowers (*matai*) and sometimes also heaps of warm sweetened milk-rice. There is a great deal of minor variation in the rituals, depending on the individual traditions of each family, but there is unanimous agreement that once a household has made an offering to a protective deity such as Mariyamman, a divine contract has been established. Every year thereafter, the goddess will expect a similar offering, and several of my Tamil friends told me tales about the dire consequences which ensued when households in their neighbourhood had been lax in the performance of their annual rituals 'for Ammal'. A household may also institute special vows and restrictions: for the past three generations my Tamil landlord's family has prohibited chickens and eggs from the residential compound for fear of angering the household goddess Katanacciyamman.

Moorish Domestic Worship: The religious life in Moorish households conforms to the orthodox demands of Islam, including daily prayers, annual Ramzan fasting, and (when possible) pilgrimage to Mecca. The amplified voice of the muezzin calling the faithful to prayer can be heard even in the Hindu neighbourhoods of Akkaraipattu. For men, attendance at the mosque, especially for the Friday *jumma* prayers, is strongly urged and can be only discretely evaded. The mosques are all-male preserves; thus, although men have the option of praying individually and privately at home, women have no choice but to do so. The Moorish household becomes a focus of collective devotional activity principally on the occasion of religious holidays, when local Koranic experts are invited to sing a *maulud*, a chanting of the texts and stories associated with some scriptural event, e.g., the birth of the Prophet Mohammed. On such an occasion, neighbours and friends will be invited, and refreshments will be served afterward. Men of religion are also summoned to a Moorish home to recite prayers marking various rites of passage, such as infant tonsure on the 40th day after birth. The walls of Moorish dwellings are often hung with calendars depicting scenes of the black-shrouded Kaaba in Mecca, as well as with framed copper *accarams*, protective Muslim talismans inscribed with sacred words and numbers, which, like the Hindu accarams inscribed by the Tamils, serve to ward off malevolent spirits (pey, picacu, and djin).

In some Moorish households there is an echo of the domestic Hindu goddess cult in a sporadic ritual practice called *Taymarukku ceyra*, ('doing it for the *Taymar*'), another form of propitiating supernatural 'mothers' (*tay*, mother). Sometimes the ceremonies take place at the seashore and sometimes at home, and their aim is often to counteract skin eruptions and fever symptoms caused by the 'heat' of an angry female supernatural. Because they are conducted more or less surreptitiously by groups of Moorish women, I was never invited to witness a Taymar ritual. They are reportedly performed in response to individual illnesses and household misfortunes, rather than on a regular annual basis.

Measures Against Household Sorcery: There are of course rationalists and sceptics in the community, but most Moors and Tamils share an even greater commonality of beliefs about the immediate supernatural environment, a world of nocturnal ghosts and greedy spirits which can cause illness and misfortune for anyone in their path. Aside from adventitious encounters with pesky spirits, the threat of intentional sorcery (*cunivam*) is a concern to many people. For personal prophylaxis against both stray spirits and sorcery, Tamils and Moors sometimes wear protective inscribed accarams in cylindrical silver lockets tied around their neck, arm, or waist. However, it is an entire house and compound which is frequently the target of sorcery, a deliberate magical attack performed by a *mantiravati* (sorcerer, 'reciter of mantras') on behalf of an enemy or jealous party. In the face of inexplicable household misfortune, a typical suspicion would be that an evil copper accaram, together with a secretly obtained scrap of the victim's clothing or exuviae (hair, nail clippings, etc.) had been buried under the outer gate of the compound or in the ground in front of the doorway to the house. The technology of sorcery is believed to consist in the power to 'tie' or 'bind' (*kattu*) malevolent spirits through the magical formulae (*mantirams*) instilled in, and inscribed upon, the buried talisman and thereby force them to harm the victims as they repeatedly pass over the buried charm. The prescribed remedy is for a friendly mantiravati to 'cut' (*vettu*) the spells which bind the evil spirit to its task, and to use intermediary spirit possession to enable this spirit to point out the physical location of the buried charm, which is then unearthed and nullified.[18]

[18] The sorcery remediation rituals which I witnessed were highly theatrical night-time events involving one or more friendly mantiravatis who entered a trance in order to communicate with and/or embody the opposing spirit. The culminating event was usually for the mantiravati to dig—while still in trance—for the hidden charm, which he eventually plucked from the bottom of a darkened (and sometimes water-filled) hole for everyone's inspection.

Assuaging Souls of the Dead: In their obligations to departed souls, both the
Moors and the Tamils accept similar supernatural assumptions and are
bound by similar ceremonial rules. The spirit or soul (*avi*) is believed to
hover around its former household until the period of mourning and death
pollution is over: the 31st day for Tamils and the 40th day for Moors. On the
final day of this mourning period, food is cooked and offered to guests, to
ritual experts, and to needy persons in the community. Among the Tamils
this observance is called *amutu* (or less commonly, *cirattam*, Sanskrit
shraddha), and it includes a number of food offerings which are explicitly
directed at appeasing the soul and sending it off to the supernatural domain
where its accrued karmic merit will be balanced and its eventual reincarna-
tion determined. Among the Moors the corresponding observance is called
kattam; although no special offerings are made by Moors explicitly to the
dead soul, Muslim prayers are recited and a communal meal in the name of
the deceased is offered to everyone in attendance. On subsequent anni-
versaries of the death, Hindu and Muslim households enact ritually similar
observances (justified in different theological terms) which transfer religious
merit to the deceased soul, until more recent deaths gradually displace
earlier ones in the memory of the living. Premature neglect of a death
anniversary, however, can cause an angry soul to cause household misfortune
and suffering until the 'deficiency' (kurai) is rectified. Apart from these
death commemoration events, neither the Tamils nor the Moors maintain
any organised cults of household, lineage, or clan ancestors.

Pollution and Propinquity

One of the features commonly associated with patrilineal descent organisation in India is the shastric concept of *sapinda* (Manu V, 59 in Buhler 1969),
or the community of shared exogamy and shared death pollution. Even the
Nayar *taravad* is reported to follow a matrilineal version of this rule (Gough
1959, 1961: 323–24), which obviously serves as an important marker reinforcing the corporate identity of the unilineal descent unit. In eastern Sri
Lanka, where matriclans do not maintain a corporate control of lands or real
property and where awareness of sub-lineage segmentation is not particularly
well-developed, there is a corresponding lack of strong consensus concerning
the spread of death pollution (*tutakku*) within any strictly defined 'unit' of
kinship. I found that local theories to explain the path of death pollution
were surprisingly varied and contradictory, but matrilineally-slanted interpretations tended to outnumber patrilineally-slanted theories 2: 1, despite a
fairly large residual cluster of bilateral and idiosyncratic viewpoints
(McGilvray 1982a: 56–57). What emerges from all this, however, is not a
principle of death pollution which reflects strict matrilineal descent reckoning.

In addition to a matrilineal descent component, many local people in Akkaraipattu discussed death pollution as if it were something concommitant with the field of social relations which is centred on the matri-uxorilocal household cluster. Rather than using concepts such as sapinda (a Sanskrit word no one recognised) or emphasising a strict line of unilineal descent, they mentioned natural ties of love (*anpu, pacam*) between people who reside close by and with whom one has frequent social interactions. In most people's minds, this amounts to a functional description of the matri-uxorilocal kindred centred on a cluster of ancestral houses, an aspect of Tamil/Moorish matrilineal organisation which strongly resonates with revisionist views of the Nayar taravad as a 'house-and-land unit' rather than as an African-style unilineal descent group based upon ancestral blood (Moore 1985). There is widespread agreement that a man's wife, his parents, his brothers and sisters, and his children will be polluted by his death. Beyond these immediate relations, there is a tendency to trace death pollution matrilineally *both* from the dead man's sisters *and* from his daughters. Physical propinquity and social interaction are contributing factors in many minds, as is shown by the fact that a dead man's matri-uxorilocal son-in-law is also polluted, but not his daughter-in-law, who resides elsewhere.

Honour, Law and Matriliny

Enough has been said about the relative weakness of matrilineal lineage and sub-lineage segmentation, about the lack of economic resources at the disposal of matriclans, and about the diffuseness of matrilineal death pollution concepts to pose questions about 'what' matriliny is and 'where' it resides in this society. At the same time, it must be noted that matrilineal reasoning extends even to the domain of Hindu caste affiliation, where the children of cross-caste marriages (sometimes fully sanctioned alliances between the two major Tamil landowning castes, Mukkuvar and Vellalar, see McGilvray 1982a: 84–86) are assigned to the caste and matriclan of their mother. The question of matrilineal ideology is further complicated by the discovery that there is no underlying concept of unique matrilineal blood, bodily substance, or reincarnated soul which is perpetuated by membership in the matriclan, such as, for example, Malinowski reported among the Trobriand Islanders (1922: 70–71; 1954: 215–37). Nor is there a recognised matriclan ancestress or even an organised cult of a tutelary deity for the matriclan as a whole.

Corporate matrilineal interests do exist, but they are largely vested in traditional rights to display politico-religious marks of honour at household rituals, or to sponsor 'shares' of communal religious ritual at mosques and temples, or to hold certain leadership roles in the local caste system, in the

mosque, or in the temple. Matrilineal consciousness in this region of Sri
Lanka is imbued with titles and symbols of hereditary rank and privilege
bestowed by kings and conquerors of the past, displays of hierarchical group
privilege which at one time were associated, no doubt, with real political
power but which are nowadays perpetuated mainly in ritual performance.
These marks of honour which are transmitted matrilineally to succeeding
generations are conceptualised not as outer indices of some inner matrilineal
bodily substance shared by members of the clan, but rather as legal rights
inherited according to the matrilineal law or enactment (*cattam, erpatu*) of
the Mukkuvar chiefs who acquired hegemony over the east coast in the 13th
century. The local term which expresses the matrilineal idea is *tay vali*
('mother-way'), which is cognate with Malayalam *tavali*, recorded by Gough
(1961: 334; also Mencher 1962) as the word for a segment within the larger
Nayar taravad. Here, however, the expression is employed as if it were a
principle of law historically associated with the Batticaloa region. All of this
evidence seems to point to stronger affinities with south Indian concepts of
royal honour and royal gift which have recently been discussed by Dirks
(1987) as well as to more obvious parallels with the Malayo-Indonesian
concept of *adat* as customary—in some places even matrilineal—village law
(de Josselin de Jong 1960; Kato 1982; Swift 1965), than it does to connections with Hindu ethnosociological concepts of shared substance or
biomoral codes for conduct (Daniel 1984; Marriott 1976).

IV
Case Studies of Household Dynamics

The Ideal Pattern—More or Less: Nilam and his Sisters

One of the very first persons I met when I began my fieldwork in Akkaraipattu in 1969 was Nilam, an unmarried Moorish teacher of English in the
local Muslim high school who miraculously managed to find me a dry vacant
house to rent in the aftermath of a monsoon flood. We have been close
friends ever since, enabling me to trace each of his sisters' marriages and
finally his own marriage and subsequent employment as a temporary English
teacher in the Sultanate of Oman. Nilam's family, although not really
wealthy, is highly respected in the community and thus has a good deal of
social status to protect through strategic marriage transactions. His father, a
retired civil servant, is the official Muslim Qazi or magistrate for matters of
Islamic marriage, divorce, and inheritance. As the eldest son of a family in
the town of Kalmunaikudy, 20 miles to the north, he had married the eldest
daughter of an influential Akkaraipattu public works contractor, and

eventually, after retirement from a migratory civil service career in various parts of the island, settled back into his wife's natal house. By then he had a very large family of nine children, and what was worse from the standpoint of dowry, all but two of his children were daughters.

Just as his wife's parents had chosen him for his cleverness, his reliability, and his civil service pension, so he and his wife carefully recruited their own first son-in-law, Hussain, who was working as a statistician for the Central Bank in Colombo. Hussain also happened to be related to his bride, Fareena, as her FZ's stepson (a classificatory cross-cousin), thus adding the further ingredient of kinship solidarity to a union which had many other socio-economic virtues. He and Fareena were given a deed to the ancestral house in Akkaraipattu, along with some prime paddy land south of the town and some cash (I do now know the amount), but since Hussain's work and residence were in Colombo, they eventually agreed to swap the ancestral house for title to a vacant lot across the street. This meant that the ancestral house could be offered, along with 2.5 acres of paddy land and Rs. 5,000 cash, as a dowry for the second daughter, Zohora, when she married Jauffer, a local schoolteacher. By strict order of birth, Nilam would have been the third child to marry, but when I met him in 1969 he still had five unmarried sisters, a father on a meagre civil service pension, and a brother far too young to help earn money for the dowry fund. But by this time Hussain, Nilam's elder brother-in-law in Colombo, had begun to prove his worth: he agreed to take in one of his wife's younger unmarried sisters, Nilofa, on the understanding that he would eventually ensure that she found a respectable marriage. With this burden lifted, Nilam still had the major responsibility of building the dowry funds for three of his younger sisters. His very youngest sister (still unmarried) would have to be the eventual responsibility of his younger brother, he told me.

When I first knew Nilam in 1969–71, he occupied the southern bedroom in the ancestral house. His second 'bil', Jauffer the schoolteacher, lived matrilocally with Nilam's second eldest sister, Zohora, in the 'inner room' of the house, while Nilam's parents and unmarried siblings slept in the front rooms or in various other areas of the house. When I returned to Akkaraipattu for additional fieldwork four years later in 1975, I found that Nilam's parents had moved into a brand new dowry house they had just constructed on a segment of the original compound immediately next door to Jauffer and Zohora, who were now running their own uxorilocal nuclear household in the ancestral house, except for Nilam's continued occupation of the southern bedroom. The 'inner room' of the new house sheltered Nilam's younger sister Saleema and her new husband Farook, the northern room housed the other unmarried sisters, the southern bedroom was for Fairoz, Nilam's eldest sister's son, and the front reception area was where Nilam's

father, mother, and younger brother slept. On my next visit to Sri Lanka in
1978 I found that Nilam's parents had shifted domicile once again. They
were now living in a rented house across the lane with their recently married
daughter Zahira and her new husband Gafoor, who had agreed to the
marriage after receiving a firm pledge that a new house would eventually be
constructed for him on a lot already purchased (from his brother-in-law
Jauffer, in fact) for that purpose.

As the money gradually accumulated (from paddy harvests, pensions, and
Nilam's salary as an English teacher) to complete Gafoor's house, Nilam's
parents began to make plans for their last two daughters' dowries as well as
for their own eventual retirement. With vacant building lots near the old
ancestral house nowadays both high-priced and rare, they decided to purchase several spacious parcels of land in a former coconut plantation (*tottam*)
on the northernmost edge of town, perhaps a mile away. With three
daughters married and established in a group of houses clustered around the
old maternal homestead, Nilam and his parents shifted their attention to a
new enclave which would be constructed on the *tottam* property. In 1979
Nilam's parents granted him permission to marry a Colombo Muslim schoolteacher, Shukri, whom he had first met at the Teacher Training College in
Jaffna in 1971 and to whom he had considered himself informally betrothed
for at least five years. It is considered unusual for an east coast man to marry
a west coast woman, because west coast women do not typically bring with
them the substantial real-property dowries which east coast men are
accustomed to receiving in lieu of inheritance. However, this marriage was a
'love match' which had surmounted serious obstacles from both families:
Nilam had to obtain dowries and husbands for several of his unmarried
sisters, while Shukri had to wait until her older unmarried sister found (with
Nilam's eager assistance) a man to her liking. Even so, Nilam's marriage to
Shukri disappointed his mother's brother, who had hoped to arrange a
cross-cousin marriage for his own daughter, who was 20 years younger than
Nilam.

When both Nilam and Shukri were able to obtain employment as school-
teachers in the Sultanate of Oman in 1981, any lingering doubts about the
wisdom of their marriage were dispelled. When I inquired whether his
parents now looked to him for the funds required to secure husbands for his
remaining two unmarried sisters, Nilam wrote back jokingly: 'Yes, I am
expected to send an oil well from here [Oman]!' In the conventional east
coast household pattern, a man's premarital financial obligations to his own
sisters would normally be replaced by post-marital obligations to his wife
and her sisters. However, because his wife is a Colombo-born 'outsider'
whose sisters are already married, and because his affluence as a school-

teacher in Oman is obvious to everyone, Nilam has been expected to continue assisting his unmarried sisters with their dowries. Around the same time, Nilam's eldest brother-in-law, Hussain, obtained employment in Iraq, so there were now two sources of overseas funding. As it turned out, Nilam and Shukri had to provide the largest share of the dowry for sister number five, Nilofa, who, it had been originally understood, would be the sole responsibility of senior brother-in-law Hussain. Hussain did, however, contribute significantly toward the wedding costs of sister number six, Fareena. The dowry houses for all three of Nilam's youngest sisters will be in the new 'tottam' enclave, thus effectively fissioning the sisters into two spatially distinct matrilocal clusters. Here, too, Nilam's parents plan to live out their days, possibly with the youngest daughter when she is finally married, or perhaps in a modest house of their own located in a corner of their daughters' property. The solution planned for Nilam and Shukri when they eventually return from Oman will be to maintain two houses, one of which they have already purchased in Akkaraipattu and one to be built on a lot they have acquired in Colombo. During the period while brother-in-law Hussain was in Iraq separated from his family, Nilam's eldest sister and her children were living in Nilam's Akkaraipattu house. Since 1984, this house served as the temporary sororolocal residence of sister number five (Nilofa) and her new husband, and of sister number seven (Nihara) and her husband, while their respective dowry houses were being erected with Nilam's financial assistance on the 'tottam' property.

While Nilam and his sisters offer an example of how the ideal matri-uxorilocal residence pattern is put into practice, it is also obvious that special circumstances and infusion of Persian Gulf earnings have played an important role. Without the foreign money which Nilam and Shukri have invested in the family, it is obvious that the younger sisters could never have been as well-dowered. Even then, Nilofa and Fareena were both over 25 years of age when they married, a reflection of the rising age of marriage throughout Sri Lanka. But even in the absence of money from the Gulf, this family would have sought to make the best possible matrilocal marriages for their daughters, and I think the outcome, although considerably delayed and certainly much less affluent, would have been more or less the same.

Pragmatism and Parental Power: Ratnam's Daughters

The large family of Ratnam, a retired Tamil postman with whom my family and I lived in 1975 and 1978, afforded an opportunity to record some pragmatic variations in the marriage and residence pattern. Ratnam has nine children, the three eldest of whom are daughters whose marriages occurred close to the time of my fieldwork. Although Ratnam and his wife are of high caste and matriclan rank,[19] they must get by financially on Ratnam's modest government pension, because the rainfed irrigation tank which formerly watered their paddy land is no longer maintained, and squatters now cultivate the tank ! ottom. Their major asset is a large, well-situated residential compound in Division 7, containing Mrs. Ratnam's maternal dowry house and one new dowry house which Ratnam had built in anticipation of future need. His eldest son is now beginning to earn money as an apothecary's assistance, and there are four other younger sons who will eventually be able to ensure the marriage of the youngest daughter. A bit earlier, however, when his sons were not yet old enough to contribute to the dowry fund, Ratnam had faced a major problem in securing husbands for his three older daughters. The marriage of each daughter was unorthodox in some way, showing how the ideal system must sometimes be forced to adapt to the real world.

Contrary to the cultural norm which stipulates that elder daughters should marry before younger, it was Mahesvari, Ratnam's third daughter, who married first. Normally, elder daughters will object to such violation of seniority, in part because it threatens to deplete the dowry assets available for their own marriages and in part because any irregularity in the order of marriages will appear suspicious in the eyes of potential affines. However, in this case, Ratnam was given an offer he could not refuse, a 'love match' proposal which would cost him relatively little, which would be correct according to the Dravidian kinship categories, and which would also conform, more or less, to the matri-uxorilocal ideal. His daughter's suitor, Sajipati, was the only child of one of Ratnam's classificatory sisters, a respected widow in the neighbourhood, so he was both a classificatory cross-cousin to Mahesvari and he already had a house (his mother's) in which to live. Ratnam ended up giving Mahesvari a cash dowry of Rs. 2,000, two water buffaloes, an empty residential lot, and three acres of land. Because Sajipati offered to marry Ratnam's daughter without the need for a dowry house, and because the virilocal couple would be living only five minutes' walk from the bride's maternal home, the arrangement appealed to Ratnam and his wife and was unopposed by the other daughters. While we lived with Ratnam, Mahesvari came to visit her parents regularly, bringing along her infant daughter and occasionally her husband as well.

[19] Among the Tamils of Akkaraipattu, a pattern of cross-caste marriage alliance exists between two high-ranking matriclans, one of which is identified with the Vellalar caste and one of which is identified with the Mukkuvar caste, and children are assigned the caste affiliation of their mother. In this instance, Ratnam is a Vellalar (*Maluvaracan kuti*) and his wife is a Mukkuvar (*Panikkana kuti*). A political myth sanctions this cross-caste marriage alliance (McGilvray 1982a: 84–86).

All along, Ratnam's greatest concern had been to find a husband for his eldest daughter, Rajalakshmi, who had the highest level of education (secondary school certificate) and also the highest expectations for her future groom. Over the years, Ratnam had investigated several potential sons-in-law, but each had been flawed in some respect (too old, too un-educated, or not employed in a sufficiently prestigious occupation). A new dowry house had been constructed next to the ancestral home, but with no marriage on the horizon, Ratnam first rented it to a visiting postmaster and then to me. While the whole family was striving to find a groom for Rajalakshmi, a quite unforeseen series of events unfolded which resulted in the early marriage of Mani, the second daughter.

One day, it seems, a distant male cross-cousin of Mani's (her FMZDS), Seenitamby, arrived at the Ratnam house, indicating that he had quarrelled with his mother and that he needed a place to eat and sleep. Assuming this to be a temporary visit, Ratnam dutifully welcomed Seenitamby as befitted his classificatory sister's son and found him a place to sleep. However, when several months passed and Seenitamby showed no sign of moving out, the neighbours began to whisper about this unmarried cross-cousin living in the same house with Ratnam's two unwed daughters—and Ratnam saw that something had to be done. Ratnam broached the possibility of a marriage to Rajalakshmi, but she was nor receptive, given Seenitamby's age (40 years) and lack of education. So Ratnam and his second daughter apparently realised that, given Rajalakshmi's legitimate prior claim on dowry resources, the alternative for Mani was likely to be an extended spinsterhood. Later it was learned that Seenitamby had intended all along to force a marriage with one of Ratnam's daughters. In terms of dowry, Seenitamby indicated that he would happily settle for a verbal promise of the old house and three acres of useless parched land. This would leave the new house for Rajalakshmi when she eventually found a husband, which she did about a year later.

Everyone knew that Seenitamby was a bit eccentric, but for the first nine months of his marriage to Mani everything went well. Then he began to behave autocratically and jealously, even demanding that Mani not visit her sister in the house next door without his permission. Ratnam eventually compiled a list of grievances against his matrilocal son-in-law which in-cluded stinginess, poor financial judgement, lack of trust, neglect of Mani's gynaecological problems, refusal to eat Mani's cooking (and thus disrupting her diet, since wives eat after husbands), irrational hostility to his wife's sister's husband, and highly suspicious behaviour which suggested to some people an interest in sorcery. At this point in the saga I, my wife, and my 18 month-old son entered the Mani/Seenitamby household to reside for three months in 1978. We were given the inauspicious, but vacant, southern bedroom. I quickly learned that Ratnam was watching his son-in-law very carefully. He had originally intended to write a deed transferring to Mani and Seenitamby the ancestral house and the three acres of useless land, but now he was glad he had not done so, since it seemed possible that Seenitamby might even try to sell off the property and then abscond with—or perhaps abandon—his wife.

The final straw was Seenitamby's behaviour on the night that Mani's elder sister's baby died. The death was abrupt and totally unexpected, probably a case of sudden infant death syndrome, coming just after Rajalakshmi had brought her firstborn home from the hospital. It was not until the next morning that I learned that Seenitamby had forbidden Mani to go next door to console her bereaved sister whose baby had just died.

Ratnam and his wife told me that something had to be done, but they waited for Seenitamby's next transgression before acting. Several weeks later, when Seenitamby prevented Mani from visiting her younger sister Mahesvari, whose little girl was sick, Ratnam angrily confronted his son-in-law. With several witnesses present, including Seenitamby's elder brother, Ratnam publicly told him to leave the compound, stating that there was a point when one must stand up for one's daughters. Seenitamby threatened to take Mani away with him, but Ratnam said that he would allow it only if she were willing (which she was not). With no legal rights to any of the Ratnam family property, and with few allies even in his own maternal kin group, Seenitamby tried to maintain a foothold by leaving behind some belongings, but he was finally forced to vacate the house completely after a few days.

The price of this debacle for Mani was that she might well never find another husband, so she continued to wear the gold wedding tali around her neck indicating that this was an indefinite separation, but not a divorce. A month passed, and Seenitamby's family began to send female emissaries to test the climate for a reconciliation. Meanwhile, my wife and I took Mani to see a gynaecologist in Batticaloa, and the good news was that Mani might be pregnant. Finally, following two months of discreet domestic diplomacy with Seenitamby's kinsmen, Ratnam felt there was evidence of a change in Seenitamby's attitude and behaviour. I had been away for two weeks conducting fieldwork in another part of the district, so when I returned to the Ratnam compound I was surprised to learn that Ratnam had cast me in the role of the divorce court judge. Mani, her visibly chastened spouse Seenitamby, and an audience of invited witnesses were eventually summoned into my presence as I sat on a sack of paddy. In my most dignified and inflated Tamil, I asked first the husband and then the wife whether each was prepared for a reconciliation, and the answer was yes. My fieldwork ended a few days later, so I was unable to observe how the marriage went thereafter. However, a letter from Ratnam eight months later relayed the good news that Mani had given birth to a healthy child and that Mani and Seenitamby were doing well.

Upstaged by her younger sisters, Rajalakshmi was the last of the three older daughters to marry. But her patience was rewarded when Ratnam finally located an unrelated but suitably high status groom for her. He was Sivagnanaselvam, the branch manager of a government cooperative store ('coupon *katai*'), who had already broken off marriage negotiations with four other families, mainly because they could not supply a satisfactory dowry house. A nice 'modern-style' house—not an old-fashioned ancestral dwelling—was apparently the most important of Sivagnanaselvam's dowry requirements, and fortunately that was the one thing that Ratnam could offer. When Ratnam heard that this highly desirable groom might be receptive to a proposal of marriage to Rajalakshmi, he acted fast. Knowing that the groom had already backed out of four marriages, Ratnam hired a car to take the wedding party directly to the district *kachcheri* in Amparai in order to avoid a two week delay in clinching the deal at the local marriage registrar's office. The actual wedding took place seven months later.

The groom (who was often referred to by his occupational title, 'Manager') had been raised by his mother's sister's husband, a Hindu priest. This meant that he was the only strict vegetarian in Ratnam's compound, definitely a burden for Mrs. Ratnam who therefore had to do twice as much cooking during the matrilocal adjustment period. Apparently he wanted to assert superior ritual status in his wife's household, as shown by his decision to sleep and eat alone in the inner shrine room alongside images of the Hindu gods whenever his wife was in a state of pollution. Whatever his foibles, however, Sivagnanaselvam was the dignified high status son-in-law whom Ratnam clearly needed as his eventual successor in the matricentric household cluster; as far as I was able to discern while I lived next door, Rajalakshmi's new husband received deference, or at least polite avoidance, from everyone in the compound. Soon after his eldest daughter's marriage, Ratnam began to discuss with me his plans to build a small thatched hut in a shady corner of the compound where he and his wife would 'retire' when they vacated their youngest daughter's dowry house.

The Enclave Solution: Ismail Stores

I have already remarked that real estate prices and a general shortage of vacant building lots in the older neighbourhoods of Akkaraipattu have forced many families, particularly those with numerous daughters, to acquire sites for constructing dowry houses in cheaper neighbourhoods on the outskirts of the town. However, with comfortable financial resources it is still possible to acquire a prime location on which to build a dowry house for one's daughter, and if money is no object it is possible to establish a complete matrilocal enclave. I am aware of two Moorish brothers, owners of a large dry goods establishment ('Ismail Stores') and a local-style cigarette factory ('Ismail Beedi'), who have done this. In keeping with local parlance which freely assigns such metonymic nicknames, I will refer to these two brothers jointly as 'Ismail Stores'.

After their marriage, the two brothers found themselves residing in immediately adjacent houses which had been provided as dowry for their wives, who were themselves sisters. In view of the fact that the brothers were partners in a, major enterprise, their marriage to two sisters probably served to reinforce their shared interests and may have lessened the likelihood of conflict between their wives. Such an arrangement has no particular advantages from a dowry point of view.[20] In any event, as their daughters began to attain womanhood, Ismail Stores gradually acquired ownership of the entire 'block' of residential land on which their houses sat, an extremely valuable parcel bounded on all four sides by lanes. In preparation for each daughter's marriage a new dowry house was erected, until the vacant lots were filled up, at which point a high masonry wall was constructed encircling the entire block (Figure 3). For a while, this cluster of new houses provided high quality rental accommodation for a number of professional workers temporarily posted to Akkaraipattu, but now that the daughters are beginning to marry, the houses are fulfilling their original purpose. There will not be much vacant space to build houses for the granddaughters in this dense matrilocal enclave, but at least the present generation can enjoy what most people would consider an expensive but perfect solution to the matrilocal housing problem.

A Husband Gradually Acquires Authority and Autonomy

A matrilocal son-in-law enters his wife's house as an honoured guest, but he is also under scrutiny. As his reliability and deportment gradually validate the dowry investment which his in-laws have made in him, as the members of his household demonstrate their domestic self-sufficiency, and especially as his wife begins to bear children, the son-in-law takes on greater authority and autonomy within his own nuclear family. Because of their propinquity and often shared social or economic interests, the wife's parents and siblings always retain some leverage over his actions, but the balance of domestic power shifts more toward the husband/son-in-law. I noted this in several specific instances when sons-in-law had ultimately quarrelled with their

[20] When a brother/sister pair are married to another brother/sister pair, the marriage is termed an exchange marriage (*marrukaliyanam*). It is recognised that this type of union can be advantageous from an economic point of view, because both families will have an interest in agreeing on a lower over-all level of dowry expenditure.

Figure 3: Walled Dowry-house Enclave Constructed by the Two 'Ismail Stores' Brothers, Ismail and Meera Mohideen

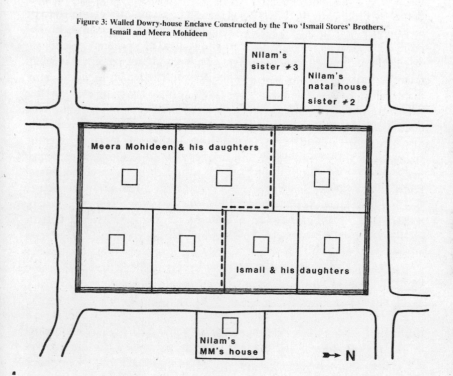

wives' parents and had subsequently exercised their right to order changes in the living arrangements.

But a Household also Needs Matrilateral 'Support'

Among both the Tamils and the Moors, the matri-uxorilocal residence pattern implies close physical propinquity between a wife, her sisters, her mother, and her mother's sisters. This is not regarded as merely an incidental by-product of the residence and dowry system, it is considered to be an essential ingredient for a successful marriage and a happy household. The point was made quite convincingly when I learned of a Moorish doctor who was having a difficult time finding a suitable groom for his sister. It seems that the doctor's parents had initially been married matrilocally in Sammanturai, but later (for unspecified reasons) their father insisted that his wife and children return with him to his home town of Sainthamaruthu. The doctor and his sister were therefore raised in the absence of the close matrilateral kin (mother's sisters and their children) who would normally reside in a cluster of neighbouring houses. Both the parents are now deceased, and the Moorish doctor, who is himself married, faces the responsibility of finding a good match for his younger sister. Although in other respects she is an extremely eligible bride (wealthy brother, excellent dowry), her prospects have been dimmed by the fact that she lacks a matrilateral female kin group which would normally give her assistance and advice as a new bride. One promising young man with whom her brother broached a marriage proposal is reported to have declined the offer because he feared that he and his wife would not enjoy the 'support' (*his* English word) normally furnished to newly married couples. This makes sense when one remembers that a new son-in-law will normally expect some special treatment from his wife's family and that the wife's final 'on-the-job training' as a cook and housekeeper is normally given by her mother and married sisters *after* the wedding. Probably even more important in the long run is the valuable assistance which a woman normally receives from her mother, her maternal aunts, and her married sisters at childbirth and during the period of early infant care.

V
Concluding Remarks: Female Autonomy
in South Asian Households

If one had to epitomise rural South Asian domestic and marital relations in only a few words, one would doubtless emphasise patrilineal descent ideology, joint patrilocal residence, and exclusive (or at least disproportional) inheritance of real property by husbands and sons rather than by wives and daughters. There are also numerous patriarchal and androcentric aspects of the textual South Asian religious and intellectual Great Traditions (Hindu, Islamic, and Buddhist) which tend to subordinate women in both domestic and ritual contexts. However, we must not overlook the important ethnic and regional exceptions and variations on these Indic themes, including matrilineal descent patterns in parts of Kerala and Assam, bilateral kinship institutions among the Kandyan Sinhalese, not to mention the hybrid Sri Lankan Tamil/Moorish system I have described in this chapter. Such examples invite us to consider, by way of comparison, some of the most significant factors which restrict or enhance female domestic autonomy in South Asian households. Despite the obvious difficulties of assessment, I would contend that both externally-generated holocultural comparisons as well as internal ethnographically-grounded analyses point to a relatively higher level of domestic autonomy for Tamil and Moorish women on the east coast of Sri Lanka than in many other parts of South Asia. Let me summarise the external cross-cultural evidence first.

Based upon a sample of 66 matrilineal societies drawn from Murdock's *Ethnographic Atlas* (1967), Alice Schlegel (1972) has advanced the hypothesis that, in matrilineal societies where either a woman's husband or her brothers hold positions of strong unilateral authority in the household, such women enjoy *less* personal autonomy than they do in matrilineal societies where husbands and brothers jointly *share* authority over women. Schlegel argues that as male domestic authority divides, it also declines absolutely, giving women greater personal latitude and domestic influence. In view of the autonomy which is eventually accorded to a son-in-law as the head of his own nuclear household, I would have to classify the Sri Lankan Tamil/Moorish system as one of 'weak husband dominance' using Schlegel's own coding categories (1972: 145–47). However, it should be noted that very few of the features associated with this authority pattern are found in the Batticaloa region, while several characteristics strongly correlated with Schlegel's 'neither dominant' household type—in which domestic authority is divided between husbands and wives' brothers—are in fact prevalent here, including matrilocal residence, wives' sharing in the control of household property, absence of sororal polygyny (1972: 22, 64–68, 71, 86–87). Overall, Schlegel's study suggests a strong functional association between matriliny, matrilocal residence, women's participation in property control, weak or neither dominant male authority patterns, and relatively high female autonomy. Most of these ingredients are found in some form in the Tamil/Moorish household system of eastern Sri Lanka.

On a more detailed ethnographic level, the Tamil/Moorish household system invites comparison with female authority patterns in other parts of

Sri Lanka and South Asia generally. Admittedly, from the perspective of Western industrialised society, Tamil and Moorish women would not appear particularly independent or autonomous. Yet within the comparative universe of South Asian kinship and household patterns, let us note that the Tamil/Moorish wife is free from the burdens of: ·

- A domineering mother-in-law (e.g., Hobson 1978)
- An authoritarian elder brother such as the old-style Nayar *karanavan* (e.g., Fuller 1976: 58ff.).
- Patrilocal isolation from her mother, maternal aunts, and sisters (e.g., Lewis 1958).
- Sanskritic ritual severance from her descent group and transubstantiation to her husband's lineage as his metaphysical 'half-body' (e.g., Inden and Nicholas 1977: 39ff.).
- Widespread wife-beating and Brahmanical *pativrata* rules of wifely asceticism and subordination (e.g., Obeyesekere 1963; 1984: 430ff.).
- Exclusion from, or unequal rights to, inheritance and control of real property (Hindu *Mitakshara*, Muslim *Shari'at*).

In contrast to most regions of South Asia, these traits, together with other general features of the Tamil/Moorish matri-uxorilocal household pattern, suggest some of the reasons for a *relatively* greater level of female domestic autonomy and influence, not to mention lower female infant mortality (Miller 1981) and protection from homicidal 'bride-burnings' (Bordewich 1986), than in patrilineal/patrilocal regions of the subcontinent. This type of comparison can be useful, particularly if it helps to correct stereotypic text-based assumptions about South Asian marriage and household values, such as Obeyesekere's improbable theory that Hindu goddess cults in eastern Sri Lanka are generated by a severe 'Sanskritic' ideology of patriliny, wifely subordination, and female repression (McGilvray 1988; Obeyesekere 1984). The data I have presented here show rather conclusively that an awareness of textually-prescribed Great Tradition ideological factors must be combined with local ethnographic studies of actual kinship practices, domestic norms, property relations, and residence patterns in order to gain a truer understanding of South Asian households and their relationship to the larger society.

● ● ●

References

Banks, Michael Yaldwyn. 1957. The Social Organization of the Jaffna Tamils of North Ceylon, with Special Reference to Kinship, Marriage, and Inheritance. Unpublished Ph.D. Thesis, Cambridge University.

Barnett, Steven A. 1970. The Structural Position of a South Indian Caste: Kontaikkatti Velalars in Tamilnadu. Unpublished Ph.D. Thesis, University of Chicago.

———. 1976. Cocoanuts and Gold: Relational Identity in a South Indian Caste. *Contributions to Indian Sociology* 10: 133–56.

Beck, Brenda E.F. 1976. The Symbolic Merger of Body, Space, and Cosmos in Hindu Tamil Nadu. *Contributions to Indian Sociology* 10 (2): 213–43.

Bordewich, Fergus M. 1986. Dowry Murders. *The Atlantic* 258 (1): 21–27.

Brito, Christopher. 1876. *The Mukkuva Law, or the Rules of Succession among the Mukkuvars of Ceylon.* Colombo: H.D. Gabriel.

Buhler, G. (ed.). 1969. *The Laws of Manu.* New York: Dover Publications, Inc.

Burling, Robbins. 1963. *Rengsanggri: Family and Kinship in a Garo Village.* Philadelphia: University of Pennsylvania Press.

Caplan, Lionel. 1984. Bridegroom Price in Urban India: Caste, Class, and 'Dowry Evil' among Christians in Madras. *Man* 19 (2): 216–33.

Daniel, E. Valentine. 1984. *Fluid Signs: Being a Person the Tamil Way.* Berkeley and London: University of California Press.

David, Kenneth. 1973. Until Marriage Do Us Part: A Cultural Account of Jaffna Tamil Categories for Kinsmen. *Man* 8 (4): 521–35.

de Josselin de Jong, P.E. 1960. Islam versus Adat in Negri Sembilan (Malaya). *Bijdragen Tot de Taal-, Land- en Volkenkunde* 116 (1): 158–203.

Dirks, Nicholas B.. 1987. *The Hollow Crown: The Ethnohistory of an Indian Kingdom.* Cambridge: Cambridge University Press.

Farmer, B.H. 1957. *Pioneer Peasant Colonization in Ceylon: A Study in Asian Agrarian Problems.* London: Oxford University Press.

Fruzzetti, Lina M. 1982. *The Gift of a Virgin: Women, Marriage, and Ritual in a Bengali Society.* New Brunswick: Rutgers University Press.

Fruzzetti, Lina M. and Akos Ostor. 1976. Seed and Earth: A Cultural Analysis of Kinship in a Bengali Town. *Contributions to Indian Sociology* 10: 97–132.

Fuller, C.J. 1976. *The Nayars Today.* Cambridge: Cambridge University Press.

Goody, Jack and S.J. Tambiah (eds.). 1973. *Bridewealth and Dowry* (Cambridge Papers in Social Anthropology 7). Cambridge: Cambridge University Press.

Gough, Kathleen. 1959. Cults of the Dead among the Nayars. *In* Milton Singer (ed.), *Traditional India: Structure and Change*, pp. 240–72. Biographical and Special Series X. Philadelphia: American Folklore Society.

———. 1961. Nayar: Central Kerala; Nayar: North Kerala; Tiyyar: North Kerala; Mappilla: North Kerala. *In* David M. Schneider and Kathleen Gough (eds.), *Matrilineal Kinship*, pp. 298–442. Berkeley: University of California Press.

Harrell, Stevan and Sara A. Dickey. 1985. Dowry Systems in Complex Societies. *Ethnology* 24 (2): 105–20.

Hiatt, Lester R. 1973. The Pattini Cult of Ceylon: A Tamil Perspective. *Social Compass* 10: 231–49.

Hobson, Sarah. 1978. *Family Web: A Story of India.* London: John Murray.

Inden, Ronald B. and Ralph Nicholas. 1977. *Kinship in Bengali Culture.* Chicago: University of Chicago Press.

Kato, Tsuyoshi. 1982. *Matriliny and Migration: Evolving Minangkabau Traditions in Indonesia.* Ithaca and London: Cornell University Press.

Leach, Edmund R. 1961. *Pul Eliya, A Village in Ceylon: A Study of Land Tenure and Kinship.* Cambridge: Cambridge University Press.

Lewis, Oscar. 1958. *Village Life in Northern India.* New York: Vintage.

Madan, T.N. 1962. Is the Brahmanic Gotra a Grouping of Kin? *Southwestern Journal of Anthropology* 18: 59–77.

Malinowski, Bronislaw. 1922. *Argonauts of the Western Pacific.* London: George Routledge and Sons.

———. 1954. Baloma: The Spirits of the Dead in the Trobriand Islands. In *Magic, Science, and Religion and Other Essays.* Garden City: Doubleday Anchor.

Mandelbaum, David G. 1972. *Society in India.* 2 vols. Berkeley and London: University of California Press.

Marriott, McKim. 1976. Hindu Transactions: Diversity without Dualism. *In* Bruce Kapferer (ed.), *Transactions and Meaning: Directions in the Anthropology of Exchange and Symbolic Behavior,* pp. 109–42. ASA Essays in Social Anthropology 1. Philadelphia: ISHI.

McGilvray, Dennis B. 1974. Tamils and Moors: Caste and Matriclan Structure in Eastern Sri Lanka. Unpublished Ph.D. Thesis. University of Chicago.

———. 1981. The Matrilineal Viracaiva Priests of Eastern Sri Lanka. *In* M. Arunachalam (ed.), *Proceedings of the Fifth International Conference-Seminar of Tamil Studies: Madurai, Tamilnadu, India, January 1981.* Vol. II, Section 11: 73–84. Madras: International Association of Tamil Research.

———. 1982a. Mukkuvar Vannimai: Tamil Caste and Matriclan Ideology in Batticaloa, Sri Lanka. *In* Dennis B. McGilvray (ed.), *Caste Ideology and Interaction* (Cambridge Papers in Social Anthropology 9), pp. 34–97. Cambridge: Cambridge University Press.

———. 1982b. Sexual Power and Fertility in Sri Lanka: Batticaloa Tamils and Moors. *In* Carol P. MacCormack (ed.), *Ethnography of Fertility and Birth,* pp. 25–75. London: Academic Press.

———. 1982c. Dutch Burghers and Portuguese Mechanics: Eurasian Ethnicity in Sri Lanka. *Comparative Studies in Society and History* 24 (1): 235–63.

———. 1983. Paraiyar Drummers of Sri Lanka: Consensus and Constraint in an Untouchable Caste. *American Ethnologist* 10(1): 97–115.

———. 1988. Sex, Repression, and Sanskritization in Sri Lanka? *Ethos* 16(2): 1–29.

Mencher, Joan P. 1962. Changing Familial Roles among South Malabar Nayars. *Southwestern Journal of Anthropology* 18: 230–45.

Miller, Barbara D. 1981. *The Endangered Sex: Neglect of Female Children in Rural North India.* Ithaca and London: Cornell University Press.

Moore, Melinda A. 1985. A New Look at the Nayar Taravad. *Man* 20 (3): 523–41.

Murdock, George Peter. 1949. *Social Structure.* New York: Free Press.

———. 1967. *Ethnographic Atlas.* Pittsburgh: University of Pittsburgh Press.

Nadaraja, Tambyah. 1972. *The Legal System of Ceylon in its Historical Setting.* Leiden: E.J. Brill.

Obeyesekere, Gananath. 1963. Pregnancy Cravings (Dola-Duka) in Relation to Social Structure and Personality in a Sinhalese Village. *American Anthropologist* 65(2): 323–42.

———. 1984. *The Cult of the Goddess Pattini.* Chicago: University of Chicago Press.

Parry, Jonathan P. 1979. *Caste and Kinship in Kangra.* London and Boston: Routledge and Kegan Paul.

Pfaffenberger, Bryan. 1979. The Kataragama Pilgrimage: Hindu-Buddhist Interaction and its Significance in Sri Lanka's Polyethnic Social System. *Journal of Asian Studies* 38: 253–70.

Ryan, Bryce. 1950. Socio-cultural Regions of Ceylon. *Rural Sociology* 15: 3–19.

Schlegel, Alice. 1972. *Male Dominance and Female Autonomy: Domestic Authority in Matrilineal Societies.* Human Relations Area Files Press.

Swift, M.G. 1965. *Malay Peasant Society in Jelebu* (L.S.E. Monographs on Social Anthropology 29). London: Athlone Press.

Tambiah, H.W. 1954. *The Laws and Customs of the Tamils of Ceylon.* Colombo: Tamil Cultural Society of Ceylon.

Tambiah, S.J. 1958. The Structure of Kinship and its Relationship to Land Possession and Residence in Pata Dumbara, Central Ceylon. *Journal of the Royal Anthropological Institute* 88 (Part 1): 21–44.

———. 1973. Dowry and Bridewealth and the Property Rights of Women in South Asia. *In* Jack Goody and S.J. Tambiah (eds.), *Bridewealth and Dowry*, pp. 59–169 (Cambridge Papers in Social Anthropology 7). Cambridge: Cambridge University Press.

Trautmann, Thomas R. 1981. *Dravidian Kinship.* Cambridge: Cambridge University Press.

Yalman, Nur. 1967. *Under the Bo Tree: Studies in Caste, Kinship, and Marriage in the Interior of Ceylon.* Berkeley: University of California Press.

7

Households and Social Identity: Domestic Group, Domestic Space and Ritual Contexts Amongst Indians in Malaysia

David J. Mearns

Introduction

IN ONE sense the overall argument of this paper might well be summarised as a reconsideration of a large and hoary old theoretical problem. That is the extent to which 'culture' remains relatively autonomous with respect to the economic and political processes in which it is embedded. The particular concern here is to examine the relationship between meanings located within a cultural complex, the formation of ideologies and ethnic identities, and the processes of reproduction of a 'social formation'. The population considered comprises those people labelled 'Indian' for Identity Card purposes in Melaka, Peninsular Malaysia. I concentrate on the nearly 70 per cent of such people who claim Hinduism as their religion and who originate in southern India.

In the course of considering how social identity is created, it becomes necessary to take into account two further aspects in the analysis of Malaysian social life. These are taken up only briefly in the discussion. They are those processes which define 'class fractions' in Malaysia and those factors which inhibit the emergence of class consciousness. These are important in so far as they are linked to the major issue which is an examination of those processes which inhibit the emergence of a logically possible alternative consciousness, one which is continually debated in Malaysia, that of membership of a single, strong ethnic group. For those encompassed by the label 'Indian', such an emergent identity might be thought potentially to provide the required basis for rendering politically cohesive an otherwise disparate set of people. Alternatively, such an identity might appear to some writers (e.g., Abner Cohen?) as a natural outcome of the representation of shared interests in an arena of competition for scarce resources. However, it will be argued that for particular cultural and social reasons neither perspective is adequate to explain what has been and is taking place in Melaka. It will be shown, for example, that the social *category*, Indian, does not even relate unproblematically to an actual interest group in this context. Nor is it likely to become such an unequivocal interest group given the local understandings as these operate in and through the household or domestic group.

The position taken here assumes that Indians in Melaka as social actors, individual or group, are involved in urban processes which are not susceptible to their *direct* and conscious manipulation at the level of basic structure. The reasons for this have been elaborated elsewhere (Mearns 1982). In this paper, it will be argued that the processes which reproduce cultural forms, i.e., systems of belief and practice, and which take place largely in the domestic setting, are nonetheless central to understanding the reproduction of the social formation at large. The cultural forms which have the capacity to affect the wider social structure within which Indians find themselves, albeit to a limited degree, are such things as caste and religion, as well as gender and ethnicity. Ethnicity itself is a complex phenomenon which, like the other three sets of relations, is, of course, only partly constituted by culture and in the domestic context. It is precisely how and in what sense the constitution of ethnic identity is or is not achieved as one of the major aspects of overall social identity, which is the concern of this argument. It is an integral part of the approach here that Indian conceptions of the environment, including the superhuman environment, be incorporated into the analysis. However, the first concern is with conditions of a more mundane sort which are more amenable to direct observation.

The Domestic Group

For the purposes of this argument, the notion of domestic group refers to that set of people, normally resident in one dwelling, who pool at least part of their income, divide their labour, and share food on a regular basis, in such a way as to constitute a recognisable unit to both the analyst and the local population.[1] The most common terms used locally, by Tamil and Malay speakers, best translate as 'my house'. Most frequently, ties of descent (or filiation) along with affinity provide the ideological basis of the group. However, the prime definitional characteristic is the cooking and sharing of

[1] This is not to ignore the strictures of such writers as Wong (1984) by assuming an economically or socially bounded unit somehow isolated from other such units. Remittances, for example, are an important component of income in many Indian homes.

food. Such a group may contain or, more rarely, be made up entirely of unrelated (i.e., non-kin, non-affinally linked) members but such cases are unusual.

I am concerned to show the relation between the structure of domestic organisation and the investment of imposed social categories with meaning. Categories such as 'Indian' are given or not given flesh and bones by the actions and conceptions of the people so categorised. In particular, I shall maintain that the understandings actors have of domestic space is crucial to the analysis of the social significance of such categories. These understandings may be conscious or unconscious, comprising 'discursive' or 'practical' knowledge, in Giddens' (1979) terms. Nevertheless, as socially produced 'cultural forms', their shared patterns provide the basis for the identification of unity and division within a category.

Creating Domestic Space

The aim of this section is to consider how the patterns of ownership and distribution of capital in Malaysia are subsumed in, and interpenetrate notions of, the nature of domestic space contained in Indian culture. Indeed, it will be argued that the Indian domestic group and its encompassing social space are ordered according to structural principles which are such that they ultimately produce significant contradictions in relation to the structuring properties of the wider social context. These become apparent in the actions of individuals and groups located in social processes at concrete historical junctures.[2]

The location of housing and the general use of space in the town of Melaka is only now beginning to break out of the patterns established in the colonial period. Indian housing is, of course, part of this trend and present patterns of distribution of Indians consequently mark some important changes, especially in the case of upwardly mobile middle class Indians. However, inasmuch as there still exist foci of Indian populations, a clear class- and ethnically-based ideology, made manifest in colonial practices, was found to account for many of the important defining characteristics of Indian patterns of residential location. Incorporated into these ideological positions was a version of the colonialists' knowledge of the Indian caste system employed as a subtle form of social control mediated, on the colonial capitalists' behalf, by other Indians.[3] The point is that cultural and ethnic

---

[2] One such appears in the transition to manufacturing capitalism where employment opportunities for young women occur at a time when those for young Indian men are diminishing. This has seriously undermined existing patterns of domestic organisation amongst working class Indians.

[3] See Mearns (1982: Chapter 2) for a fuller discussion of this.

anderstandings are necessarily entailed in the essentially class-based differentiations manifested in the built form of Melaka, now as in the past. These differentiations in turn had their dominant rationale in the expansion and reproduction of capital.

For the purposes of the preliminary stages of this analysis, I shall operate with the sub-categories which members of the population comprising the 'Indian' census category themselves most commonly employ in self-reference. It is precisely the reproduction of such sub-categories as meaningful social distinctions which is at the heart of the final conclusions of this analysis. Thus, adopting this heuristic position is perhaps to put the analytical cart before the horse. The way in which actors reproduce categories in the course of their social lives and the structural principles which lie behind the process is what I shall now attempt to uncover.

The Ceylonese[4]

The sub-category 'Ceylonese' contains those 'Indians' with the highest levels of both wealth and education. Ceylonese Tamil domestic contexts in Melaka may be grouped according to two major distinctions with respect to the ownership and transmission of the houses. The Ceylonese recruits to the colonial economy of Malaya moved into the plantation industry or into the colonial public service, at clerical, supervisory and junior management levels. As such, their early accommodation was provided by their employers.

In the early days, many Ceylonese settlers retained clear property rights in the Jaffna peninsula in Ceylon, where the vast majority of them originated. Domestic property among the higher castes in Jaffna was and still is mostly obtained at marriage. Wealthy members of these castes donate a house and its land, with sundry other property, as part of a daughter's dowry.[5] Initially, therefore, many of those who migrated as married men, or who returned to be married, had these property rights in Jaffna together with an intention of eventually returning there, though the timing of their return was often in the indeterminate future. In practice, by the time of my research, most of the migrants had come to the conclusion that their interests and those of their children would be best served by remaining permanently in Malaysia, and many had ceded their land in Sri Lanka to relatives. It was very rare to find a Malaysia-born Ceylonese under the age of 50 who felt that he or she retained any land rights in Jaffna.

In the early days, wives were not only recruited from Ceylon but also returned there to give birth, at least for the first child. Roughly coincident

---

[4] The Tamils of Melaka who come originally from what is now Sri Lanka do not generally adopt the term Sri Lankan in reference to themselves. They see this as a Sinhalese usage.
[5] See Pfaffenberger (1977) for a description of contemporary Jaffna.

with the cessation of the practice of wives returning to Ceylon to give birth, came an increase in the incidence of Ceylonese purchasing land and houses on the private market in Malaysia. Ceylonese themselves suggested two main rationales for this: many report that they initially sent surplus income back to Ceylon to improve or increase family property held there. When the conditions of their life in Malaysia had become clearer and they had estab- lished families there, they stated that they felt that a better investment was to obtain property where they were resident.[6] This, they pointed out, remained convertible should they decide at a later date to return to Ceylon. The secondary reasoning in informants' expressed views was an often vague statement about the advantages of owning one's own house and thereby avoiding both debts to others and the control inherent in tied housing. This was deemed especially the case when 'you have a family'.

The analytical importance of the move to ownership of domestic property resides primarily in the logic of marriage practices as they are even in contemporary Ceylonese Tamil culture. Most fathers in Melaka saw matters resolving themselves into two alternatives for their daughters. The choice was seen to be between gaining tertiary-level educational qualifications or accepting the 'traditional' pattern of marrying at a younger age with a good dowry which would ensure, it was to be hoped, a marriage into a 'good family' locally.[7] The idea was that a good education, particularly one which led to the professions, and more especially, one which led to a medical career, would of itself ensure that a girl was able to marry well.

A Ceylonese girl who chose not to or was deemed unable to pursue her education to the tertiary level relied on her parents to find her a suitable husband. This normally meant a man from a known equivalent sub-caste of the Vellalars, above all.[8] The normal pattern was for parents to look first for spouses who were themselves in the professions. Despite attempts by some reform groups, such men could in general command high dowries throughout

[6] At the time of my research, most urban Ceylonese families were living in houses bought by the head from his savings, partially accrued as an employee in a colonial undertaking. A few, however, remained resident in government quarters' while others had gained living space in the manner described later.

[7] As indicated in Mearns (1982: Chapter 1), immigration regulations effectively preclude the recruitment of male marriage partners from Ceylon, though it is still possible to bring a Ceylonese bride into the country.

[8] There are cases recorded in my field notes of men of lower Vellalar sub-castes and even of lower castes (i.e., Koviar), according to the Jaffna caste system (see Banks 1957; David 1972; Pfaffenberger 1977), successfully obtaining brides from 'higher' sub-castes, reportedly because wealth and occupational status had transcended caste rank as a dominant criterion of marriageability in the contest of a reduced pool of men of the correct age. Acceptance of these marriages was always somewhat equivocal, however, as were those cases of Hindus marrying Christians which I recorded, though the latter were all of people originating in high castes according to informants.

Malaysia. Kin and affinal networks ensured that eligible men would receive offers from several parts of the nation and their dowries normally consisted of the minimum of a large house.

The major point for the purpose of the present analysis, is that two consequences follow from the patterns which emerged in the historical development of Ceylonese practices of property transmission and marriage. Both mark the effect of contradictions between prior cultural forms and a contemporary social formation, in which the Ceylonese culture in question is subordinated politically to that enacted by dominant others.

The first consequence was the creation not only of private property in Malaysia in the form of housing, but also the creation of private domestic contexts, for a generation of individuals who, if not born there, had spent most of their lives there. We shall return to the implications of this more fully in what follows. The second consequence was that, possibly to an even greater extent than in Ceylon itself, young women became the primary source of, or more accurately, medium for, the transmission of capital wealth. This mainly took the form of housing which remains the major form of property owned by most Ceylonese (though later, some bought land and engaged in petty commodity production). This property was usually placed, at least initially, in the woman's name. Women's control of the domestic domain is still greater in the second generation of Ceylonese than in the first generation, where rights to domestic space were a product of the husband's social status, derived from his position in the occupational structure of the colonial economy. Informants suggest, however, that the significance of the transformation, which is in effect a return to previously preferred patterns of transmission, are tempered by the lack of supply of 'good' husbands and the inflation of dowries into which this has resulted. Well-qualified Ceylonese men are still able to gain access to considerable property on marriage.

The uxorilocal residence pattern, at least in the early years of a marriage, contrasts Ceylonese with the patterns of other younger Indians in the town. Moreover, their houses, though accounted for largely in the three major middle class areas of the town form, at best, clusters of a very loose kind.

There exists then a clear class difference between Ceylonese and most other Indians in terms of the ownership of property *and*, incidentally, the use of it as capital for the production of rent. This is overlain by the cultural differences which place women in a different structural location in the Ceylonese community. We shall return to a further discussion of the differences in the control and ordering of space within dwellings. This is also fundamental to an understanding of the reproduction of social differentiation within the category 'Indian'. However, outwardly there is little to distinguish Ceylonese middle class houses from the South Indian or, indeed, the Chinese equivalent, either in style or location (see also Mearns 1982).

As is the case of almost all cities, in Melaka, status and class position are to some extent marked by the style and location of housing. However, Indian status is a complex problem as even Dumont (1970) warns. Housing, of itself, represents a reflection and source of reproduction of only one aspect of status in this context. Status for Indians, as we shall see, is created in practices which relate to cultural understandings which are peculiarly 'Indian', and which are not necessarily in consonance with the understandings of others in Malaysia who are not defined as Indian. I hasten to add that I am arguing not for two or more different kinds of status, but rather for status, insofar as it is socially relevant for Indians, to be a complex of various processes. These processes engage ideas entailed in caste, class and ethnic relations. In order to understand the meaning of Indian houses as elements of social reproduction and transformation in relation to the urban processes, it is necessary to examine the nature of 'domestic space' in a more restricted sense, and to focus on its internal relations.

Ceylonese Tamil houses in Jaffna are renowned for their high fences, cleared compounds and defence of privacy (see Banks 1957; David 1972; Pfaffenberger 1977). In Melaka, the high walls and fences which block inquisitive and dangerous eyes are often missing, although there is always a carefully tended garden, where nature, if allowed to remain at all, is under tight control and restricted to grass and a few ritually important plants. In this, Melaka practice does replicate the concerns of the Jaffna household. This garden, if not enclosed by a high wall, is usually surrounded by a substantial wire fence or metal railings. It usually has an imposing gate which is normally kept shut. The main entrance doors to the house are also normally kept shut and unlike the Melaka Chitties, to whom we shall return, or the Indians of the 'labour lines', the Ceylonese generally do not use the area in front of the house as a place to sit and chat in the evenings, nor as a place for casual interaction with friends and relatives at the weekends and on holidays. To put it another way, the boundary between inside and outside is made clearer in practice for the Ceylonese than is the case for any other set of Indians.

Labourers

By way of contrast, south Indian labourers find themselves in a very different position. Urban Indian labourers, mainly recruited from Tamil Nadu, were housed for the most part in barrack like 'labour lines'. These were owned by the government in the early days of British colonial economic expansion as part of the controlled reproduction of labour power (see Mearns 1982). But Melaka, like other Malaysian metropolitan centres, has experienced a continual migration of Indians into and away from its environs such that a significant population arose which was not directly accommodated by the state. Many of the later migrants into the town came from rubber estates in the rural hinterland of the Melaka state and they mobilised kin or 'native place' links and networks in order to create access to land in close proximity to people they knew. This tendency had the consequence of producing clusters of non-state housing around those government quarter areas where Indians were predominant. The pattern persists into the modern context (see Mearns 1983). Many of these homes are rented and even those owned by labourers are modest by comparison with the Ceylonese.

Cultural Passages

Let us examine the cultural parameters within which domestic space is ordered. The area surrounding any Indian home in Melaka is conceptually an area of danger. The danger is thought to reside primarily in the potential for invasion of, and interference in, the domestic domain. Around each house, a number of incorporeal beings, spirits, unsettled ghosts of ancestors or residents, and malevolent deities are thought to reside or to visit regularly, attracted by the effluvia of everyday family social life. These are 'impure' (asuttam) beings whose force lies in their potential for usurpation of normal relations within the home. These latter relations extend beyond those between human members of the household and beyond those between the human household members and the divine beings, to those between household members and outsiders entering the home. The impure spirits may also usurp relations between an individual's mind and his normal social and bodily self.

Some of these beings are deemed to have an active desire to create havoc and may only be resisted through correct, regular rites ensuring the beneficient presence of the family deity (kula devam).

However, the space in front of the house is not merely a point of vulnerability to what is often termed the 'supernatural' forces. It is also an area where nature, in the form of animals, decaying vegetables and polluted humans, is likely to appear in close proximity to the home, even when precautions are taken. Of the south Indian and Ceylonese houses in the town, very few retain the raised platform or verandah (thinai) which is traditional in the higher caste house construction of parts of south India. Most modern houses have a porch and verandah at the ground level, if they have any, on which are placed rough wooden benches or outdoor chairs. Amongst working class people this is a place where men, especially, may congregate in the evenings and late afternoons after returning from work.

Men will often rest here before taking their evening bath and meal. The bath is a prerequisite for lighting the lamp before the images of the deities in the household shrine. This is the shortest form of *puja* (worship) possible, and it is the duty of the household head to perform it before the evening meal is taken.

Men who are still 'dirty', that is, men who are unwashed and therefore physically *and* ritually unclean, and strangers whose caste and ritual conditions are unknown, may often remain on the verandah until the circumstances are deemed to have altered either as a result of bathing or of new knowledge of their ritual status. Some individuals may never enter the house proper at all if the head is not at home, or if the person is suspected of being of a low caste or polluted by recent association with death or a similar extreme situation. In the case of higher castes visiting lower castes, the verandah may be as far into the domestic space as the higher caste member may be prepared to penetrate. On the other hand, an 'outsider' whose ritual status is known or deemed unproblematic, may be accorded the privilege of entering across the threshold into the first room or 'hall' of the house. Not to allow such an individual to enter could, under certain circumstances, be construed as an insult. Thus, Ceylonese being visited by other Ceylonese would normally expect that the visitors could enter the hall, as almost all the Ceylonese in Melaka are known to be of equivalent Vellalar caste status.

The cultural practices I am describing are not, of course, adhered to with the same degree of circumspection by all Indians in the modern urban context. In the homes of many educated Indians, including the wealthy Ceylonese, domestic space is more open to outsiders than the above description might suggest, especially to members of other ethnic groups who are of an equivalent social standing in terms of occupation, education and wealth. Although, Ceylonese do not typically encourage such interaction. Here, the principles I describe apply more to the relations between 'Indians' of known low caste rank and those of higher caste, rather than between 'Indians' and those who have no caste status. This is important in the discussion of the role cultural systems play in the reproduction of social relations and the social formation precisely because the conception of domestic space which cultural principles order, divides Indian from Indian, and to a lesser extent, Indian from outsider.

Entering the hall of all Indian (Hindu) houses involves passing under a string of mango leaves (*thoranam*) pinned across the lintel. Above this is usually a picture which most commonly represents the goddess Lakshmi, the female deity whose special association is with wealth, prosperity and general personal and familial well-being. Mango leaves, like the whole tree itself, have very potent and 'multivocal' or 'multivalent' (Turner 1967) symbolic import in the religious system of Tamils and other south Indians. In all cases, the essential quality is of a positive valency. The mango, like sandalwood, is a powerful tree which attracts the gods. It symbolises fertility, fruitfulness and coolness. These are strong values antipathetic to the polluting, deathly forces which pervade 'uncivilised' areas.

The thoranam and the image of the deity are installed at the rite of passage which transforms a building into a house habitable by human beings. This puja is centred around the installation of the family deity (i.e., the patrifilially-inherited kula devam) in his or her new domain and preferably into the shrine.

More immediately there are two principles of the cultural organisation of the Hindu house which might be seen to stand in contradiction to the principles organising mundane space in the social system at large. Firstly, a pervasive principle of Hindu space is that it should be maintained to welcome the beneficent forms of the divine and turn away the malevolent forces. This renders even bodily personal space, as will be discussed more fully later, as well as the home, *a potential temple*. Indeed, the successful incorporation of the deity demands that it be treated in precisely this manner. In turn, this creates domestic space in the form of housing as a context where the 'rational' economics of commodity exchange are totally inadequate as a mode of explanation of the patterns of property transmission, let alone of utilisation of household space.

The second contradictory aspect which has already been briefly mentioned and which is to some extent integral to the understanding outlined above, is the Hindu material life as predicated on the continuing promulgation of the correct relationship between the divine forces and the human. It is not merely the individual human, but the social order of which he or she is a part, which he or she has the prime responsibility for reproducing according to the correct principles. The apparent cultural inversion of the materialist approach which makes all material life subject to the forces of insubstantial conceptions embodied in ritual practice, is familiar enough in the literature of the anthropology of religions. The argument that these cultural activities are mere mystifications, which obfuscate the 'objective' reality of the principles which organise the social formation, would here be totally misleading. What such an approach would miss is the complexity of the relationship between social practice in the form it is found amongst actual human actors, and the structuring properties which lie behind the categorical analysis of a 'mode of production' or of even a 'concrete social formation'. The way in which Hindus conceive of and act in their domestic space may not fundamentally alter the relations of exploitation inherent in a capitalist-dominated social formation, but they do significantly affect the form that exploitation takes and its possibilities of reproduction. They also affect the limits of the penetration of the forces of the capitalist mode of production and its cultural concomitants into the lives of those whose labour reproduces the system. More specifically, the understandings of the cosmic and social orders which are being reproduced in cultural performances act in particular ways to inhibit the formation of class-based identities. This is not simply because class interests are obscured by general cultural superstructures, but because this particular superstructure represents interests which are thought to transcend 'this-worldly' concerns and which render them correspondingly less important for the Hindus who share the ideology. The manner in which Hindus in Malaysia *experience* and express their experience of the forces of a 'world system' are both fundamentally altered by their cultural context.

In order to elaborate the points I am trying to make, I shall briefly consider the structuring principles which order domestic space from the threshold inwards by means of a detailed description and analysis of a house belonging to one Indian family, in this case working class, 'Melaka Chitties'.[9] I shall consider it comparatively in terms of variations in form found amongst other Indians. While there are many different styles of houses with different ground plans, I shall maintain that Indian houses are essentially arranged spatially according to the same set of structural principles. More-over, what would appear as major differences, residing at the level of class-based variations in access to resources, may be shown to engender minor transformations rather than fundamental distinctions in meaning or organising principles.

In the case of the Chitty family house, and most other working class houses, the space one enters in the act of crossing the threshold is that which is the most formally constructed of all domestic space. This is true both in symbolic and material terms. A guest being received there enters and is then made to sit on the most expensive items of furniture which the family is likely to own, usually a vinyl or cloth covered suite, set around a coffee table. These might rarely be used by the family except when guests are in the house. In this respect the 'hall' superficially resembles the English 'parlour' as described by Lawrence (1981).

On the west wall of the 'hall' of the house is the wooden family shrine, consisting simply of an enclosed shelf and housing the household deities, in both pictorial and sculptured forms. As with many houses in Melaka, the Melaka Chitties cannot normally afford the luxury of devoting a complete room to the images of the deities, where the space is used only for worship. Most middle class Indians, and almost all Ceylonese, set aside a screened area if not the whole room, known as the *pusai arai*, or puja room, where a number of images are kept and regular offerings made by the head of the

household. Such a room, where possible, is usually located at the heart of
the domestic space, at a point where it is not only most protected from the
dangers of the invasion of polluting forces from outside the house, but also
from the polluting potential of normal household processes of birth, living
and dying.

Though Ceylonese and other middle class Indians may not have their
family shrine there, the hall remains the place where guests are received *and*
contained and it is the location for domestic rituals to which outsiders are
invited.

The Melaka Chitty houses, and almost all working class Indian homes,
contained within this hall at least a small 'gallery' of family portraits, most
commonly photographs of recently dead ancestors and family or household
members. Patrilineal relatives of the head of the house, and their spouses,
were often prominent (usually at least his F, M, and often FF and FM). The
latter, especially the father and mother of the present head, were often
stationed above the lintel of the door which led from the hall into the
interior of the house. The 'images' are garlanded and offered the *arathi*
(flame offering) of the camphor lamp as part of the daily or, at least, the
Friday puja to the shrine of the deities.

This space is commonly that used for performing rites to ancestors and to
recently deceased household members, especially anniversary rites. During
the mourning period of 16 days, the shrine will be closed and at least while a
corpse is present the photos of ancestors and deities will be turned to face
the wall. Melaka Chitties mark a difference in their own cultural practice in
this area too. They and they alone of the Indians in the town perform two
annual sets of rites (*parichu*) for the ancestors which involve elaborate
offerings of food and a puja in the hall area. One of these sets occurs at the
time (Bhogi Pandikai), on the eve of Thai Pusam the 'harvest festival', when
many other Indians perform an anniversary sequence. It involves the offering of
foods including meat, and the favourite items of consumption of the deceased
kin and household members being honoured. These may include alcohol
and cigars. The second set of rites can occur at any time during a month
known as Bulan Parichu and involves the offering of a range of fruits with
some vegetarian curries. On both occasions, guests from within and outside
the community will visit and share in a meal which will include items from
which the ancestors have taken the essence or 'smell'. On these occasions
the shrine to the deities is closed and the space becomes the archetypical
expression of the continuity and reproduction of the domestic core.

Now, it should be noted at this point that the normally 'taken for granted'
world of practical activity in the domestic space is occasionally confronted
by reflective moments when the assumptions underlying the action are
brought to the surface. Such occasions can occur during ritual when a

transgression of norms for practice takes place. One minor transgression I observed was when some noisy laughing children entered the hall space during an annual ancestor rite and were quickly quietened. They made an elaborate show of tiptoeing through to the front of the house and the verandah where guests were assembled. On another occasion a son of one house was reprimanded for standing in the front doorway. He was told that he could be preventing the ancestors from entering. Informants elaborated these points to show how ancestors should be left in peace to consume the offerings. They could take offence and depart if proper respect is not shown and might not even come if confronted by inappropriate behaviour.

In a recent trend, Indians have begun to offer an 'open house' to friends on their ethnic public holiday of Deepavali when guests are brought into the hall and served food and drink. The shrine is normally closed at this time and Indians self-consciously expose their lifestyles and homes to the often reflective gaze of outsiders, including members of other ethnic groups.

The vital point for this argument is that the ancestors as spirits or spiritual potentialities are contained with the divine presence and accepted human 'strangers' in the most formally structured space within the house. More-over, just as Lakshmi protects the entrance to the house as a whole, and to the house as 'temple', so the immediate ancestors protect the entrance into the more mundane space of the house where ordinary human life is lived. In a sense, the whole house is a domain of the deity, but especially that area where the spiritual forces of the universe are most pervasive; while the ancestors have the area within, where internally-generated pollution is a real potential. Each must seek to ensure that the force of one does not unduly invade the other.

In fact, the relationship of this space to the rest of the house is a complex one, implying as it does the parallel, but inverted spatial order of the Hindu temple (see Mearns 1982: Chapter 5) with similar conceptual relationships to surrounding space. Unfortunately for the analyst, the structure of organ-isation of Melaka Indian house space does not have the neat mirroring form of 'le monde renverse' which Bourdieu was able to discern for Kabylie (Bourdieu 1970; 1977). However, I shall argue that, like the Kabylie house, the relations embodied in the domestic space of urban Indians in Melaka do in some important senses provide a 'matrix of perceptions, appreciations and notions' (Bourdieu 1977: 83). This matrix in turn provides one of the major cultural bases for understanding the social world in which Indians are engaged. This is emphatically not to suggest that it is the sole basis of cultural orders and social understandings, or that it stands in grand isolation from other forces which affect perceptions or order processes of social reproduction.

In Turner's terms (1974), the house and temple are both 'arenas', concrete settings in which 'paradigms become transformed into metaphors and symbols', but I would go further: the space in and around the house enters and orders social relations directly from the perspective of those inhabiting it in such a way as to belie its metaphorical status and to constitute a basic 'reality'. I shall argue that Indians operate with what Giddens (1979) terms a 'practical consciousness' of their social world which derives in large measure from their conscious and unconscious understanding of their domestic space. This practical consciousness comes about not from theorising but from regularities of practice. Actors reflect on their practices in varying degrees, of course, but most of what takes place in the domestic context is what phenomenologists would term part of 'the-taken-for-granted world' of Indians. Indeed, I would accept that it is the processes of reproduction of the practices and the relations of the taken-for-granted world which constitute the very identity 'Hindu' or 'Indian' and distinguish it from other social identities available to Malaysian citizens.

It is appropriate here to recall that the very symbolism of the house and that of the human body are closely related. Both are entailed in the symbolic structure of the south Indian Hindu temple (see Mearns 1982: Chapter 5), as are notions of the human bodily form in relation to that of the divine. Beck (1976) traces more systematically than I am able to do here (or indeed an ordinary Indian in Melaka would be able to trace), the ideal Tamil understanding of bodily orientation in cosmic space, and its relations to architectural orientation. The fundamental orientations are, of course, shared in terms of their primary significance and there is no need at this point to repeat Beck's points. The particular conceptions I would wish to emphasise for the purposes of this discussion are the importance of the head and the notion of 'being allowed inside' (Beck 1976: 219). I would also like to extend Beck's analysis by elaborating upon the commonly heard Indian aphorism that 'the body is a temple', and relating that point to the analysis of the connection between the house and the temple forms.

As with the body, the house is a spatial enclosure, the central and pervasive meaning of which resides in the need to control entry and egress. In a global perspective, such concerns are certainly recorded in other ethnographic contexts, for example, that described by Littlejohn (1960; 1963). However, in Malaysia, Indians reproduce the basis of a larger cosmological scheme as much through their domestic practices as through their more public performances. Incorporated in the practices of each domain are sets of relationships and concepts which may be usefully considered as being founded on, and evidence for , 'structuring principles' in Giddens' terms. These principles provide the basis for interaction and, therefore, the reproduction of regularised practices of everyday life which, in turn, are the only basis for determining that the same principles are in fact governing social behaviour.

The reproduction of spatial relationships and their meaning relates dialectically to the apparently fixed form of Indian social relations through time. Where, as I have argued (Mearns 1982), Indian social relations are transformed by the effects of power relations inherent in the processes of colonisation, decolonisation and the formation of a new nation-state enmeshed in a world capitalist system, it is still possible for these changes to be 'externalised' from the point of view of changes to the structural relations of the domestic and religious domains. That is to say, though the form of the physical dwelling and its location in geographical space are determined by forces of the wider social formation, external to the culture of Indians per se, the structure of the relations that organise internal domestic space remain essentially the same. Similarly, it has been argued in my discussion of temple space (Mearns 1982: Chapter 5) that the internal ordering of space and meaning stand outside the forces which determine the existence or location of temples in Melaka's urban context. Where wider changes impinge directly into the domestic domain, as we shall see, not only conceptual but also spatial transformations occur which transform the reproductive possibilities of the system. This is because contradictions are made manifest which are resolved both by interpretive shifts and by changes in the material organisation of social life. Nonetheless, it will be argued that these transformations must always be given both meaning and direction in terms of the 'matrix of perceptions' inherent in the relations which pre-exist them, in a continuous dialectic.

I shall now return to the conceptual base of the perceived relationship between the house, the body and the temple. The head is the main point of entry into the body; amongst males it is normatively the only point of entry. The head is simultaneously the controller of what may penetrate further into the body's inner space. So, in the house, the household head, ideally male, is labelled 'headman' (*talaivar*) and is deemed to be responsible for determining who shall enter the house space, in particular the space at the point of entry, a room which amongst the Ceylonese is called the *talaivacal* or head room (see Pfaffenberger 1977: Chapter 3). In controlling who or what may enter the house through the region which is most susceptible, the head of most Indian households also protects the honour and well-being of those divinities and ancestral spirits deemed to control the successful continuity of the normal relations of the household and its reproduction through time.

In Hindu theology, self-realisation, the recognition of and identity with the divine within, is the precursor of ultimate escape from the constraints of the human body and rebirth of the soul (*atma*). Explicitly, the tradition of yogic control of the worldly body and the consequent achievement of internal physical and spiritual harmony are one path whereby the prior conditions for escape from the human world may be achieved. The parallels with the home are recognised in varying degrees of articulation by Melaka Hindus who conceive that the maintenance of internal household harmony is similarly dependent upon carefully controlled relations between the household and the outside world. This in turn ensures the spiritual and physical progress of the household members. Both the external relations and the internal relations may be directly disrupted by the actions of often ill-defined supernatural intervention which may appear capricious until its cause is discovered. That cause is frequently determined to be the giving of offence, often inadvertently, to divine beings. The mundane social world of human interaction is deemed to be very similar and the household's harmony may be disrupted by the intervention of offended outsiders, or by acts of the members which lead to social stigma.

For Indians in Melaka, two major sources of danger are conceptualised. One stems from the idea of the invasion of outside forces into guarded space—religious, domestic and personal; the other from the effects of 'natural' processes of everyday human living, which generate vulnerability partly, but not entirely, by virtue of their polluting capacity. Outside forces are uncontrollable, or barely so, and are unpredictable. They are attracted by the 'smell' of human activity taking place within the house, varying from cooking odours to the less humanly accessible smell of pollution. They might be human, superhuman or animal agents, acting consciously, with malice perhaps, or simply unaware of the consequences. Conceptually they represent real physical danger and this is why so much care must be taken in the control of household space and the activities it encompasses.

As with all Hindus, Melaka Indians conceptualise all matter and exudations emerging from any orifice of the body as dangerously powerful. This power is normally equated solely with pollution in the literature (see especially Dumont 1970). However, controlled exudations such as the expulsion of breath in the form of a *mantra* (a good example would be the universal *OM* or *AUM*) or in the practice of Hatha Yoga, have positive power. Similarly, the ascetic retention of semen enhances the power of the *sannyasi* not only by the avoidance of a polluting bodily fluid, but because semen has powerful creative potential.[10] Creation through the loss of semen is obtained at the cost of a diminution of the donor's strength in normal procreation.[11]

Therefore, the containment of the sources of greatest potential pollution and most danger at the rear of the house, away from the domain of both ancestors and the divine, is part of an even larger concern to exclude as

[10] Frequently repeated versions of divine creation myths usually involving Shiva, but also other deities, describe how a lesser divinity, sometimes malevolent, was formed from an illicit ejaculation, often simply onto 'mother' earth.

[11] In Indian conceptions, semen is a form of blood. For a discussion of the significance of blood, see Beck (1972) and Barnett (1975).

many of the sources of internal disharmony as possible. Such disharmony is not simply a matter of concern in terms of the relations of individuals within the house, or even their health, both of which are important enough considerations, but of the long-term fortunes of the household both physically and spiritually. A major source of potential disharmony which may be generated from within is thought by males to reside in women, especially among some more 'orthodox' Ceylonese. Women are a prime cause of invasion of spiritual forces into the human world amongst all Indians, of course, especially in the context of menstruation and childbirth. However, Banks (1957), David (1972) and Pfaffenberger (1977) all report the extent to which Vellalars in Jaffna also seclude their women on the basis of their presumed propensity to seek illicit sexual relations, should the slightest opportunity present itself. Women are, therefore, mostly confined to the domestic domain, and to the rear of the house at that, and are encouraged to leave the house as little as possible and never unchaperoned. No men, other than 'blood' relatives, should enter the woman's domain and no stranger should enter the house at all unless the head is there to greet him in the 'head room'.

Pfaffenberger (1977: 156) describes the vulnerability of women, especially at times of menstruation, to sorcery and to the influences of Rahu and Kethu, the nodes of the moon, who as minor deities are thought to be able to produce infertility. There is then, a double-edged aspect to this; women produce the 'faults' (*kurran*) which make themselves and the house vulnerable through the natural processes of their daily lives. Moreover, they are thought to exacerbate this potential through uncontrolled 'natural' desires. Yet, at the same time, women are the symbolic centre of the home and the acknowledged reproductive base of society. Pfaffenberger notes how in Jaffna it is the woman who is to be the centre of the home, whose birthdate is required for the correct performance of the construction ritual of a new house. Thus, the reproduction of the family, at both the levels of physical and social existence, and the status of the head and his whole family, depends crucially on women. The process begins, from the point of view of each new household, with the status of the family from which the woman as a bride comes, and the size of the dowry she brings. It continues through her conduct and the number and gender of her children, to her role as primary socialiser. The overlap between the symbolism of the house and that of the body is clearest in the central role women play in the control of the kitchen and the production of food. What enters the body, and who enters the core of the house, determines individual and family well-being and creates the necessary conditions for the successful reproduction of both.

Control of the bodies of women ensures for men that what is socially reproduced is a legitimate and status-enhancing family structure. However, men must also control their own bodies and their products, as well as the material conditions for the reproduction of the household, insofar as this is possible. This dual problem is dealt with in Melaka by the demarcation of the area beyond the rear of the house as an area of containment of the inevitable pollution of everyday life. Here are found the toilet, often the bathroom, and the location of any domestic animals such as chickens or goats. It is through the door to this rear area that a person returning from a funeral should enter, bathing before entering the rest of the domestic space.

In Melaka, as in Sri Lanka, the Jaffna Vellalars and other Ceylonese who aspire to their status, are deemed particularly conservative in matters of pollution and the seclusion of women. Paradoxically, it would appear, it is also the Ceylonese who have educated their children up to the tertiary level in many cases and begun to encourage them to enter the professions of teaching, medicine and the law. As I suggested earlier, the Ceylonese themselves often see this as a contemporary necessity for ensuring a 'good marriage' given the competition for men. Other Indians often characterise the change as one based on economic motivation of a more mundane sort. In this, they are sometimes supported by Ceylonese parents who say that young men educated in Malaysia now see women as an economic resource who should not be wasted 'in the home'. Young men say that nowadays it is important that one should have a wife who is at least capable of conversing with visitors and who knows a little of the 'outside world'.

Amongst Melaka Chitties, there is an important difference at both the conceptual and physical levels which means that the control of dangerous forces generated by or through women does not necessarily require the extent of seclusion found in the 'orthodox' Ceylonese context. By virtue of their control of what might be termed 'local' or peri-domestic space, the Chitties are able to contain the activities of women largely within the *kampong* which they own. The kampong is constituted of domestic units which are interlinked in a complex set of cognatic and affinal relations such that in close proximity to any domestic unit will be several closely related others. Almost all these units are contained in the area delineated by the three important Hindu temples which define the Chitties socially as well as geographically. Within this space, which I would argue is conceptually an extension of the domestic space contained by the house, the activities of women are able to be monitored and controlled by the Chitties in such a way as to ensure the reproduction of a collective identity which is deemed 'respectable'. The denigration of one unit is the denigration of all related units which, in effect, means the whole community.

It is undoubtedly true that the increased standards of education, and the consequent mixing with others from different communities, has had a major influence on the attitudes of women towards their present and future roles throughout the 'Indian' population of Melaka. However, almost all the

Chitty women who have work outside the kampong, and most of those I interviewed from other working class Indian houses, stated that they would expect to revert to the pattern of the domestic- and kin-centred life of their mothers, on or soon after their own marriages. Their present jobs were seen either as necessities, or irresistible opportunities to make their parents' lives easier and to give their own married futures a better start than they might otherwise expect. Never was there expressed a desire to escape the structures of domesticity and the concomitant narrow range of interaction and social relations which Ceylonese 'career women' were likely to project as a motive for their action. Where it was possible to find several 'independent' Ceylonese women beyond the normal age of marriage, this was extremely rare amongst working class women.

Working class women as a category, that is, the wives and daughters of men involved in unskilled or skilled manual work, clearly have the highest proportion of their number engaged in regular jobs. Indeed, the recruitment of Tamil women even into heavy manual work has been a feature of employment patterns in the estates and in the urban areas of Malaysia since the earliest days of their migration. The relationship to domestic organisation and to caste has to be understood in discussing the reproduction of patterns of female employment amongst the various class categories of Indians and within any class category.

The structuring principles of Indian domestic space, once occupied, are fundamentally the same for all classes. However, the private ownership of house and land, or the 'right' to what is collectively owned, as in the case of Chitties, constitutes a different order of relationship to the production and reproduction of the relationships it encompasses from that achieved in rented public or private property. In the past, recruitment patterns engaged in by government utility employers enabled working class families in the labour lines to assume the residential continuity and security of income for a relatively unproblematic reproduction of domestic relations. Men often succeeded their fathers as the 'tenant' of a particular dwelling provided by the employer on the father's retirement. This was made possible by the preference given to sons of loyal workers in the allocation of jobs as I have described elsewhere (see Mearns 1982: Chapters 1 and 2).

Increasingly in the era since independence, Malay-dominated government bureaucracies have sought to redress what they define as an unfair imbalance in the allocation of both urban jobs and urban public housing. A direct result of this policy has been the greater uncertainty of occupational and residential continuity amongst Indians. It is recognised that working class Indians have the highest rates of unemployment of any ethnic group in Malaysia, and highest proportional representation in the category 'urban poor' (see *Third Malaysia Plan* 1976: 143, and MIC 1975). Those families who have left the labour line accommodation have mostly sought cheap rented accommodation in the area or, in a small proportion of cases, been given the opportunity to purchase 'low-cost housing', that is, cheap, government subsidised housing. In most cases, therefore, Indians from the working class occupational category accept the situation of present or potential disruption of preferred patterns of domestic organisation. It is a mark of status and achievement that the woman married to the head of the house, and if possible, their daughters, should not *need* to work. Thus, the families which can be shown to have raised their occupational status and income levels in comparison with those of the parent, not only seek a new location and outward form of domestic space, but also attempt to organise the division of labour within the domestic group according to models which derive from a perception of the relations of men and women of higher castes and class positions, particularly those of the Vellalar Ceylonese, and the Malayalis of managerial levels.

From the point of view of the present analysis, then, a rise in social standing tends to mean the increased isolation of domestic units and the greater containment of women within the domestic domain. However, where high status and income levels have existed in previous generations, education for women is stressed and a pattern of the emergence of women from the domestic domain and engagement in occupations with status equal to or superior to that of their fathers is in the process of developing. As yet though, this trend is too new, and there are too few cases of women with careers who have married and had children, for clear conclusions to be drawn on the long-term effects of the reproduction of Indian social relations, either within or beyond the domestic context, for this relatively privileged section of the population.

Indians housed in government-supplied accommodation constituted the first proletarian population proper in Melaka, as I stated earlier, and also constituted small concentrations of an almost exclusive ethnic category, that of the south Indian Tamils. It is perhaps not surprising, therefore, to discover that some marriages took place on a local basis and that networks of kindred developed within certain labour lines as well as between them. However, there were limitations to this pattern because of the juxtaposition in the original allocations of members of different castes and people from different natal places. At the same time, people of the same caste and from the same natal places were often to be found in nearby urban areas or in the estates of the immediate rural hinterland. Thus, Indian working class kin and affinal networks tend to be spread wider within the state than those of any other category of Indians. These factors explain in part the failure of these populations to reproduce the sort of peri-domestic space created by the Chitties, let alone the village or hamlet organisation of their original homes.

Nonetheless, the people of the artificial clusters of workers' houses, or perhaps more appropriately, the bureaucratically-created clusters, have attempted to create their own sense of community in some cases. In one specific case, this process involved the building of a communal temple at the heart of the housing area. Internal disputes and the gradual erosion of Indian dominance of the area have somewhat confounded these efforts, but there is still an important sense in which the people concerned were responding to an ascribed identity, that of 'low caste' Indian (the adjectives being most significant to other Indians and the noun to other ethnic groups). They in fact responded with an attempt to transform isolated households into a united social grouping and spatial formation focused on the symbolic core of the divine force deemed necessary for the successful reproduction of any Hindu group.

There do exist contradictory aspects between the perceptions of the ordering of space contained within the culture of Indians, and the principles ordering relations in the wider domains. I do not believe either to be entirely independent, nor do I unequivocally assign a status of greater objectivity or reality to either. The fundamental consideration from the point of view of understanding the position of Indians in Melaka and the reproduction of social divisions within the wider social formation, is the problem of where one stops the explanatory efforts and considers that a sufficient account has been constituted.

It is my opinion that an analysis of the cultural patterns of Indians in the manner being pursued here is one way in which to consider the role of actors in the reproduction of culture. This facilitates the analysis of the ways in which cultural transformations are generated in the course of social life, and thereby leads to a greater understanding of what I consider to be the goal of social anthropological analysis. This is to relate the distinctiveness of sets of human beings to the processes which operate to deny their distinctiveness. In other words, the aim of this procedure is to argue that rather than simply being passive products of social forces entirely beyond their control, Indians in Melaka shape the impact of those forces, to an extent limited by the contemporary relations of international capitalism in its particular Malaysian form. The shaping of the impact I have spoken of derives not from isolated individuals, of course, but from sets of people who operate distinctively in terms of their cultural traditions and practices. This is not to suggest that a reified phenomenon 'culture', or indeed, another called 'society' or 'international capitalism', operates in any sense independently. The concept of culture that I wish to promote in this paper is one of a set of relations of symbolic orderings and understandings of the world, which evolve to maintain their relevance to the world in which they are located, and which, in the process may act to transform the direction of the world's social evolution as a whole. Thus, the relations of a capitalist mode of production based on an international division of labour (see Froebel, Heinrichs and Kreye 1980) cannot be understood in any concrete social formation except in relation to the cultural contexts in which it operates.

Elsewhere (Mearns 1982), I have shown how cultural prejudices, as one aspect of ethnic relations, gave the colonial and post-colonial relations of production their particular form. Now I am arguing that similar processes operate at the micro level of domestic relations to give form to the local social relations of production, exchange and distribution, in such a way as to reproduce cultural and social divisions which, amongst other things, prevent the emergence of a class struggle operating at either the political or ideological level, and to prevent the economic class struggle from transcending those barriers which mark *fractions of classes*. It is the ethnic dimension which most completely accounts for the perpetuation of these circumstances but ethnic identity is only one aspect of a wider consciousness of social identity, much of which is generated in relation to domestic ideology and practice.

In most societies the building of concepts of 'self' and 'group' identity begin and take their shape in the context of households and domestic relations. Relations between households, particularly those of mutual aid and support (see Wong 1984) must be considered in understanding how these concepts are reproduced and extended and how they relate to the broader social processes in which they are encapsulated. The experience which individuals and sets of people gain in their location as members of a domestic group in large part determines how they conceptualise 'people like us'. The process is a dialectical one which entails situational shifts in identity and changes in the perceived and 'objective' relationships between households and between them and the forces of society which seem to act independently of them. However, one could not understand the ways in which the Malaysian economic system and its ethnic and gender division of labour operate and reproduce without understanding how they relate to these contexts of actual human interaction.

It is the household which is basic to the continuity and transformation of the meaning of a Hindu/Indian identity and of the sub-ethnic identities such as 'Melaka Chitty'. It is often the relations within and between households which determine the saliency of a particular identity and the capacity to sustain it. Unless one were to understand the processes which allow the continual re-emergence of divisions within the category Indian, divisions based on place of origin, caste, class and class attitudes, style of Hinduism, and so forth, one could not hope to understand the dynamics of the Malaysian social system. That system itself operates in terms of ethnic divisions which relate in a complex fashion to class divisions. Indians within

258   David J. Mearns

that system are located at various levels in the class structure but are
collectively subordinate to two other ethnic groups. The incapacity of
Indians to create and maintain a consistent collective identity or consciousness in the face of such a social location can only be adequately understood
by starting from the 'inside' and by examining how culture plays its part in
establishing various group patterns of thought and interaction. Only then
can we understand how these forms subvert a single response to the 'outside'
which so determinedly seeks to impose its shape upon the experience of
people who are so much more than mere units of 'labour power'.

● ● ●

References

Banks, M.Y. 1957. *The Social Organisation of the Jaffna Tamils.* Unpublished Ph.D. Thesis,
    University of Cambridge.
Barnett, S.A. 1975. Approaches to Changes in Caste Ideology in South India. *In* B. Stein (ed.),
    Essays on South India, pp. 149–80. Delhi: Vikas Publishing House, and Honolulu:
    University of Hawaii Press.
Beck, B.E.F. 1972. *Peasant Society in Konku: A Study of Left and Right Sub-castes in South
    India.* Vancouver: University of British Columbia Press.
Beck, B.E.F. 1976. The symbolic Merger of Body, Space and Cosmos in Hindu Tamil Nadu.
    Contributions to Indian Sociology 10(2): 213–43.
Bourdieu, P. 1970. La Maison Kabyle ou le monde renverse. *In* J. Pouillon and P. Maranda
    (eds.), *Echanges et Communications,* pp. 739–59. The Hague: Mouton.
Bourdieu, P. 1977. *Outline of a Theory of Practice.* Cambridge: Cambridge University Press.
David, K. 1972. *The Bound and the Nonbound: Variations in Social and Cultural Structure in
    Rural Jaffna, Ceylon.* Unpublished Ph.D. dissertation, University of Chicago.
Dumont, L. 1970. *Homo Hierarchicus.* London: Weidenfeld and Nicolson, Ltd.
Frobel, F., J. Heinrichs and **O. Kreye.** 1980. *The New International Division of Labour.*
    Cambridge: Cambridge University Press.
Giddens, A. 1979. *Central Problems in Social Theory. Action, Structure and Contradiction in
    Social Analysis.* London and New Jersey: Princeton University Press.
Lawrence, R.J. 1981. The Social Classificatiion of Domestic Space. A Cross-cultural Case
    Study. *Anthropos* 76 (5/6): 649–64.
Littlejohn, J. 1960. The Temne Space. *Anthropological Quarterly* 36(1): 1–17.
————. 1963. The Temne House. *Sierra Leone Studies* 14: 63–79.
Mearns, D.J. 1982. Religious Practice and Social Identity. Unpublished Ph.D. Thesis, Uni-
    versity of Adelaide, Australia.
Mearns, D.J. 1983. Residence, Religion, Ethnicity and Social Change Amongst the Indians of
    Melaka. *In* K.S. Sandhu and P. Wheatley (eds.), *Melaka: The Transformation of a
    Malay Capital c. 1400–1980,* pp. 212–38. Singapore: OUP.
Mearns, D.J. 1984. Chitty Melaka: Hindus, 'Indians' or Marginal Malaysians? *Contributions to
    Southeast Asian Ethnography* 3, December, pp. 72–83.
MIC (Blueprint): Dasar Ekonomi Baru Dan Malaysia Indian: Ratindak MIC. 1975. Kuala
    Lumpur: MIC Head Office.

Pfaffenberger, B. 1977. *Pilgrimage and Traditional Authority in Tamil Sri Lanka*. Unpublished Ph.D. dissertation, University of California, Berkeley.

Third Malaysia Plan 1976–1980. 1976. Kuala Lumpur: Government Press.

Turner, V. 1967. *The Forest of Symbols*. Ithaca, N.Y.: Cornell University Press.

———. 1974. *Dramas, Fields and Metaphors*. Ithaca and London: Cornell University Press.

Wong, D. 1984. The Limits of Using the Household as a Unit of Analysis. *In* J. Smith, I. Wallerstein and H.D. Evers (eds.), *Households and the World Economy*, pp. 56–63. Beverly Hills: Sage Publications.

Notes on Contributors

John N. Gray is Senior Lecturer in Anthropology at the University of Adelaide. He studied anthropology at Northwestern University and the University of Hawaii where he received his Ph.D. in 1976. Since 1973, he has made a number of extended field trips to Nepal. His publications cover a variety of interests: sacrificial and exorcistic rituals, mode of production and its relation to social hierarchy, kinship and hypergamy, and , of course, the household. Prof. Gray has recently extended his interest in comparative systems of hierarchy by conducting research in rural Scotland.

Pauline Kolenda is Professor of Anthropology at the University of Houston. She is the author of *Caste in Contemporary India, Caste, Cult and Hierarchy* and *Regional Differences in Family Structure in India.* Her articles have appeared in many scholarly books and journals, and she has conducted extensive field work in various parts of India. Prof. Kolenda's research interests include studies of kinship, family, caste, women and South Asia.

Vivienne Kondos is a lecturer in the Department of Anthropology at the University of Sydney. Her publications cover a variety of interests: the issue of the operation of statecraft in the traditional polity of pre-revolution Nepal; Hindu metaphysical questions and gender relations. Dr. Kondos is currently working on a book on *Traditional Hindu Culture, Power and the State: The Nepalese Example* and is editing a collection on *The Politics of Ritual.*

Dennis McGilvray is Associate Professor of Anthropology, University of Colorado, Boulder, U.S.A. A graduate of Reed College and the University of Chicago (Ph.D. 1974), he has also taught at Santa Claxa, Cambridge and Cornell. Since 1969 he has been studying the social organisation, ethnomedical ideas, and religious rituals of the Tamil-speaking Hindus and Muslims of eastern Sri Lanka. Prof. McGilvray's publications include *Caste Ideology and Interaction* as well as articles and chapters on Tamil ethnomedical beliefs, the Eurasian Burghers of Sri Lanka, and Untouchable caste identity. His essay entitled 'Sex, Repression, and Sanskritization in Sri Lanka?' received the 1987 Stirling Award for psychological anthropology.

David J. Mearns is currently Lecturer in Anthropology at the Universtiy College of the Northern Territory, Darwin, Australia. He was educated at Manchester University and at the University of Adelaide, where he received his Ph.D. in 1983. Dr. Mearns' major research has been among overseas Indians in Melaka, Malaysia. This has led to publications on urban ethnicity, religious practice and social identity, caste and class, and the Malay-speaking Melaka Chitty Hindu population. He is the author of *Ethnicity*, a coursebook for Deakin University, Australia.

Ursula Sharma was educated at London University where she graduated in sociology from the London School of Economics and completed a doctorate in anthropology at the School of Oriental and African Studies. She taught sociology at the Delhi School of Economics and now works at the University of Keele where she is Senior Lecturer in Sociology in the Department of Sociology, Social Anthropology and Social Work. Dr. Sharma conducted extensive research in India, especially in Himachal Pradesh, mainly on women's work and the household.

Sylvia Vatuk is Professor of Anthropology at the University of Illinois at Chicago. She studied anthropology at Cornell University, the University of London's School of Oriental and African Studies, and Harvard University, receiving her Ph.D. degree in 1970. She has made a number of extended field trips to India, beginning in 1966. A book, *Kinship and Urbanization*, and numerous articles in professional journals and edited volumes have resulted from this research. Prof. Vatuk is currently engaged in a project that combines ethnographic and documentary data to examine the history of a south Indian Muslim family, within the context of the past 200 years of social change in the region.

Index